MAKING CLIMATE LAWYERS

ENVIRONMENT AND SOCIETY
KIMBERLY K. SMITH, EDITOR

Making Climate Lawyers

Climate Change in American Law Schools, 1985–2020

Kimberly K. Smith

UNIVERSITY PRESS OF KANSAS

© 2024 by the University Press of Kansas
All rights reserved

Published by the University Press of Kansas (Lawrence, Kansas 66045), which was organized by the Kansas Board of Regents and is operated and funded by Emporia State University, Fort Hays State University, Kansas State University, Pittsburg State University, the University of Kansas, and Wichita State University.

Library of Congress Cataloging-in-Publication Data

Names: Smith, Kimberly K., 1966– author.
Title: Making climate lawyers : climate change in American law schools, 1985–2020 / Kimberly K. Smith.
Description: Lawrence : University Press of Kansas, 2024. | Series: Environment and society | Includes bibliographical references and index.
Identifiers: LCCN 2023028995 (print) | LCCN 2023028996 (ebook)
  ISBN 9780700636396 (cloth)
  ISBN 9780700636402 (ebook)
Subjects: LCSH: Climatic changes—Law and legislation—United States—History. | Climatic changes—Study and teaching—United States—History. | Law schools—United States—History.
Classification: LCC KF3819 .S65 2024 (print) | LCC KF3819 (ebook) | DDC 344.7304/6—dc23/eng/20231002
LC record available at https://lccn.loc.gov/2023028995.
LC ebook record available at https://lccn.loc.gov/2023028996.

British Library Cataloguing-in-Publication Data is available.

Printed in the United States of America

The paper used in this publication is acid free and meets the minimum requirements of the American National Standard for Permanence of Paper for Printed Library Materials Z39.48-1992.

Contents

Preface vii

Introduction 1

1. Making Environmental Lawyers 15

2. The Birth of Climate Law 51

3. The Changing Landscape 85

4. The Great Transformation, 2000–2010 111

5. Making Climate Lawyers, 2011–2020 141

Conclusion 173

Appendix A: List of People Interviewed 183

Appendix B: Law School Environment-Focused Centers 187

Notes 189

Bibliography 215

Index 237

Preface

In 1988, I entered law school at the University of California in Berkeley unsure of what to expect but excited to start the adventure. Unlike many of my peers, I loved law school. Berkeley Law School* offered an extraordinarily rich learning environment, a cadre of engaged and brilliant students, and plenty of opportunities to pursue my intellectual interests. My three years there had a profound impact on my development as a scholar and a teacher. And yet I graduated in 1992 having learned nothing about the climate crisis. This book is an attempt to understand this puzzle: environmental policy experts knew about global warming by the 1980s, but my law school apparently did not. How could an institution with the mission and resources of Berkeley fail to anticipate the greatest environmental challenge of the twenty-first century?

The answer, of course, is not simple. It is rooted in how educational institutions operate—not only in the structural features of colleges and universities but also in the historical development of law as an academic field. Understanding those features in this country's educational system goes a long way toward understanding its slow response to climate change and to complex global problems more generally. I hope this book will help to explain the barriers to change facing law schools, as well as how those barriers are being overcome. I'm happy to report that Berkeley is now one of many law schools that have embraced the mission of making climate lawyers—legal professionals who will help to lead us toward a more sustainable and resilient future. That is the story this book highlights.

Many people contributed to researching this story. I would like to thank Moses Jehng, my research assistant, for his substantial contributions to this work. I also received valuable assistance from librarians: Sean Leahy at Carle-

---

*Many law schools have a common name that differs from the official name. Throughout this book, I have used the official name when I first mention a law school.

ton College, Eric Taylor at the University of Wisconsin Law Library, and the library staffs at the University of Minnesota Law School and University of Michigan Law School. John Dernbach helped me to conceptualize this project, and Mark Lemley offered valuable insights on how law schools operate. Mark Kanazawa, Annette Nierobisz, and Bill North read the manuscript carefully and provided very useful feedback, as did the two reviewers for the University Press of Kansas, Michael Ariens and Noah Hall. Finally, I'd like to thank everyone who granted me an interview for this project. Environmental law professors deserve much greater recognition for their role in increasing our capacity to govern together our common world. This book is dedicated to them.

MAKING CLIMATE LAWYERS

Introduction

In 2016, Katharine Hayhoe, an expert in climate science, wrote a short piece on climate change for *Ecowatch* magazine. That piece included the following paragraph:

> For more than 150 years, we've known that mining coal and burning fossil fuels produces heat-trapping gases. For more than 120 years, we've been able to put numbers on exactly how much the Earth would warm if we artificially increased carbon dioxide levels in the atmosphere. And it's been more than 50 years since the President's Council of Advisors on Science and Technology formally warned a U.S. president—Lyndon B. Johnson—that building up carbon dioxide in the atmosphere would "almost certainly cause significant changes" and "could be deleterious from the point of view of human beings."[1]

The piece as a whole is a clear and accessible overview of the history of climate science, but this paragraph bothered me. I couldn't help asking: "Who do you mean by 'we,' Professor Hayhoe?"

I certainly didn't know about climate change—not in 1965 (when President Johnson was briefed on the issue, one year before I was born), in 1972 (when it was discussed at the first Earth Summit), or in 1988 (when the International Panel on Climate Change was created). Not until the mid-1990s did I start thinking about global warming (as we called it then) as an issue that I might want to learn more about. Granted, I'm not an atmospheric scientist. But I am an expert on environmental policy. I've been interested in environmental issues since my youth. When I entered the University of

I

California in autumn 1988, I immediately joined the staff of the *Ecology Law Quarterly* and proceeded to take every environmental law course available, which at the time totaled only two courses. Neither one, to the best of my recollection, gave very much attention (if any) to global warming. My interest in environmental issues grew during my subsequent six years in graduate school (the doctoral program in political science at the University of Michigan). But environmental policy covers a huge territory, and I was more concerned about environmental justice—the pollution affecting marginalized communities—than in what seemed the more distant and abstract problem of global warming.

Histories like the one offered by Katharine Hayhoe—that "we've all known about climate change for decades"—are the basis for the narrative of failure that dogs the climate change issue, particularly in the United States. According to that narrative, we have known about climate change for many decades but stupidly or stubbornly failed to do anything about it. That narrative troubles me. It suggests that, as soon as climate scientists (or at least some climate scientists, with some degree of certainty) knew about climate change, the problem should have been—simply, automatically, and without much effort—taken up and addressed in a comprehensive way by the public policy community. That story fosters a completely unrealistic understanding of that community: how it is structured, how it operates, how it takes up new information and new issues. And it glosses over the fact that climate change as a policy problem challenges the public policy community in a fundamental way by undermining the basic organizing concepts and frameworks structuring American law.

This is not to fault Katharine Hayhoe, who was talking about the development of climate science. That is where most of the historical work on climate change has focused; intellectual historians including Joshua Howe and Spencer Weart have produced excellent works on the development of climate science that Hayhoe could draw on. The development of climate policy—the process by which institutions and communities that produce public policy learned about climate change and started developing policy approaches to it—has not received the same attention. I wrote this book to fill (at least partially) that gap. Specifically, I set out to understand how climate change has been taken up by the largest and most important policy community in the United States: the legal profession. By examining how climate change has been incorporated into the education of American lawyers, I will try to illuminate the pace of climate policy development and the

2 INTRODUCTION

challenges the climate problem poses to the American policy community and legal system. I also aim to replace the narrative of failure with a more encouraging story of success: the success of American law schools—among the most stolid, conservative institutions in American society—in (partially) transforming legal education to meet the necessity of creating climate policy professionals.

To approach that subject, I explore how American law schools have incorporated climate change into their curriculum, covering the period from 1985 to the present. I explain how environmental law professors created "climate law" as a domain of legal specialization. I use this story as a lens through which to understand both the transformation of legal education since the 1980s and the nature of climate change as a policy problem.

Climate Change and American Law Schools

First we have to place the emergence of climate law as an area of legal knowledge within the context of the transformation of American law schools. Since 2000, American law schools have become major sources of policy innovation, as evidenced by the proliferation of centers, institutes, programs, and clinics aimed at connecting policymakers with law students and legal scholars, as well as by the growing number of clinical courses focused on advising policymakers and the increase in interdisciplinary seminars and problem-based learning in law schools. Legal professionals have been advocating for this sort of interdisciplinary, policy-oriented interaction between law schools and the policy world since the creation of law schools in the late nineteenth century. But that reform agenda did not have a substantial impact on legal education until the first decade of the twenty-first century. Accordingly, we will explore the barriers facing professors who seek to engage in this kind of interdisciplinary, problem-oriented pedagogy and how those barriers were and can be overcome.

Climate policy is a good subject for this investigation because global environmental problems are one of the most visible areas in which law schools have created new interdisciplinary, policy-oriented programs and centers. To take just one well-known example: the Sabin Center for Climate Change Law at Columbia Law School works with Columbia's Earth Institute to produce interdisciplinary research, thereby offering a rich set of resources, including a database of climate litigation, a regulation/deregulation tracker, a climate law blog, and numerous reports and other publications. It is an invaluable resource for anyone interested in climate law. But the Sabin Center was created in 2009, which poses an interesting puzzle. Climate change was placed on the global policy agenda in the mid-1980s. Indeed, we can point to a specific year: the 1985 Vienna Convention organized by the World Meteorological Organization, which issued the first scientific report explicitly calling on policymakers to develop a policy response to climate change. That event led to the creation of the International Panel on Climate Change in 1988 and the first international climate agreement in 1992 (the United Nations Framework Convention on Climate Change). Despite this activity, however, climate change did not have a significant presence in the American law school curriculum during the 1990s. On the contrary, in the 1999 *Harvard Law Review* symposium "Environmental Law: Trends in Education and Scholarship," only one article (by David Wirth) mentioned climate change as a topic needing to be addressed—and he addressed it as a topic in international environmental law, which many law schools did not offer as a stand-alone course.[2]

Not until the 2000s, *after* President George W. Bush announced that the United States would not ratify the Kyoto Protocol in 2001, did climate change become a major focus of curricular innovation in law schools. By 2010, many law schools were offering entire courses on climate law, and at least three textbooks on climate law were available.[3] Today, climate change has shifted to the center of the environmental law curriculum. It serves as the master frame for both pollution law and natural resource management, reducing the traditional divide between these two branches of environmental management.[4] New pedagogies (such as the interdisciplinary, problem-based seminar) have become standard in this field, posing a significant challenge to the traditional case method.[5] And many schools are establishing climate change policy centers and hosting symposia on climate change aimed at influencing policy. The puzzle is: Why did it take so long to incorporate climate change into the curriculum? What changed to facilitate the explosion of climate-related courses, programs, and centers? Did the policy context affect this timing, or does the growth of climate law owe more to changes in legal education?

These questions are interesting enough simply as a chapter in the history of American law schools. But I believe they have a deeper significance: understanding the challenges to incorporating climate change into the environmental law curriculum provides insight into the challenges of incorporating climate change into the American legal system generally. Most of the scholarship on American climate policy treats those challenges as primarily political—and the political challenges are indeed significant.[6] But there are also a host of challenges attributable to how the policy problem relates to the legal system. Dealing with climate change calls for what the climate policy experts Danny Cullenward and David Victor call "profound industrial change"—indeed, a "massive industrial transformation" of a kind that does not lend itself to "easy planning with existing policy tools."[7] It requires us to transform our entire energy system through public policy (not merely through market forces) and also to put land use policy on an entirely different basis, aiming for carbon sequestration rather than simply biodiversity or other traditional goals.[8] It will certainly require policy action at the state and federal levels—and a significant amount of this policy work must come from local governments, something that traditionally is a neglected topic in the law school curriculum. Managing the global climate system and adapting to climate change call for a suite of policies ranging across different levels of government and different areas of legal expertise, from energy law to land use to agriculture and food law to insurance law to securities law, to name just a few.[9] The climate problem requires a much more comprehensive legal reform than the kinds of problems that the environmental law curriculum was created to address. Indeed, it may even challenge the fundamental assumptions of law itself by disrupting the relative stability of ecological systems—a stability that makes it possible for us to form reasonable expectations about the future and thus form rational legal rules in light of those expectations. Environmental law professors may have been the first people to fully grasp the magnitude of the challenge to our legal system posed by climate change.

In short, if we want to explain the American policy response to climate change, we need to understand how climate change as a policy problem challenges the deep structure of the American legal system, including how that system trains the lawyers who staff the American state.

Climate Change and the American State

This study is intended also as a contribution to the literature on American political development. Most of that literature focuses on the founding era and early development of "the state of courts and parties" (approximately 1787–1870) or the dramatic expansion of the federal government in the Progressive and New Deal eras (1890–1940).[10] By the middle of the twentieth century, the American state (defined here as the partially autonomous and relatively stable collection of institutions with governing authority over a society) had proven its ability to provide domestic security, to manage social and economic problems over a geographically extensive and growing population, and to provide global leadership. American state development in the second half of the twentieth century (after the New Deal) focused on fending off challenges to the state's legitimacy by incorporating marginalized populations more fully into the national community and by growing the national economy.

But the story of the American state has entered a new phase. The twenty-first century poses novel challenges that require further (or different) state development. These challenges grow out of the technological, economic, and scientific trends that have come to define the twenty-first century. The contemporary state must cope with demands to manage not only national but also global systems: a global economy tightly connected by transportation, trade, and information; a global community demanding rising standards of living; and a global environment posing risks we have only begun to comprehend—including, prominently, climate change. How is the twenty-first century American state evolving to manage the challenges posed by these transformations?

And evolve it must. The challenges of global environmental management—such as managing climate change—are very different from most twentieth-century social problems. Obviously, they require a high degree of international coordination to address. They also require an extraordinary expansion of state capacity to gather, process, and interpret scientific information. They are wicked problems, requiring the management of complex socio-ecological systems. For example, climate change requires states proactively to drive an energy transition away from fossil fuels—a transition that will require transformations in global transportation, food, and energy systems and in local economic development and public health strategies (not to mention the potential abandonment of trillions of dollars invested in the fossil fuel economy). This is an enormous task for public policy to achieve. And yet the United States has already produced a substantial amount of policy directed at this goal. While the problem is far from solved, we are beginning to see what climate policy looks like and what kinds of laws and institutions it requires. How is the American state developing in response to this challenge?

In this volume I approach that question by focusing on one underappreciated dimension of this story of American political development: the training of the legal experts needed to create public policy aimed at managing climate change. This topic—the training of lawyers—has not received much attention either from scholars of American political development or from experts on climate policy. But it should. The American public policy system is dominated by lawyers to an extent not seen in any other nation. Lawyers are a hundred times more likely to be elected to Congress compared to any other type of citizen, and they similarly dominate state governments.[11] As the American observer Alexis de Tocqueville famously observed, lawyers *are* the political class in the United States. Understanding the American policy response to climate change thus requires us to investigate the legal profession's relationship to the climate problem: When and how did legal scholars begin addressing the climate problem? How was it conceptualized as a legal problem? Where in the organization of the legal system—to which legal specialty—did climate regulation belong? Was it a foreign policy problem, a pollution problem, a public health problem, a problem with the energy system, a problem of corporate governance, or a natural resource management problem? What if it was all of these and more—not just one problem but an interrelated set of problems involving many different socio-ecological systems? How could the policy system be mobilized to address a problem cluster that cut across conventional areas of legal specialization? And how could such a problem cluster be incorporated into a legal curriculum based on conventional common law categories?

These are the questions that had to be addressed, often in the first instance, by law professors taking on the task of teaching law students about climate change. Almost all lawyers in the United States are trained at about 203 accredited law schools, all of which share a fairly uniform approach to legal education and professional socialization. They are therefore a convenient focus for this inquiry. By examining how, when, and why these schools took up the challenge of creating climate lawyers, I aim to provide insight into the nature of climate change as a policy problem—as well as the nature of the state development needed to manage it.

Theoretical Approaches

My work is informed by two relatively new theoretical concepts in the scholarship on political development, both of which have proven useful in understanding the climate change problem: social learning and knowledge infrastructure. As an overarching framework I draw on the literature on social learning, which I define here as the long-term development of a society's capacity to manage global environmental risk. Specifically, this literature examines the development of global environmental management as a "sustained social learning process." It thus underscores the importance of learning as an agent of change. Questions guiding this research include: Where did ideas and beliefs about global environmental management come from? Why do particular actors see themselves as interested parties in this problem? How do institutions promote changes in concern and capacity that affect global environmental management?[12]

I also draw on the related literature on the development of the "climate knowledge infrastructure."[13] "Knowledge infrastructure" refers to robust networks that generate, share, and maintain specific knowledge. The climate knowledge infrastructure includes, for example, climate models and climate data, along with the institutional and technical infrastructure needed to produce them. This infrastructure, developed and supported by twentieth-century nation-states and their scientists, makes it possible to conceptualize the "global climate" as a subject of knowledge—and therefore regulation. The climate knowledge infrastructure is a key component of state development in the twenty-first century.

Climate knowledge must include legal knowledge, defined here as knowledge related to the use of legal tools, the operation of regulatory systems, and creation of legal regimes that aim to bring the climate system under the rule of law.[14] But neither the social learning literature nor the knowledge infrastructure literature gives much attention to the production of the legal expertise needed to develop and defend climate policy. Perhaps this gap is not surprising, since both literatures focus on the role of climate scientists in international climate policymaking.[15] The role of lawyers may seem less in need of explanation. But as we turn our attention to domestic policymaking (at least in the United States), it becomes obvious that lawyers capable of crafting complex climate policies—ranging from carbon trading systems to carbon offsets to wholesale urban reform—don't appear out of nowhere. In the United States, at least, law schools are critical elements of the knowledge infrastructure required for twenty-first century environmental management. How did ideas and beliefs about climate change make their way into the legal curriculum? How did law professors and students come to see themselves as parties responsible for addressing climate change? How have law schools promoted (or failed to promote) these changes in legal education?

One way to approach these questions is to conceptualize the development of climate law in American law schools as an innovation, which allows me to draw on *diffusion of innovations theory*.[16] This well-known theory defines "diffusion" as a process whereby an innovation (an idea or practice) is communicated through certain channels among members of a social system. A key insight of this theory is that diffusion takes place over time, and its adopters can be classified as innovators, early adopters (usually local opinion leaders), early majority, late majority, or laggards. Here the relevant social system (the boundary within which an innovation diffuses) is American law schools. In defining the members of that social system, however, we encounter some complexity. Who actually makes the decision to innovate? Should we focus on the law school as a whole or on individual faculty members?

These questions are related to another theoretical question: What drives curricular and pedagogical innovation? It is not my aim to develop such a theory here, but I do make some assumptions about the main drivers of the innovations I am discussing, and these assumptions help explain my focus on professors rather than the law school as a whole. I see three sets of actors in a position to influence law school curriculum and pedagogy: institutional leaders (deans, faculty governance bodies, and other high-level decision makers); individual faculty members; and students. Each set of actors has different motives and opportunities.

Administrators are concerned with the law school's competitive position relative to other law schools, as well as with keeping the school financially strong. They may also have to respond to external constituencies such as the administration of the university of which the law school is a part, the accreditation agency (the American Bar Association, or ABA), and state bar examiners. Administrators influence curriculum primarily through hiring decisions (hiring people to teach a new subject). They have less ability to influence pedagogy (how courses are taught), although they can encourage faculty to develop new teaching skills by offering grants for such professional development.

Law school professors, in contrast, have less reason to worry about competition among schools or pressure from external constituencies. Their immediate concerns are to design courses that can be taught successfully and to advance their own scholarly reputations. Traditionally, law professors are expected to teach at least one of the required law school courses, but they have some freedom to develop elective courses in their area of expertise. And because they are protected by norms of professional respect and academic freedom, they enjoy a very high degree of autonomy concerning how they teach.

Students are the least powerful members of the law school community.

INTRODUCTION 9

They have very little opportunity to influence teaching. However, they can generally choose which courses to take during their second and third years, which provides faculty an incentive to offer courses that students want to take. In addition, professors interact intensively with students and may respond to their feedback about the course or about what courses they would like to see offered.

In sum, I assume that administrators, looking to make the school appealing to potential students, may influence the curriculum through hiring decisions. Students, looking to satisfy their intellectual and career interests, may influence which courses are taught via their choices whether to enroll in certain courses. But faculty members—responding to these influences, their colleagues, and their own judgments about what subjects are important and interesting—have by far the greatest say in what is taught and how it is taught. To be sure, much of the curricular innovation I will discuss requires institutional support. Professors are hired by a school (often located in a university), and the school may choose to support or discourage curricular changes, research agendas, and other professional activities. Law professors are key actors in the shaping of legal education in the United States, but only because (or to the extent that) law schools support that agency. Thus the financial and competitive context in which law schools operate and how that context might influence innovations in teaching is important to our story, as I will discuss in chapter 3. But in general I consider the law professor to be the primary actor making the innovation decision.

Finally, in order to understand how law professors operate, I draw on a well-established body of literature on professionals as participating in "communities of practice," meaning they are engaged in collective learning in a shared domain of human endeavor.[17] Members of a community of practice engage in problem-solving, request information, seek experience, reuse assets, coordinate activities, discuss developments, document projects, visit each other, and map and identify gaps in knowledge. I use the phrase "communities of practice" to describe the law professors who are developing climate law as a curricular domain (a community of teaching practice) and also to describe the policymakers—including lawyers and legal scholars—focused on creating climate policy (a community of policy practice). Indeed, one of the observations driving my analysis is that law professors are increasingly participating in both educational and policy communities of practice, serving as a critical bridge between law schools and the policy system.

Sources and Methods

Primary sources for this study included archival materials such as reports and other documents produced by legal educators (conference proceedings, ABA reports, and the like); discussions about teaching in the law review literature and blogs (such as the Environmental Law Professors Blog); casebooks and other scholarly books used for law school courses; and syllabi collected from professors themselves and the International Union for the Conservation of Nature climate law syllabus collection. I also conducted 53 interviews with professors who teach environmental law at American law schools and with 15 students who have taken those courses since 2000. (Most of the law professors, of course, were also law students.) I also interviewed the editor in chief and vice president of West Academic, one of the major publishers of legal teaching materials.

The majority of the professors I interviewed are prominent scholars in the field, teaching at leading law schools, making them (in my view) significant historical figures with a good deal of influence in the field of environmental law. They include the authors of many of the major textbooks, directors of environmental law programs at leading law schools, and some of the most widely cited environmental legal scholars. Accordingly, I secured consent to use their names so that I could document the contributions of specific individuals to the project of creating climate law as a field. I ensured their continuing consent by inviting them to review my manuscript before I finalized it. I also included among my interviewees professors at lower-ranked law schools—not as many but enough to see how changes in the field were being taken up at schools with fewer resources and different kinds of students. I do not identify the students I interviewed, since I was seeking from them a more general sense of what their climate education was like rather than their specific contributions to the practice of climate education. I list in appendix A the law schools that the student interviewees graduated from. In order to protect their privacy, I did not collect demographic data about them, and they should *not* be taken as a representative sample of American law students in general.

An important caveat: my interest in the development of the field led me to focus on the top-ranked schools and the most prominent scholars. I do not attempt to document the teaching of climate change across the whole range of law schools. What I learned from professors at the lower-ranked and under-resourced law schools was not to assume that I knew what was going on at those schools. Many of them were far more innovative than I expected; but most of them also faced more serious constraints (like a tiny faculty) than I had understood originally. My story raises more questions than it answers about these rank-and-file schools, and I have flagged those questions where I see them.

With that caveat in mind, the story that follows begins, in chapter 1, with background on American legal education and the development of environmental law as a field. Some of this material is probably overly familiar to the average American environmental law professor, but this book is intended for a broader audience—for climate scholars, policy professionals, and others interested in the history of climate governance. Accordingly, I assume that many readers will not be familiar with American law schools, and I attempt to clarify some of the more arcane or unusual aspects of American legal education for those readers.

Chapter 2 takes up the development of climate policy in the United States, concluding by exploring how environmental law professors during the 1980s and 1990s learned about the subject and whether and how they began to incorporate it into their teaching. This chapter begins to examine the initial barriers to teaching climate law. Chapter 3 examines a significant series of changes in legal education as well as climate policy, starting in the 1990s, that set the stage for the development of climate law as a field after 2000. Chapter 4 recounts the growth of the field in law schools from 2000 to 2010, and chapter 5 brings the story up to date with developments from 2011 to 2020. Climate law now appears as a reasonably mature field. It is being taught in most if not all law schools, if not as a stand-alone course then as part of standard environmental law courses. Some schools offer multiple courses on the subject, along with clinics or other experiential learning opportunities. There are still important questions to be confronted about the further development of climate law training, and the conclusion following chapter 5 engages with the current conversation about whether law schools are approaching climate change the right way with the right tools and with the right level of commitment.

My story adds an important qualification to Hayhoe's claim that we've known about the dangers of climate change since the 1970s. *Some* environmental law professors did indeed start to learn about climate change by the late 1970s. But they were not, in general, sharing that knowledge with students. During the 1980s and 1990s, law professors faced barriers to teaching climate change that were rooted in the structure and definition of the field of environmental law and the lack of resources dedicated to environmental law. However, a number of entrepreneurial law professors did begin to innovate in this area, so the beginnings of climate law as a curricular domain emerged at this time. That domain developed rapidly during the 2000s, due in part to the increased salience of climate change as a public policy problem and in part to the increase in resources and transformation of teaching practices at American law schools beginning in the 1990s. By the 2010s, most law schools addressed climate change in an introductory environmental law course, and many offered stand-alone courses on climate law; there was a significant trend toward expanding the curriculum toward energy law and other fields important to dealing with the climate crisis.

In sum, this is a story of at least partial success. It took several decades, but American law schools have evolved into institutions capable of producing climate law knowledge and climate law professionals. To be sure, this evolution is still uneven; the environmental law curriculum is underdeveloped at some schools, and traditional teaching practices are still common. But curricular and pedagogic changes that took root during the 1990s are paying off today, increasing the capacity of law professors to prepare students to face a twenty-first century rife with problems related to climate change.

CHAPTER ONE

Making Environmental Lawyers

Where do lawyers come from? Although all scholars of the American state recognize the role of lawyers in staffing it, none of the dominant theories or histories of American state development give any attention to the law schools that produce those lawyers. Judging from the literature on American political development, one might think that lawyers simply spring into existence when needed, complete with a command of all the skills needed to craft legislation and defend it in court. In reality, of course, the American state depends on the system of legal education that evolved in the United States in the late nineteenth and early twentieth centuries to produce much of that state's staff. I therefore begin this story by exploring the role that American lawyers play in creating and implementing public policy and how they have historically been trained—or not trained—for that role.

I then turn to the rise of environmental law as a field within the legal academy. This was a fairly late development; law schools started producing environmental lawyers as we know them today beginning in the 1970s. The evolution of legal education and environmental legal education has significant implications for how law schools would take up climate law.

Lawyers and the American State

It would be hard to exaggerate the degree to which lawyers dominate the policy system in the United States. The juris doctor (JD)—the degree awarded by law schools—serves as a general credential for law careers, both private and public. It is (with a few exceptions) illegal to practice law in the United States without a license, which is awarded by state supreme courts that almost universally require licensees to hold a JD from a law school

15

accredited by the American Bar Association. What constitutes "practicing law" is sometimes debatable, but at a minimum a JD is mandatory for anyone representing any party, including a government entity, in court. Lawyers therefore hold a monopoly on certain governmental positions concerned with law enforcement and civil litigation, such as attorneys general, solicitors general, and federal prosecutors.[1] A JD is usually a formal requirement for becoming a judge as well. The federal bench and state judiciaries are firmly in the hands of lawyers—and the judiciary has an unusually important policy role in the United States, since any court can exercise the power of judicial review, overruling policy decisions by other branches of government as inconsistent with a state or the federal constitution.[2] Even more important for environmental law, the American judiciary also plays an active role in reviewing the regulatory actions of administrative agencies to ensure compliance with statutory mandates. In the United States, legal professionals usually get the final say on public policy.

They also usually get the first say on policy, since elected offices are also dominated by lawyers. There are about 1.35 million lawyers in the United States—about 0.4 percent of the population. But as of 2017, 59 percent of American presidents have been lawyers, and lawyers accounted for 39 percent of seats in the House of Representatives and 56 percent of seats in the Senate. (That figure is actually a decline from the nineteenth century, when lawyers held nearly 90 percent of congressional seats.)[3] These figures make the United States an outlier, as the political scientist Adam Bonica notes:

> By comparison, lawyer-legislators account for just 13 percent of the U.K. Parliament. The percentages are similar for other nations that inherited the English Commonwealth system of law. Canada, New Zealand, and Australia are at 15, 14, and 13 percent, respectively. The percentages for France, the Netherlands, Sweden, Denmark, and Japan are much lower, ranging from 2 to 6 percent.[4]

Moreover, lawyers dominate legislators' staff. Lawyers are disproportionately represented on both the personal staff and committee staff in the US Congress, and the Offices of the Legislative Counsel (for the House and for the Senate) are composed entirely of lawyers.[5] These staffs play a critical role in shaping and ultimately drafting legislation.[6]

State governments are also dominated by lawyers. As of the 2006 election, lawyers held 44 percent of all state governorships and 17 percent of state legislative seats and constituted all state prosecutors and chief legal officers.[7] State attorneys general in particular illustrate the influence of the legal profession in state government. A law degree is not always formally required for this office, but in practice the duties of the attorney general (which include representing the state government in court) require membership in the state bar. State attorneys general are often elected rather than appointed, so they can exercise an independent influence on state policy. Indeed, a good deal of policy reform is led by state attorneys general challenging federal policies in court or seeking change from state judiciaries.[8] Even at the municipal level, where lawyers are less prevalent among elected officials, city attorneys are still essential gatekeepers, advising elected officials on their legal powers and duties.[9]

Lawyers have a smaller footprint in administrative agencies, but they still have a direct influence on policy. The federal Environmental Protection Agency (EPA), for example, employs about a thousand attorneys (out of a total staff of about 15,000), and traditionally lawyers dominate its top positions.[10] Most EPA lawyers are in the Office of General Counsel, where attorneys provide "critical input to rules, regulations, and guidance documents" and "shape national legislation affecting the environment."[11] These lawyers are key veto points in the policy process, since they have primary responsibility for informing top-level policymakers in the agency what they are legally required to do or not do.[12] They also develop legal arguments aimed at changing the law. For example, Jonathan Cannon, EPA's General Counsel in 1998, wrote a widely circulated memo arguing that greenhouse gas (GHG) emissions were "pollutants" and could therefore be regulated under the Clean Air Act. His argument was adopted by the EPA's leadership and eventually prevailed in the United States Supreme Court (in 2007), leading to the first federal climate regulation (the 2015 Clean Power Plan).[13] The same roles are played by the 430-person Office of the Solicitor in the Department of the Interior, which manages public lands.[14] The other major federal environmental agency, the Department of Agriculture (USDA), receives legal advice from some 200 attorneys in its Office of the General Counsel.[15]

Lawyers outside government also influence the development of the state. The role of lawyer-lobbyists, representing business interests in policymaking, is well known.[16] But social movements are also often led by lawyers; indeed, a 1986 study found that more than half of professionally trained public interest activists were lawyers.[17] "Cause lawyers" pursue social movement objectives using legal tools, including litigation, lobbying, and policy development. While much scholarship describes cause lawyers as having an adversarial relationship with the state, they still serve as agents of state development by organizing and bringing resources to bear on the policymaking machinery.[18] In fact, cause lawyers frequently form collaborative relationships with policymakers, developing policies and strategies in concert. And, of course, as Douglas NeJaime documents, cause lawyers often move into government when sympathetic administrations take office.[19]

In sum, law remains a preferred path to a political career in the United States. A legal education is a valuable credential, giving one access to a variety of jobs within the state and within broader communities of practice focusing on public policy. Lawyers are essential to the staffing, operation, and evolution of the American state. But does this matter to public policy? Or are lawyers too diverse a group to generalize about?

Research on the American legal profession has concluded that we can make some important generalizations about lawyers. To be sure, law school is not the only influence on lawyers. The JD is a graduate degree, usually requiring the standard bachelor of science or bachelor of arts degrees as a prerequisite, so most students entering law school have received at least four years of instruction in the typical American undergraduate education under the liberal arts model. Nevertheless, law school leaves its mark. Mark Miller, reviewing the scholarship on the professional socialization of lawyers, concludes that law school has a significant impact on how lawyers think about and approach public policy. Law schools aim to teach students to think like a lawyer, and by and large they succeed. American lawyers share a "legal ideology" inculcated in law school that "dominates and shapes our legislative decision-making processes."[20] Specifically, lawyers are rule- and procedure-oriented practitioners, understanding the legal system as an objective, rational order. That is to say there is a basic logic to the existing system of law; some legal rules fit well into the system and others would disrupt it. Few lawyers see the existing legal system as perfect, but they do favor certain kinds of reform: they take a narrow, rights-focused approach to solving broad social problems and favor incremental reforms over radical change.[21] And they see the distribution of legal rights as the main tool of social change.

Law school therefore tends to have a moderating influence on law students, teaching them to be wary of radical social changes and concerned about maintaining the basic structure of the existing legal system. If legal education does have such an effect on America's dominant group of policy professionals, this fact has significant implications for the American state's ability to address twenty-first-century problems. These problems may require deep restructuring of many complex systems, as well as the creation of better systems for producing, verifying, and managing scientific information. We need different forms of governance and new kinds of institutions. It's not clear that merely modifying individual rights—the task that lawyers are traditionally trained for—is going to help us.

Miller's book was published in 1995. If legal education has changed since then, that should have important implications for our policy system. Thus the questions driving my inquiry: What kinds of education and training have law students been receiving since the 1990s? Has that education changed in ways that may affect how legal professionals think about social problems like climate change? Are law schools better, or differently, preparing lawyers to deal with the challenges facing the twenty-first-century state?

To begin addressing those questions, we first need to understand the American legal education that Miller and other scholars were describing: the traditional law school as it existed up until 1990 or so. Happily, there is a rich body of scholarship on the history of law schools in the United States, and one of the major themes in that literature is whether legal education is or should be aimed at preparing students for their role in staffing the American state.

History of Legal Education

Today, American law schools are a powerful force in American society. There are about 200 ABA-accredited law schools, and they produce almost all the lawyers practicing in American society, including the large cadre of legal experts staffing federal, state, and local governments.[22] Much of the scholarship on the history of legal education in the United States focuses on how law schools evolved to acquire this monopoly on legal education and the development of its signature pedagogy: the case method.[23]

Rise of the Harvard Model

The story begins with the founding of law schools in the nineteenth century as an alternative to the legal apprentice system (by which lawyers were trained in law offices by practitioners). Initially these schools followed the standard lecture model characteristic of most higher education in the United States in the late nineteenth century. But early in the twentieth century that method gave way to a new approach to legal education pioneered by Harvard Law

School and advocated by Harvard's dean, Christopher Columbus Langdell: a three-year program focused on training students in analysis of common law doctrine through the case method (sometimes called the "case-dialogue" or "Socratic dialogue" method). This method has evolved over time, but basic features of the Harvard model still shape legal education: a curriculum focused on private law and a pedagogy focused on teaching students how to analyze doctrine by reading appellate court decisions.[24]

Under the Harvard model, the curriculum is designed to introduce students to the major areas of *private law*, or the law governing relations between private citizens, such as contracts, property, and torts. Criminal law, constitutional law, and civil procedure, which could be characterized as *public law* courses (concerning laws governing the legislative and executive branches and the creation of public policy), usually round out the standard first-year curriculum. However, the curriculum as imagined by Langdell and his acolytes focuses on training lawyers to serve private clients: the goal is to understand the rules as they apply to private actors rather than to evaluate how well the rules serve public values. This focus on private law has important consequences for understanding the relationship between law schools and the state. But it was never an uncontroversial focus, as discussed below, and an important theme in curricular debates challenges private law's dominance.

The private law orientation, however, was reinforced by the case method of pedagogy. Under this method, students do not learn legal rules by reading legal treatises or by studying how laws are made. Neither do they study the aims and methods of public policy. They may not even spend much time reading statutes. Rather they read opinions written by appellate judges applying legal rules to cases. In class, a good deal of instruction consists of asking a student to present a case (explain the facts, the legal issue and applicable legal rules, and the judge's reasoning). The professor may then ask the student a series of questions about the case and the judge's reasoning, usually focusing on how different facts or a different interpretation of the rule might change the analysis. Assessment typically consists of one final exam, requiring students to identify the legal issues raised in hypothetical fact situations and explain how the relevant legal rules would apply.[25]

This form of instruction has certain important features. It does a good job of teaching students doctrinal analysis and how to apply legal rules to fact situations—which is no small matter, since there is little of this sort of training in the typical undergraduate curriculum in American colleges and

20 CHAPTER ONE

universities. This method also works reasonably well with large classes. Law schools can therefore train large numbers of students with a small faculty (and no expensive equipment), making law schools inexpensive to operate.[26] However, the case method doesn't teach law students how to do many of the tasks that lawyers perform, from drafting legal documents to handling clients to running a law firm. Training in those tasks is left to law firms, resulting in a division of labor that has characterized legal education in the United States throughout the twentieth century and (to a lesser extent) today. Students are expected to spend their two summers in their three-year law school program doing internships at law firms, which introduces them to the practical dimensions of legal practice. If the students do well, the firm usually offers them employment after graduation, committing itself to a good deal of additional training of new associates. To be sure, periodic movements to offer clinical education in law school (most prominently in the 1960s) led to the creation of law clinics and skills-based courses in most law schools by the 1970s. Nevertheless, the bulk of the practical skills of lawyering are expected to be learned on the job after graduation.

This division of labor persisted in part because it freed law professors from skills-based courses and allowed them to focus their teaching and research on the analysis of doctrine.[27] Thus the standard model of legal education also helped give definition to the academic discipline of law, which came to be understood as the study, critique, and development of legal doctrine as represented in the decisions of appellate judges. Indeed, the bulk of legal scholarship even today consists of analyzing appellate decisions. This model served the needs of law schools pretty well, providing them with a clear and intellectually respectable mission that does not compete with other academic fields and that can be carried out on the scale necessary to supply the public's increasing demand for legal services. And it helped them to gain a near-monopoly on legal training by the 1950s. By that time, most states required that lawyers hold a JD from an accredited law school (as well as passing a state bar exam) to be admitted to practice.[28]

The success of the standard model of legal education was supported as well by external organizations that influence legal education in the United States.[29] The most important of these is the American Bar Association, which is currently the only accrediting agency for law schools.[30] Accreditation standards cover everything from curriculum and faculty credentials to financial and other institutional resources. The ABA therefore has an important influence on what and how law schools teach. State bar associations also influence curricula, since most students expect law school to prepare them to pass the bar exam. The National Conference of Bar Examiners was founded in 1931 to encourage more uniformity in bar exams, which led to the creation of the Multistate Bar Examination in 1972, now used by 33 states (although exams usually also include some state-specific questions).[31] The legal education infrastructure also includes the Association of American Law Schools (AALS), which provides support for law school administrators and professional development for law school professors. And, of course, publishers of law textbooks (usually called "casebooks") must also be included in the ecosystem of legal education.[32]

This legal education landscape has evolved since 1970. Consolidation in the legal academic publishing industry, particularly in the 1990s, has left this niche populated by only a few companies, the most prominent being West Academic, Carolina Academic Press, and Aspen Publishing. Professional associations concerned with legal education have also proliferated, most of which meet at the AALS's annual conference. These include, for example, the Society of American Law Teachers, founded in 1972 to promote a more progressive agenda for law teaching; the Clinical Legal Education Association, incorporated in 1992 to promote clinical education; and the Association of Legal Writing Directors, formed in 1996.

In the 1980s, however, these other organizations had not yet made much impact on the law school curriculum. American law students at a full-time law school in 1985 could expect to take a standard suite of courses during their first year (contracts, torts, property, civil procedure, criminal law, constitutional law, and generally a moot court and legal writing course). During their second and third years they could choose from a set of elective courses, most of which would use the same case method used in first-year courses. The electives available would likely include some statute-based courses, such as tax and environmental law, as well as a few seminars. However, students would be advised to fill their schedules with "bar courses"—courses on subjects tested on the bar exam, such as estates and trusts, negotiable instruments, and the law of corporations. They might take a legal clinic, which would likely focus on providing basic legal services to underserved communities. The top students might also be chosen to work on a law review, which provides a basic introduction to conducting legal scholarship. Students would receive additional training through summer internships at a law firm (some of which have well-developed, and well-paid, internship programs). The very best students might work as a clerk in a judge's office for a year or two after graduating, but most law students could expect to spend several years in private practice, even if they hope to eventually work for a government agency or teach law.

Challenging the Harvard Model

Much has been written about the deficiencies of the Harvard model of legal education, including its focus on producing lawyers to serve the business community, its failure to diversify the student body, and the high-pressure, competitive atmosphere it encourages. For this analysis, the most relevant critique concerns the goals of legal education: Should law schools focus on training lawyers to minister to private clients (as most lawyers do)? Or should they aim to prepare students for the role that lawyers play in staffing the state and crafting public policy? Advocates of the second, broader view of the goals of legal education have two major criticisms of the standard model: It doesn't teach practical skills necessary to serve the modern administrative state; and it doesn't prepare students intellectually to join public policy communities of practice.

The first criticism reflects the general neglect of practical skills in law school, but it focuses on the skills involved in making public policy, such as drafting statutes and administrative regulations, evaluating policy, and negotiating with diverse stakeholders. These are skills that even traditional legal clinics (focused on serving private clients) usually did not attempt to teach. They constitute what advocates for a broader vision of legal education called "legal process": how legislatures and administrative agencies operate, from the creation of public policy through statutes, regulations, and guidance documents to implementation, enforcement, and policy assessment.

The second criticism, concerning the intellectual training of law students, posits that the standard model encourages students to see law as an autonomous system governed by its own logic, largely independent of broader social forces. This is the "American legal ideology" that Miller summarizes: students are taught to care about the internal consistency of the legal system but not its impact on society. This sort of preparation results in legal experts trained to read copious amounts of judicial opinions, master complex legal rules, and apply them to fact situations—but they remain wholly unequipped to consider the wisdom or necessity of those laws, much less to envision radically different alternatives to the existing system. Education reformers have tackled this deficiency by calling for law schools to teach more social and policy science and even political philosophy. A broader curriculum based in the social sciences, they hope, would provide students with a greater ability to analyze law's impact within society and think critically about the principles guiding state action. Today we characterize this as a call for a more interdisciplinary education, although in the early twentieth century it was the nature of law as a discipline itself that was under debate.

This critical perspective on the standard model has a long history. Langdell's court-centered and private law–based model was in fact a response to a competing vision (offered by Lester Frank Ward, for example, in his 1883 *Dynamic Sociology*) of law as socially informed government regulation produced by legislatures.[33] Throughout the early decades of the twentieth century, reformers (often associated with the Legal Realist movement) called on law schools to broaden their vision of legal education. For example, Felix Frankfurter's 1915 address to the ABA encouraged law schools to see themselves as training students for a public profession and as "participating in a great state service" by developing the law.[34] Alfred Reed's 1921 report on the state of legal education (sponsored by the Carnegie Foundation) echoed that idea. Lawyers, argued Reed, "are part of the government mechanism of the state." Noting that "a large proportion of our legislative and administrative officials, and virtually all of our judges, are chosen from among this practically ruling class," he insisted that "their functions are in a broad sense political."[35] The concept of law as a public profession resonated with the emerging concept of the university as the training ground for servants of the administrative state, producing administrators and experts committed to disinterested state service in the public interest.[36]

This vision of law school as training for statesmanship had significant implications for the legal curriculum. For Frankfurter, for example, it required a broader focus than the case method permitted. Legal education should be aimed at the development of a social consciousness that could relate law to the whole of society.[37] For Reed, students needed to study legal history and jurisprudence, to see the legal system as a whole.[38] For Roscoe Pound (dean of Harvard Law School from 1916 to 1936), lawyers should be trained to assume the role of social engineer, to see law as "a doing of things" rather than discernment of a fixed order of values.[39] In practice, reformers usually sought to embed legal education in the social sciences, history, and political philosophy.[40]

But that program wasn't popular with law students and most law faculty. Consider Frankfurter's attempt to implement that vision in his Harvard courses. As described by the legal historian Willard Hurst, who took Frankfurter's public utilities course in the mid-1930s:

> [The course] undertook to relate public utility law, statutory law, and what the courts did with it to what was going on in the general economy of the country. It was in some ways a strange course. The students often called it the case of the month course, because it proceeded so slowly. But that in itself was instructive because Frankfurter would relate the case to the legislative process and to the state of the economy. He would just squeeze so much out of it. But the method usually bothered the students a lot since like law students today they figured they were getting their education according to the number of pages in the casebook they covered.[41]

A Harvard colleague, Professor James Landis, shared Frankfurter's interest in teaching legal process, and Hurst was stimulated by Landis's course on legislation. But he described the rest of the curriculum as "abstractly doctrinal as it is possible to get." He cited as an example his contracts course (taught by a titan of contract law, Samuel Williston), in which he learned nothing about how the business world operated. Similarly, his course on mortgages "never mentioned the idea of a mortgage moratorium, which was going on all over the United States and was moving toward the Supreme Court as a major constitutional issue."[42] As the historian Laura Kalman explains, despite Roscoe Pound's reformist rhetoric, in practice he followed Langdell's philosophy of legal education and favored courses that could be taught via the case method. While he did teach a course in jurisprudence aimed at cultivating a broader view of the law, it was aimed at graduate students from outside the law school.[43]

Harvard proved a tough nut to crack. Elsewhere, as the historian Robert Gordon notes, a small number of law schools did attempt some pedagogical innovation, trying to create a more interdisciplinary curriculum that would put legal doctrine into conversation with emerging social sciences and also prepare students for civil service positions: "Ernst Freund . . . was a pioneer advocate of such a policy-enriched law school curriculum [at the University of Chicago Law School]. Brandeis . . . taught a progressive policy course on law at M.I.T. in the early 1890s. Woodrow Wilson tried for years to start a law school at Princeton that would include a public and administrative law component."[44] More ambitious efforts to promote a policy-oriented, social-scientific approach to legal scholarship and teaching were initiated at Yale, Johns Hopkins, and Columbia during this early period, and the fate of those efforts illustrate the obstacles to the reform project.

Columbia Law School, for example, was a leader in integrating sociology and law by the 1920s. It had established a legislative drafting service in 1911 (which is still in operation), and Professor Herman Oliphant made use of its services in the 1920s, when he was working with labor leaders to revise the law of industrial disputes.[45] This is the kind of engagement with public policy that reformers hoped to see at law schools, and Columbia during this decade looked like a promising alternative to the Harvard model. A group of faculty influenced by legal realism led an effort to reorganize the curriculum to incorporate more social and policy science, resulting in what the historian John Henry Schlegel calls "The Great Curricular Debate"—the "most searching review of the law school curriculum ever undertaken."[46] The debate resulted in a proposal to completely reform the curriculum in 1928, organizing it around "functional" topics like industrial relations, family relations, and business associations and integrating relevant sociological and economic literature into their study.[47] But the plan never won support from a significant number of faculty members or the president of the university, and it was never implemented.[48] Schlegel suggests that the university president was primarily interested in preserving "the income that Columbia derived from its horde of law students," but he also builds a case that the proposal's interdisciplinary approach to law came up against the well-established field definition and professional identity of law professors: faculty members were worried that such radical reforms would (in the words of the historian Brainerd Currie) "impair the professional training afforded by the school and turn Columbia into a mere research institute for the 'scientific' study of law as an aspect of social organization."[49] Although Columbia Law School did hire several social scientists in the 1930s, students seeking a law degree were restricted in their ability to take the nonlegal courses offered by those faculty members.[50]

A similar fate awaited the Institute for the Study of Law at Johns Hopkins. Founded in 1928, the institute was an innovative attempt to create a graduate school of jurisprudence aimed not at producing lawyers (Johns Hopkins had no law school) but to further empirical research on the legal system. It aimed to be the "research institute for the 'scientific' study of law as an aspect of social organization"—the same idea that Columbia's faculty

26 CHAPTER ONE

had rejected. Although the institute produced a surprising amount of research before it was dissolved in 1933, it wasn't able to develop a coherent intellectual justification that would persuade the Johns Hopkins faculty or funding organizations to support it, and it did not last long enough to have an impact on legal education.[51]

Yale Law School also had high ambitions for developing a curriculum based on sociological jurisprudence. By 1931 its teaching staff included an economist, a historian, a professor of psychiatry, and a social statistician. It also established a joint program with Harvard Business School and experimented with the first-year curriculum. As at Columbia, students seeking a law degree weren't allowed into many of the nonlegal courses. But according to Kalman, Yale did develop a curriculum that, by the 1940s, was permeated by the influence of sociological jurisprudence. Even at Yale, however, the faculty put up considerable resistance to changing their teaching methods and professional identity, and by the 1950s much of the traditional curriculum remained in place.[52]

Reform efforts continued during the 1940s and 1950s, but the more radical proposals continued to be defeated by the professional identity of law professors as masters of doctrine and by the social and institutional demands of mass-producing lawyers to serve the business community.[53] The most ambitious reform proposal came from Harold Lasswell and Myres McDougal, whose 1943 *Legal Education and Public Policy: Professional Training in the Public Interest* called for the deep integration of the social sciences into the study of law with the aim of preparing law students for their future role as policy experts. Lasswell offered a truly interdisciplinary approach to policy-making—but his "policy science" remained somewhat marginalized even within the social sciences and was largely ignored by law professors.[54]

To be sure, law schools continued to harbor innovative legal scholars who insisted on bringing their broader interdisciplinary approach to law into the classroom, but their isolated efforts had little impact on the overall curriculum. The experience of Willard Hurst at University of Wisconsin Law School is instructive. Hurst came to University of Wisconsin Law School in 1937, where he aimed to create a course in legislation similar to Landis's course at Harvard. His dean, Lloyd Garrison, was supportive and in fact collaborated with him in creating the course. He took as his focus the evolution of the law of industrial accidents, from its common law origins to the modern statutes and administrative regulations. That course, he recalled, deeply involved me in law teaching that amounted to teaching legal history and economically focused and institutionally focused legal history. We tried to depict the relative influence of the bar, the judges, and then the legislators and the lobbyists and then the administrators on what evolved, all very much of an institutional emphasis, but all coming back to an emphasis on the impact of these factors on the law's relation to something outside of the law.[55]

But like Frankfurter, he found that students didn't like the course because "it wasn't a law course in their point of view" (although they often reported years later that it was one of the more useful courses they had taken in law school).[56] Clearly Hurst was sensitive to student opinion, but (relying on the faculty autonomy discussed in the introduction of this book) he didn't let their views stop him from continuing to teach the course. The course did build a constituency over time, but it didn't dislodge the standard model. Neither did Hurst's legal history scholarship challenge the dominance of doctrinal analysis in law reviews.[57]

To say that radical reform efforts failed, however, does not mean the reformers had *no* impact on legal education. Law school curricula did evolve slowly over time, and during the post–World War II period the idea of law as a profession aimed at government service as much as tending to private clients had begun to find its way into legal education. While Columbia and Yale did not pioneer an entirely new model of legal education, they did continue to offer courses steeped in sociological jurisprudence. The University of Chicago famously became the home of an influential law and economics tradition. More generally, casebooks increasingly incorporated materials beyond appellate opinions.[58] Seminars became more common, and some schools experimented with legal clinics.[59] External influences reinforced these trends. Importantly, the New Deal had brought several law professors into the upper levels of civil service, and enactment of the Administrative Procedure Act in 1946 made administrative practice even more central to legal practice. Accordingly, administrative law entered the law school curricula as an elective course during the postwar period. The proliferation of international treaties after World War II also prompted greater interest in international law, which became an elective available at some law schools. By the 1960s, even Harvard had started offering more nontraditional courses.[60]

This additive approach to curriculum development, however, did not displace the core (required) curriculum or the case method of pedagogy. On the contrary, administrative and international law courses typically relied on the case method to a surprising degree, considering how ill-suited these subjects are to this pedagogical method. Thus in the 1950s and 1960s, the Ford Foundation and the Russell Sage Foundation took up the reform banner, developing funding programs that aimed to foster greater engagement between law as an academic discipline and the social sciences. In 1956, the Ford Foundation gave a grant to Harvard to create a summer law and society program. The University of Wisconsin Law School (thanks to Willard Hurst) also enjoyed support from the Ford Foundation, and it received a grant from the Russell Sage Foundation to create a center for law and society (one of four such grants).[61] These efforts did bear some fruit, and law and society took shape as an interdisciplinary specialty within the social sciences. But law and society scholarship rarely found its way into the law reviews read by legal academics. On the contrary, its social science methodologies—locating the forces shaping legal doctrine outside of the legal system—is deeply at odds with the traditional assumption of legal scholarship that law develops according to its own internal logic. Thus the law and society field did not have much impact on legal education, even at the University of Wisconsin.

Skills-based education also remained undeveloped in law schools until the 1960s. During that turbulent decade, a movement to provide legal services to poor communities led to a call for law schools to create clinics in underserved communities, where law students could learn practical skills while advancing social justice.[62] This movement also was supported by the Ford Foundation, and eventually it found a more favorable reception in law schools. In 1968, the foundation created the Council on Legal Education for Professional Responsibility, and within a year half of all law schools had clinics.[63] But once again, clinical courses were simply added as one of the many electives students might take in their second or third year. Clinical education was not (yet) required by the ABA or bar associations.[64]

In sum, the Harvard model proved remarkably resilient. It survived repeated challenges to transform legal education from a focus on doctrinal analysis to a more complex exploration of law in society, law as a tool of statecraft, and law as a means of solving social problems. That resilience is due to several forces. Some of the more obvious are:

- economic and institutional pressures to train a large number of lawyers each year, which requires large classes and leaves faculty with little time to devote to pedagogical experimentation;

- the familiar path-dependence and feedback loop in professional training that constantly reinforces professional identity and field definition—law professors like to teach the way that they were taught and do the kind of research they were taught to do;
- disciplinary gatekeeping by law reviews and law school hiring committees, ensuring that law professors and legal scholarship would continue to focus on doctrinal analysis by favoring that sort of scholarship (just as other scholarly fields also practice this sort of gatekeeping by *disfavoring* scholarship that focuses solely on doctrinal analysis, thereby reinforcing the isolation of law professors from the rest of the academy); and
- until the 1950s, the lack of sustained external funding supporting reform programs.

This was the story of legal education as of the 1980s and the point at which most of the historical scholarship on legal education stops. But as I will explain, law schools have undergone a significant transformation since 1990, including pedagogical and curricular innovations, an increasing focus on clinical education, the proliferation of interdisciplinary centers aimed at influencing public policy, and the emergence of new areas of law connected to new policy problems (such as regulating the internet and managing the global environment). Law school hiring practices, the changing financial context of higher education, and the internet have all contributed to these transformations. I will explore what this transformation means for the teaching of environmental law. But first I need to explain the evolution of environmental law itself, which was not even a recognized subfield of law until the 1970s.

Making Environmental Lawyers

The law school curriculum is not static. True, law as an academic discipline is similar to economics, in that there is a body of basic principles that applies across all subjects of analysis and doesn't change very much over the decades. Those basic legal principles concern things like how to apply precedents and interpret statutes; who may bring a cause of action; what kinds of evidence can be used in court; what sorts of remedies courts may order; and similar foundational issues. Some courses focus on these rules, but students also take many subject-area courses like criminal law, bankruptcy, family law, and the like. However, students traditionally did not (and were not encouraged to) specialize in one of these subject areas while in law school. The

30   CHAPTER ONE

goal was to understand the basic structure of the legal system by viewing it through the lens of different subject areas.

Nevertheless, law schools early on learned the value of allowing students to choose electives based on their interests and explore at least some topics in as much depth as permitted by their short (three-year) training period. The law school curriculum accordingly changes along with student and faculty interests, with the faculty developing new courses as new areas of regulation and litigation emerge—often in response to student interest. Environmental law is one of those areas. It emerged out of the environmental movement, finding its way into the law school curriculum during the 1970s through the collective efforts of entrepreneurial law professors.

History of Environmental Law

What we now call "environmental law" consists of two bodies of law, concerning natural resource management and pollution control, rooted in the common law principles of property and tort.[65] Policies concerning natural resource management were originally based on common law property principles. Put simply, under the nineteenth-century American legal system natural resources were owned either by a government or by a private party and were subject to the same legal rules governing other kinds of property. To be sure, the common law recognizes different kinds of property and different ways of holding it. During the nineteenth century, natural resources such as water and wildlife were treated by courts as "trust" property, a kind of collective ownership. State governments held these resources in trust for the use of their citizens, and the earliest conservation policies (such as limits on hunting and fishing) were aimed at carrying out this trust responsibility. Pollution control, by contrast, was rooted in tort law. Pollution was treated as a nuisance or harm imposed on a property owner, subject to the same rules governing other kinds of torts. Here, too, governments had a special responsibility, since state and (depending on state law) some local governments could declare certain uses of property to be public nuisances and therefore illegal per se. (Examples include open-air markets or street vendors who blocked streets, unsafe housing that posed a fire threat, and prostitution and gambling businesses.) Thus most nineteenth-century pollution policies simply declared an undesirable land use to be a public nuisance. Lawyers did not need to master complex statutory or administrative schemes to advise their clients, and even lawyers advising governments could rely on their understanding of the common law.[66]

The Progressive Era conservation movement, emerging in the late nineteenth century and reaching its peak in the first two decades of the twentieth, had a significant impact on policy and prompted a good deal of environmental litigation—but it did not result in the emergence of environmental law as a distinct field. This period did witness some evolution in legal doctrine as federal courts shifted away from property principles and began treating state natural resource policies as based on the *police power*, defined as the state's general power to regulate both public and private behavior to serve the general welfare. But that distinction was less significant to the practicing lawyer compared to the growing complexity of new state and federal regulations governing the exploitation of natural resources, including oil and gas. This was big business, with enough money at stake to spur the creation of legal experts. Such experts did not look like what we today call "environmental lawyers," however, since their primary aim was to help businesses gain access to natural resources.

At the same time, another kind of legal expert was beginning to appear within new and expanding government bureaucracies. Government lawyers played a critical role in laying the foundation for modern environmental law during the Progressive Era.[67] In addition to crafting and enforcing new regulatory schemes, they were embroiled in decades-long battles with the courts to legitimate government power, especially federal power, to protect natural resources under the United States Constitution. In the environmental domain, that effort resulted in judicial acceptance of a federal natural resource authority based in part on the *property power*, defined as the constitutional authority (conferred in Article IV, sec. 3 of the Constitution) to manage federal property. Additional power to regulate natural resource exploitation was found in federal control of interstate commerce (the basis of most federal regulations of water resources) and the federal government's power to implement treaties. Efforts to extend federal power to regulate pollution had little success, and pollution law remained largely a matter of state law until the 1970s. But the campaign to conserve water, wildlife, forests, and mineral resources on public lands required federal and state governments to maintain a cadre of lawyers with special expertise in the emerging legal field of natural resource law.

Consider, for example, Robert White Williams, the nation's foremost authority on wildlife law during the first half of the twentieth century. Williams graduated from Northern Indiana Law School in 1898. He worked in a private law firm until 1902, when (probably motivated by his keen interest in ornithology) he entered government service as an assistant in game law (laws regulating hunting and fishing) for the Bureau of Biological Survey. In 1907, he moved to the US Department of Agriculture, joining the staff of the USDA's Solicitor's office and remaining there for 22 years, being promoted to Solicitor in 1920. This move brought Williams into the legal discussions of conservation policy driven by the United States Forest Service, which had been transferred to USDA jurisdiction in 1905. The agency under Gifford Pinchot (the first head of the Forest Service) and his successors was the most important generator of conservation policy in the federal government during the Progressive Era. In his capacity as an expert on game law, Williams weighed in frequently on wildlife management issues raised by Forest Service policy. Perhaps most important, he was a major voice in the long and contentious debate over whether state or federal laws governed hunting in federal forests. He testified to Congress on this issue and authored legal opinions that circulated widely among federal agencies concerned with wildlife, and he influenced litigation strategy when the issue came to the Supreme Court in the 1920s.[68] In 1929, Williams returned to the Biological Survey (renamed in 1940 to the US Fish and Wildlife Service) as supervisor of wildlife refuges in Southeastern states. He held various positions in this agency and was named Chief Counsel for the agency shortly before his death in 1940. The official obituary issued by the Fish and Wildlife Service called "Judge" Williams "a noted conservationist." But it did not describe him as an environmental lawyer or characterize his specialty as environmental law.[69] Why not?

One reason, of course, is that the term "environmentalist" wasn't coined until later. But it is not just that the term itself wasn't in use; the concept of "the environment" itself was not widely available during this period. I don't wish to overstate this point. The *ecosystem concept* was certainly in use during Williams's day, and we do find the more progressive conservation policymakers and legal experts grounding their arguments in a systemic understanding of natural resources.[70] But the policy community of practice typically did not frame its object as "the environment" as opposed to "wildlife," "forests," or "water resources." In Williams's day—at least if the early conservationist Aldo Leopold is to be believed—one could formulate goals for wildlife policy without giving any thought to what forest or water policy should aim for. Leopold's criticism of that view began to have broad public impact after the publication of *A Sand County Almanac* in 1949. Today, the environmental policy community better understands the deep interconnections among natural systems; one could hardly formulate wildlife policy without starting from a broad vision of what we want for (and from) the natural environment as a whole. Williams's expertise, in contrast, was more narrow. He was consulted on matters of wildlife, but we do not find him involved in debates about federal management of water resources, management of the public range, or other conservation issues. He did not claim expertise in that broad, complex set of natural systems we now call "the environment."

But this is not the only reason that we can't characterize Williams as an environmental lawyer. An equally important reason has to do with Williams's relationship to the state. Williams was, through and through, a civil servant. His boss, Ira Gabrielson (director of the Fish and Wildlife Service) said of Williams that "his life was patterned on the highest ideals of public service."[71] He served seven presidents—from Roosevelt to Roosevelt, five Republicans and two Democrats. That professional identification as a public servant is actually at odds with the professional identification of many modern environmental lawyers. As Paul Sabin has argued, environmental law took shape in the 1960s as a movement *against* the state.[72]

Using the legal system to influence government action was not an invention of the 1960s, of course. There were many long, complex, and expensive lawsuits between and among state governments over air and water pollution during the Progressive Era, and conservation activists began targeting administrative agencies to prevent the construction of hydropower dams in the 1940s and 1950s.[73] Taking advantage of the new federal Administrative Procedure Act and other statutes allowing more systematic public input into federal policy, conservation activists during this midcentury period used litigation to elaborate and test agencies' environmental decision-making processes.[74] But the environmental movement of the 1960s dramatically increased this sort of environmental activism, leading to the emergence of environmental law as a coherent field and of the environmental lawyer as a professional identity located outside the administrative state.

Two key developments distinguish this new legal field from the older natural resources specialty exemplified by R. W. Williams. The first, of course, was the conceptualization of the environment as a subject of policy. This conception is rooted in the science of ecology and the understanding of nature as a complex system vulnerable to perturbation by human action—ideas popularized by Aldo Leopold and Rachel Carson (author of *Silent Spring*), among others. According to Richard Lazarus, the phrase "environmental law" was coined at the Airlie House Conference on Law and

34   CHAPTER ONE

the Environment in 1969. The conference was organized by a group of law professors including Sheldon Plager (University of Illinois College of Law), George Lefcoe (Yale Law School), and Joseph Sax (University of Michigan Law School), along with the leading practitioners Malcolm Baldwin, William Van Ness Jr., and Wallace Bowman. Attendees included men (and two women) who would become the leading scholars in the field, including the organizers, Dan Tarlock (Indiana University School of Law), Nicholas Robinson (Pace Law School), and David Currie (University of Chicago Law School), as well as several litigators and policy advocates interested in developing a new field focused on protecting the natural environment.[75] This conference helped to crystalize for the legal community the new, broader understanding of the goal of natural resource policy as aimed not at "conserving resources" but at preventing "environmental decay."[76]

That understanding was reflected in one of the main outcomes of the conference: the Environmental Law Institute (ELI). Beginning in 1971, the ELI published the first environmental law reporter, a serial set that collected appellate decisions and administrative materials related to what was now identified as "environmental law." The first issue of the reporter provides a useful view of the contours of the emerging field. It included appellate decisions in a number of cases brought to preserve scenic landscapes such as *Citizens to Preserve Overton Park v. Volpe* and *Sierra Club v. Hickel*; articles discussing the new National Environmental Policy Act (NEPA); an announcement of a new federal permitting program regulating water discharges; appellate decisions in interstate pollution cases; discussion of new Internal Revenue Service guidelines for public interest law firms; an announcement that the reporter would be publishing environmental impact statements (EISs) required by NEPA; and even an appellate decision on determination of federal water rights, heretofore consider a highly specialized area of practice.[77] This list illustrates the broad dimensions of the emerging field, covering pollution control and natural resource policies as they relate to conservation, along with relevant developments in administrative and even tax law. In addition to the reporter, the ELI served (and still serves) as a center for legal research, policy innovation, and professional development for environmental lawyers.

But the ELI would have had few cases to report if not for two other key developments during this period. First, environmental laws were evolving. A spate of federal statutes increasing protection for natural lands appeared in the 1960s: the Wilderness Act (1964), the Land and Water Conservation

Fund Act (1964), the Highway Beautification Act (1965), the Wild and Scenic Rivers Act (1968), the National Trails Act (1968), and legislation creating Redwood National Park and Cascades National Park (1968). These statutes built on the federal conservation policies of earlier decades. But starting in the mid-1960s, the federal government finally took up pollution control in a series of increasingly aggressive policies: the Clean Air Act (1963), the Motor Vehicle Pollution Control Act (1965), the Water Quality Act (1965), the Clean Water Restoration Act (1966), the Air Quality Act (1967), the National Environmental Policy Act (1970), the second Clean Air Act (1970), the Resource Recovery Act (1970), the Clean Water Act (1972), the Environmental Pesticide Control Act (1972), the Resources Conservation and Recovery Act (1976), and the Toxic Substances Control Act (1976). In addition, the federal government updated and expanded its general land and wildlife management regime with the Wild and Free-Roaming Horses Act (1971), the Marine Mammal Protection Act (1972), the Marine Protection, Research, and Sanctuaries Act (1972), the Coastal Zone Management Act (1972), the Endangered Species Act (1973), the Eastern Wilderness Act (1974), the Energy Policy and Conservation Act (1975), the Federal Land Policy and Management Act (1976), the National Forest Management Act (1976), and the Fishery Conservation and Management Act (1976).

These laws would require an army of lawyers with special expertise to implement them, guaranteeing the growth of this sector of the American bar. A second development further shaped the nature of that sector: the founding (between 1967 and 1971) of a set of environmental public interest law firms aimed at influencing government agencies through litigation and lobbying. Like the early legal clinics, these organizations were funded in large part by the Ford Foundation,[78] and they included major players in environmental policy: the Environmental Defense Fund, the Center for Law and Social Policy, the Natural Resources Defense Council (NRDC), and the Sierra Club Legal Defense Fund.[79] Fueled by skepticism toward the New Deal administrative state, these law firms provided the emerging group of environmental lawyers an institutional base outside the state and served not private business interests but the public interest (as defined by environmental advocacy groups). Included in this emerging community of practice were law professors, who provided a body of legal scholarship with a pronounced reformist orientation. For example, eschewing mere doctrinal analysis, Joseph Sax, at University of Michigan Law School, provided environmental advocates with a primer on litigation strategies in his influential

36 CHAPTER ONE

Defending the Environment: A Strategy for Citizen Action.[80] He also wrote an influential article on public trust doctrine, focused on the strategic value of the doctrine for serving the goals of the environmental movement.[81] Legal scholarship in the field was by and for this sort of environmental advocacy. Indeed, even the scholarship that has developed in reaction to the movement (such as so-called free market environmentalism) accepts the premise that the job of an environmental lawyer is to pursue legal reform in order to protect the environment from degradation.

To be sure, now that the field is established, practitioners may identify themselves as environmental law experts but focus on defending industry, just as traditional business lawyers did. But environmental law began as a field defined by the problem of environmental degradation and by a belief that the solution required mobilizing citizens outside the state to exert pressure on agencies, counterbalancing the influence of well-heeled corporate interests. Environmental lawyers were originally part of the new breed of cause lawyers whose professional identities were rooted in furthering a social cause rather than simply providing professional services to clients. They might move in and out of the state, but in contrast to someone like R. W. Williams, their service to the state is conditional. As professional crises at the Environmental Protection Agency during the administrations of Ronald Reagan and Donald Trump illustrate, many environmental lawyers have a difficult time serving any administration whose policies don't further their cause.[82]

A good example of this generation of environmental lawyers is Alan Miller, who would become a leading expert on climate finance and policy. Like R. W. Williams, Miller has devoted his career to environmental policy—but as an environmental advocate rather than solely as a civil servant. He has worked from within public interest law firms, academic appointments, and nongovernmental organizations, as well as some governmental positions. Graduating from Cornell University in 1971 with a degree in government, he attended University of Michigan Law School. There he encountered Joseph Sax, who had a significant impact on his career. Although Sax taught only one course on environmental law at Michigan, Miller also undertook independent study with him (writing about the Michigan Environmental Protection Act, a policy Sax advocated for). In addition, Sax encouraged him to do a semester in Washington, DC, with the Center for Law and Social Policy (one of the public interest law firms funded by the Ford Foundation), where he worked on issues of international environmental law. Miller also received funding from the Ford Foundation to pursue a joint masters degree in public policy along with his JD (an initiative promoted by Sax).

At Sax's urging, Miller went on to do an internship with ELI, which offered him his first job after law school. His work for ELI focused on energy issues, including solar energy. A Fulbright scholarship took him to Australia in 1977 to investigate their solar energy policies. With this international experience on his résumé, he went on to work at the NRDC from 1978 to 1984, working on the problem of stratospheric ozone depletion. He was then hired by the World Resources Institute to work on the emerging climate problem, from which position he participated in some of the early international negotiations on climate change. In 1986, he took a teaching position at American University, beginning a teaching career that took him to Widener University Delaware Law School and then, in 1990, to the University of Maryland School of Law. He then founded the Center for Global Change, directing it for seven years. Like many climate policy professionals, he kept one foot in the academy, teaching a term as a visiting professor at Duke University School of Law and summer courses at Vermont Law School, as well as contributing to a major casebook on environmental law. But he has spent much of his career in governmental and nongovernmental organizations such as the Global Environment Facility and the World Bank Group as an expert on climate policy.[83] Throughout this varied career, Miller forged a professional identity as an environmental policy expert and advocate—not simply representing clients or governments but moving in and out of different (mostly nonprofit public) institutions, using his legal, scholarly, and teaching skills to promote policies he believed were in the public interest.

Miller may be unusually successful, but this model of environmental law practice—moving among public interest law firms, academia, governmental and nongovernmental organizations while promoting policy innovation using one's legal and policy expertise—is what many aspiring environmental law students hope to achieve. And as Miller's story illustrates, environmental law professors are often following this career track themselves in addition to helping students find their way onto it. But at what point in this story did law schools start guiding students toward this sort of career? When and how did environmental law so conceived become part of the law school curriculum?

If law schools merely responded to policy developments, one would expect that environmental law would have entered the curriculum only after all of those federal statutes were enacted to provide a comprehensive regulatory system for students to master and help clients to navigate—after 1972 or 1973, perhaps. But on the contrary, by 1972 the legal scholar Frances Irwin reported that there were already 120 courses in environmental law being offered in American law schools and 122 faculty members teaching them.[84] The first environmental law casebooks appeared in the 1960s: Daniel Mandelker's 1963 *Managing Our Urban Environment* and Bill Shaw's 1965 *Environmental Law: People, Pollution, and Land Use*. This timing offers an instructive precedent, since climate law also emerged in advance of any federal regulatory regime. Where did these environmental law courses come from? And what did they look like?

Development of Environmental Law Education
A student entering law school in the 1950s and eager to follow in R. W. Williams's footsteps would have taken a course titled "Natural Resources Law." This was a relatively new field; the first natural resources casebook, *Cases and Materials on the Law of Natural Resources*, was published by Clyde Martz in 1951.[85] That student might also have taken a new course in administrative law, which became a standard offering only after enactment of the federal Administrative Procedure Act in 1946.[86] These courses would have provided the foundation for a career either advising businesses involved in natural resource extraction or working in a government agency tasked with regulating them. There was no third option—or at least none that law schools were able to prepare students for.

By the 1970s, the landscape of environmental legal education looked entirely different. Frances Irwin's 1972 survey of new environmental law courses found that Harvard Law School, Indiana University School of Law, University of Michigan Law School, and Stanford Law School were the early adopters, leading a wave of innovation that spread rapidly to other schools. Also among these early adopters were Lewis & Clark Law School,[87] which founded the *Environmental Law Review* in 1970, and UC Berkeley Law School, which established the *Ecology Law Quarterly* in 1971.[88] Arnold Reitze started an influential environmental law program at George Washington University Law School in 1970, which was notable for offering the nation's only LLM[89] in Environmental Law. That program helped to train Pat Parenteau, who went on to direct Vermont Law School's famed environmental law program; Michael Blumm, who led the development of the Lewis & Clark Law School program; and other prominent environmental law scholars such as J. B. Ruhl, Kim Diana Connolly, and Sandra Zellmer.[90]

The earliest environmental law courses are notable for the extent to which they departed from the standard model of legal education. They used Frankfurter-style, in-depth case studies, explored broad policy issues, and experimented with different kinds of clinics and interdisciplinary content. The University of Southern California, for example, created a law center that focused on education and research on the institutional framework for managing marine resources, offering services to local governments grappling with coastal management and providing legal resources to local attorneys. The law schools at UCLA and Colorado offered environmental internships (funded, once again, by the ubiquitous Ford Foundation).[91] George Washington University Law School offered short, intensive courses such as "Water Pollution: the Potomac, A Case in Point." At University of Denver College of Law, "The first-year students take an introductory course called Environment and Resources Law which explores both the legal and economic dimensions of the conflicting demands for resources and the quality of the environment. The course defines and evaluates probable effects of present policies and alternatives from the points of view of the individual, the enterprise, and the public."[92] The University of Denver's approach is a striking innovation, since the first-year curriculum is traditionally treated as sacrosanct; new courses are typically added to the second- and third-year electives.

As Irwin noted, this creativity was probably driven by the fact that there was as yet no consensus on what exactly environmental law was:

Environmental law considers the role of law in man's relationship to these surrounding systems of air, land, water, energy and life. Just as environmental science looks to various disciplines and fields for knowledge and techniques, environmental law draws on many legal specialties including administrative law, civil procedure, constitutional law, property, torts, and urban government as well as perhaps its most direct predecessors—land use planning, natural resources, and law and technology.[93]

The subject matter was so broad that it escaped the confines of a standard survey course, leading professors to experiment with different approaches. Many of them designed courses that focused on just one environmental system (air pollution, water resources management, controlling toxins, and so on). Others offered a deep dive into a single topic. For example, one well-known interdisciplinary, problem-based seminar was the collaboration between Columbia's law and engineering schools, the Legal Aspects of Noise Pollution. Taught by Cyril Harris (engineering school) and Alfred Rosenthal (law school), the course enrolled engineers and law students and focused on team-based projects. Examples of projects include the study of a nearby noise source, analysis of proposed legislation, and a mock trial of a noise case.[94] This course was still being taught in the 1980s—but by that time noise pollution was generally being treated as an occupational health issue rather than an environmental problem.

The boundaries of the field were still very much in flux during the 1970s. Joseph Sax in 1971 declared: "In the most important sense, there is no body of environmental law." Environmental problems, he thought, called for approaches other than simply applying legal rules to accepted facts; the environmental lawyer had to become a "force" for new knowledge.[95] And he might have added one more observation that they also had to become a force for new legal rules: in the 1960s, the lack of either a coherent body of case law or a well-defined body of statutes meant that those seeking to teach environmental law had to think broadly and creatively about how to prepare lawyers to help solve environmental problems.

The early environmental law casebooks illustrate the challenge of defining this emerging field. At least 17 casebooks and similar collections developed for teaching environmental law were in use before 1980.[96] Early efforts included James Krier's 1971 *Environmental Law and Policy: Readings, Materials, and Notes on Air Pollution and Related Problems* and Oscar Gray's 1970 *Cases and Materials on Environmental Law*. These were joined in 1974 by *Environmental Law and Policy: Cases and Materials* by Eva Hanks, Dan Tarlock and John Hanks and *Environmental Law* by Arnold Reitze. Shortly thereafter, David Currie offered a casebook on pollution law (1975), Richard Stewart and James Krier published their *Cases and Material on Environmental Law* (1975), and then Daniel Mandelker (1976) and William Rodgers (1977) entered the fray.

Gray's 1970 book is an early attempt to define the field. It offers chapters on protection of natural resources; standing to sue and federal preemption of state law; and a collection of "control programs," including air and water pollution control but also historic preservation laws, noise regulation, aesthetics regulation, special problems related to electric and gas utilities, and weather control. Another chapter discusses four federal agencies: the Army Corps of Engineers, the Federal Power Commission, the Department of Transportation, and the Department of Housing and Urban Development (but not the EPA, which was founded in December 1970). It also includes chapters discussing urban planning and grounds for public actions (suing on behalf of public values). From today's perspective, this is an odd assortment of topics. It divides attention, somewhat awkwardly, among federal, state, and local laws (land use planning is mostly undertaken by local governments in the United States) and shifts confusingly between statutory and common law. But it's actually a fairly sensible set of topics given the state of law in 1970, reflecting the issues that an attorney in general practice in a typical community might face. Similarly, Hanks, Tarlock, and Hanks's well-known 1974 casebook (*Environmental Law and Policy*) covered many of the above topics in addition to population control and the proposed federal land use act (which was never enacted).

Over the course of the 1970s, as described above, the federal government enacted a comprehensive set of environmental statutes, and litigation over the meaning and application of these statutes increased dramatically. This litigation fueled the development of the environmental law curriculum, which quickly gained definition and clearer (although still very broad) boundaries. For example, the persistent split between environmental law and natural resources law emerged: environmental law as taught in law schools focused on pollution control, more specifically on the new federal pollution regulation regime. Natural resources law broadened its traditional focus on resource extraction to cover new preservation policies.[97] Notably, the energy system, which was an important topic in the field early in the 1970s, had started to disappear from environmental law scholarship and teaching by the 1980s.[98] Also notably absent from the emerging environmental law curriculum was any attention to food and agriculture.

We can see these developments in the first edition of what would become one of the dominant casebooks in the field in the late 1980s: *Environmental Protection: Law and Policy*, by Fred Anderson, Daniel Mandelker, and Dan Tarlock. First published in 1984, the book begins with an introductory chapter on the origins, intellectual foundations, and legal ramifications of environmentalism, in which the authors highlight the science of ecology and welfare economics. They then devote a chapter to administrative law because, "fundamentally, environmental law is a law of judicial review of agency action."[99] This view reflects the fact that federal and state statutes implemented by agencies had by this time almost entirely supplanted common law causes of action related to environmental harms. Common law causes of action would largely disappear from environmental law casebooks

42   CHAPTER ONE

until they began to reemerge in the climate law era. Anderson and colleagues go on to cover air pollution, water pollution, and toxic and hazardous substances—the three topics they describe as "the heart of regulatory environmental law."[100] The final chapters cover the few still-relevant common law doctrines, the National Environmental Policy Act, and environmental values in land use.[101] As they explain, this organization allowed professors some flexibility to focus on either pollution control or resource management. But many topics are treated only in passing, like noise pollution, nuclear energy, strip-mining, and even the Endangered Species Act.[102]

Other casebooks took different approaches to organizing the field. Roger Findley and Dan Farber, for example, published a casebook in 1981 that included a chapter on national energy policy and another on intergovernmental relations. The chapter on energy would disappear from later editions, but intergovernmental relations would become more prominent as climate change (a multi-scalar problem) emerged as a major issue.[103] Thomas Schoenbaum's *Environmental Policy Law* (the first edition published in 1982) offered similar coverage, although it found room for strip-mining and noise pollution. But virtually all casebooks published after 1980 acknowledge the centrality of the federal air pollution and water pollution statutes, which impose complex regulatory requirements on an enormous swath of private enterprises; NEPA, which comes into play whenever the federal government issues a permit; and the fact that environmental law is mostly about judicial review of administrative agency decisions. Indeed, John Bonine and Thomas McGarity's 1984 *The Law of Environmental Protection* focuses mostly on judicial and agency interpretation of NEPA, the Clean Air Act (CAA), and the Clean Water Act plus some of the hazardous waste statutes—although it also devotes a good deal of attention to practical questions related to enforcement.[104]

As the boundaries of the environmental law curriculum took shape, the teaching of environmental law also shifted away from the earlier, innovative pedagogical approaches. With surprising speed, the standard environmental law course became a statute-based survey course, taught with the traditional case method. As Joseph Mintz noted in his review of environmental law courses in 1983, the field by then had a "settled core" of statutes, regulations, and judicial opinions interpreting them.[105] Relegated to the "penumbra" of the field were land use planning, energy law, natural resources law, the law of public land management, international law, taxation, occupational health and safety, property, remedies, torts, constitutional law, criminal law, civil procedure, and evidence. But many of those topics were also covered by other courses. Thus most law schools offered only one elective course in environmental law covering the major pollution statutes and sometimes the Endangered Species Act. Natural resource law remained on the books, covering its traditional territory with some additional attention to the new preservation statutes. Occasionally students were able to take an advanced seminar.

For many environmental law professors, this emerging field definition was more of a problem than a solution to the challenges of teaching the subject. As Mintz complained: "One of the great challenges of legal education in the environmental field is to convey the essence of this complex, fast-changing, open-textured, controversial, and scientifically sophisticated body of law and policy, in an intellectual framework which makes clear both its close relationship to cognate bodies of law and its ties to questions of economic policy."[106] William Funk's 1984 review of the four new environmental law casebooks (Anderson et al.; Findley and Farber; Schoenbaum; and Bonine and McGarity) suggested that they still demonstrated uncertainty about "what an environmental law course should be about" as well as "how best to achieve an agreed upon pedagogical end."[107]

> Is environmental law like, say, labor law, federal income tax, or securities law . . . an introductory course to be centered on one or two basic statutes? Or is it like oil and gas law or patent, copyright, and trademark law, to be offered as an upper level course primarily for students who actually expect to practice in the area and therefore aimed at teaching the substantive law? Should it be styled like "Law and Etc." courses—interdisciplinary and focused at least as much on the "Etc." as on the law? Or is environmental law more like energy law, agricultural law, or consumer law—grab-bags of different statutes (not to mention the common law) with no necessary or actual unifying themes or relationships—to be offered in a simple survey or perspectives course, lightly touching on each of the different areas, leaving to upper level courses the theory or practice as well as any real substantive law?[108]

Funk noted in particular the problem of hazardous waste regulation, where there was a "lack of case law on the subject" and also "a number of unanswered questions [that] will be faced rather quickly both by courts and Congress." He was unhappy with the casebook authors' responses to this still-developing policy area: "Identify the issue, ask some provocative questions, and move on."[109] But he didn't offer an alternative approach.

Indeed, professors struggled with teaching even the core material.[110] According to a 1989 survey sent to all environmental law professors by Joseph Sax, they were overwhelmed by the volume and complexity of the field, which meant their courses became "an encounter with statutes of numbing complexity and detail." The field itself was so broad that it was impossible to cover every important topic in one or two courses. They were also discouraged by how the growth of the field did not seem to be producing solutions to environmental problems. Sax cites Arnold Reitze at George Washington University Law School as saying: "We have been spending huge sums on marginally effective programs of pollution control . . . and we are reaching the limits of our capacity to do even that. Meanwhile, the fundamentals [of population growth and consumption] are unattended."[111] Sax and Mintz voiced an emerging consensus in the 1980s that environmental law required more courses and a different pedagogical approach.[112] It wasn't suited for the case method. On the contrary, the subject seemed to call for a more applied, problem-based approach that would teach important skills such as negotiating with stakeholders or working with environmental scientists. It required more attention to legal process and interdisciplinary competence. In short, the critique of what had become traditional environmental law echoed the long-standing critique of legal education in general: the Harvard model wasn't working.

At this point, let me enter a caveat to this bleak picture: I took my first course in environmental law at the University of California, Berkeley, School of Law[113] during the 1989–1990 academic year. The course, taught by John Dwyer, was exactly the kind of statute-based survey course criticized by Sax, Mintz, and most of the professors answering Sax's survey. I loved the course. Statute-based courses are not inherently boring or overwhelming; on the contrary, law students often enjoy learning how to puzzle through complex regulations. Much of the fun in the course lies in discovering the underlying logic that makes sense of the technical details of the regulatory scheme. And professors tended to focus on the Clean Air Act and Clean Water Act precisely because these complex regimes raised many interesting policy and legal questions, ranging from statutory interpretation to the design of regulatory instruments to the constitutional limits of federal environmental power. For example, Lisa Heinzerling (who would go on to teach environmental law at Georgetown University Law Center) took the survey course in environmental law from the prominent legal scholar Richard Stewart, a visiting faculty member at the University of Chicago, in the mid-1980s. She remembers learning a great deal about the theory of cap-and-trade, which would soon be adopted to regulate sulfur dioxide under the Clean Air Act.[114] Patrick Tolan studied environmental law at Michigan in 1989 under Jim Krier, using the Krier and Stewart casebook, and he also remembers a great deal of attention to the Clean Air Act that included extensive discussion of cap-and-trade specifically with reference to climate change (making this one of the earliest law school courses to treat climate change).[115] Cap-and-trade was at the time a cutting-edge policy innovation, and studying it in the context of an actual statute like the Clean Air Act may be more engaging than the more abstract and theoretical treatment it might get in a typical public policy or economics course.

However, during my time at Berkeley I also had the opportunity to take an interdisciplinary seminar on environmental enforcement, taught by Dwyer and Robert Kagan. Kagan has a JD (from Columbia) and a PhD (in sociology from Yale), and he holds appointments in both the political science department and the law school at UC Berkeley. He brought to the course teaching methods more common in fields like political science. Indeed, I was very much aware that this was a different kind of course; as Willard Hurst's students would say, it wasn't really a *law course*. It included graduate students in Berkeley's interdisciplinary jurisprudence and social policy program, focused on the empirical scholarship on regulatory enforcement, and was the only course in law school in which I conducted a case study involving empirical research. I interviewed litigants and explored legal documents generated in a long and successful effort to stop a landfill from being located in a fragile coastal ecosystem. I never met Joseph Sax, who was on the law school faculty at the time, but this course was likely modeled on an earlier interdisciplinary seminar taught by Sax and Dwyer on water pollution.

Sax described this water pollution seminar in detail in his 1989 article on teaching environmental law, and environmental law professors later would point to it as a model of the "deep-dive seminar."[116] The seminar was a semester-long case study of the effort to control toxic metals at a single industrial facility, the Chevron refinery in Richmond, California, on San Francisco Bay. Students worked with "fiendishly technical" documents and learned the detailed history of the Natural Resources Defense Council's efforts to get the Environmental Protection Agency to regulate toxins, tracing the regulatory history up to a 1988 stipulated dismissal of a suit challenging renewal of Chevron's permit. They also met the key stakeholders, following in "turgid detail" the 12-year effort to control metals at the Chevron refinery.[117]

The goal of the seminar was to "focus on the San Francisco Bay as part of a vast watershed that includes the San Joaquin and Sacramento Rivers, California's agricultural heartland." Students learned about urban runoff, the distinctive ecology of the South Bay, and past failed and future promising approaches to regulation. "Our hope," he wrote, "is that students come away from the seminar with some pretty solid impressions of how the bureaucracy . . . works, of the role of an active and sophisticated local citizen group (Citizens for a Better Environment in San Francisco), a national group (NRDC), and an industry that has, over the years, shifted from being quite recalcitrant to wanting to be a publicly admired pacesetter."[118] Further, he and Dwyer hoped to

> leave the students with enough knowledge about one characteristic pollution control problem to let them make their own informed judgment about the efficacy of a major regulatory statute. We try to give them enough sense of the vastness and complexity of the "real" resource, the watershed, to appreciate what it means to get to the root of an environmental problem. We hope they have some sense of what Reitze means when he talks about consumption as central to environmental problems. They can go down to the waterfront and see for themselves the demands that modern agriculture, growing cities, and contemporary industry impose on San Francisco Bay.[119]

Such courses, however, were hardly standard fare in the 1980s. Indeed, even many leading law schools lacked a well-developed environmental law curriculum in the 1980s. For example, the Loyola University New Orleans law professor Robert Verchick received his JD from Harvard in 1989, where he took only one course in environmental law. Lisa Heinzerling (who graduated in 1987) also found a limited selection at the University of Chicago Law School. Both schools were relying on visiting professors to teach the standard survey course (although they were impressive visitors: Carol Rose at Harvard and Richard Stewart at Chicago). Michael Blumm, who was hired to develop Lewis & Clark's famed environmental law program in 1978, was working on that project largely by himself during the 1980s. He created an innovative externship program for environmental law students, but the school did not expand the environmental faculty until 1990.[120] Dan Farber was the primary environmental law professor at the University of Minnesota Law School during the 1980s, and Georgetown, which now has a very ambitious environmental law program, relied on Edith Brown Weiss in the 1980s until the school hired Hope Babcock in 1991.[121] This minimal staffing was apparently typical. The AALS publishes an annual directory of law professors organized by subject, and in 1980 it identified 313 professors who taught environmental law at the 170 law schools surveyed—or about 1.8 per school. By 1990, there were 328 professors at 176 schools, or (still) about 1.8 per school. And we must bear in mind that not everyone who teaches environmental law considers it their primary field or is able to teach it every year. To be sure, during the 1990s the number of environmental law professors started to rise, to 2.2 per school in 1995 and 2.6 per school in 2000. As I discuss in chapter 2, that rise was part of a more general expansion of law school faculties that did not begin until the 1990s. Until that point, it was not unusual for a law school to have only one regular environmental law professor, maybe joined by one other who sometimes taught natural resource or land use law.

Given the minimal faculty resources devoted to the subject in the 1980s, it is understandable that the typical environmental law survey course was a large lecture or case-dialogue course focused on doctrine. The dominant approach was to teach the major statutes, or at least some of them, along with the major cases interpreting them. So perhaps it isn't surprising that, after three years studying in one of the leading environmental law programs in the country, I emerged in 1991 almost completely unaware of the problem that was about to transform the nature of environmental governance: climate change.

That curricular gap would be filled over the coming decades, as we will see. But two features of the environmental law field as it had evolved by 1990 are important to understanding how climate change would enter into the curriculum. First, environmental law as it appeared in the law school curriculum focused on federal statutes and the issue of pollution control. While most law schools did teach courses on natural resource management, that topic usually was not well integrated into the standard environmental survey (introductory) course. Energy was largely missing from the field by this point as well. These features meant that, when law professors considered how to incorporate climate change into their existing courses, they were looking first for a federal pollution control statute and were less focused on how climate change would impact natural resources. Neither were they conceptualizing their courses as focused on transitioning the energy system away from fossil fuels.

The second point is necessarily more speculative, but I think it's worth noting: almost everyone in this story so far is a white middle- or upper-class American male. This was not at all unusual; the world of American environmental policy and law was and still is overwhelmingly dominated by privileged white men. The rank and file of the environmental movement, in contrast, relied very heavily on white women, often working-class women. People of color were organizing around environmental issues as well in the 1980s, but racial and class divisions in American society led to the creation of a separate movement: the environmental justice movement, focused on the environmental problems of people of color. That movement has very gradually made its way into the law school curriculum (a story that deserves its own book). For us, the lack of diversity among the law school professoriate may help to explain the technocratic, federal policy–first approach that guided the evolution of the climate curriculum during the early years. Despite the attention paid to pollution, environmental law in American law schools was not focused on how ordinary communities, particularly poor and marginalized ones, could use the legal system to protect themselves. And despite origins in the mass-based environmental movement, environmental law as taught in law school was not focused on how lawyers could be part of a social movement. It was a field dominated by people like Alan Miller— people with impeccable environmental values but also considerable social privilege, elites who could expect to find their path into the upper levels of government and policymaking smoothed by social contacts and mentors. Climate change would first enter the law school curriculum as a problem to be solved by this elite community of legal and policy practice, using the tools they were familiar with: treaties, federal statutes, and EPA regulations. But that couldn't happen, of course, until the climate emerged as a policy problem, which is the subject of chapter 2.

CHAPTER TWO

The Birth of Climate Law

We don't have to explain why climate change was absent from the law school curriculum during the 1970s. Before environmental law or the environmental law curriculum could address the climate system, the climate system had to be invented—that is, it had to be modeled, understood, and conceptualized as an object amenable to human influence. Regulation waited on science. We thus begin the story of climate law with the familiar story of the creation of climate science. But we turn quickly to a less familiar story: the development of climate policy in the United States. This complex tale highlights the variety of policy arenas that have contributed to the early development of American climate policy: international, federal, judicial, and state and local governmental actors have all had a hand in shaping the United States' response to climate change.

That variety of governmental policy arenas provides a critical context for understanding how law schools would respond to the climate problem during the 1980s and 1990s. Climate change, in all its multidimensional and multi-scalar complexity, did not fit neatly into the categories used to organize the law school curriculum. Accordingly, it would enter that curriculum first as a topic in the subfield of international environmental law and then, in a very limited way, via discussions of federal regulation of air pollution. Its broader significance for energy and land use systems may have been understood by many environmental law professors in the 1990s, but bringing that understanding into the classroom would prove to be challenging. And addressing the serious implications of climate change for vulnerable communities would be even more difficult.

51

Climate Science

Environmental law is rooted in environmental science to a degree that is somewhat unusual in the American legal system. While legal scholars have often defended the autonomy of law from other disciplines, that autonomy has never been particularly strong in the field of environmental law. From the Progressive Era onward, environmental protection policies have been based on conceptual models of nature and humans' relationship to nature derived from ecological and geological sciences. So one of the most important forces driving the development of environmental law is the rise of earth systems science: the growing understanding of global natural systems, particularly the climate system, in the second half of the twentieth century.

A systemic view of nature—that is to say, a model of nature as a set of interconnected systems—has been integral to environmental policy from its foundations in Progressive Era conservation policy.[1] The federal environmental statutes of the 1970s and their interpretations by courts take ecosystems as the basic building blocks of nature and aim to protect them from human-induced disturbance.[2] The ecosystemic policy regime of the 1970s sought to regulate human activities with the explicit awareness of the structure and function of ecosystems, with ever-increasing recognition of biodiversity as a goal of natural resource management.[3] These policies, however, did not attempt to grapple with the nested, multi-scalar aspect of natural systems. That limitation would become problematic as earth system scientists developed models of global systems and began thinking of Earth as consisting of complex systems that varied in their spatial and temporal scales. In the 1970s, scientists forwarding that conception of the environment began to enter into conversation with the policy community (or at least some parts of that community).

The story of climate science—the creation of models of the global climate system and gradual confirmation of the greenhouse effect caused by carbon dioxide and other gases—has been told by others, so I will summarize only a few key events here.[4] Beginning in the 1950s, the World Meteorological Organization (WMO) helped to create an international scientific community of practice around understanding the global climate system. By the 1970s, these scientists had made considerable progress in modeling the climate system and documenting the greenhouse effect. For example, by 1967 Syukuru Manabe and Richard Wetherald had developed a rough estimate of the impact of increasing carbon dioxide on global temperatures, and by 1975 they had produced an estimate of the effect of doubling carbon dioxide concentrations on global temperature.[5] Their work constituted a critical advance in climate science—but their estimates remained very uncertain, as they did not take into account numerous factors such as cloudiness, seasonal variation, and topographical variations on climate. Indeed, as Spencer Weart emphasized, the development of climate science during the 1970s and 1980s did more to complicate than to clarify the climate system: "The climate began to look less like a simple mechanism than a confused beast that a dozen different forces were prodding in different directions."[6] Between 1975 and 1985, increased computing power made it easier to refine general circulation models to explore these different forces, although it was not until the 1990s that scientists were able to investigate how land, oceans, sea ice, and atmosphere interact to affect the climate. The impacts of climate change also became clearer in the 1990s, when scientists began developing regional climate models and research confirmed that oceans were becoming more acidic and that sea levels were rising.[7]

In short, we must avoid projecting our current understanding of the mechanisms and impacts of climate change back into the 1970s and bear in mind that federal regulation of even well-known air pollutants had barely begun at this point. Indeed, in comparison to the decades-long fight for federal air and water pollution regulation, it is striking how quickly climate change made it onto the federal policy agenda. By the early 1970s, scientists were already conceptualizing carbon emissions as a pollutant and climate change as a potential environmental problem.[8] Using that framing, climate scientists began communicating more regularly with policymakers in the 1970s, and the first policy initiatives aimed at climate change emerged during that decade.

The Development of Climate Policy

We can piece together the early history of American climate policy by looking at (1) the international arena and federal policies related to that sphere of action; (2) state and local policymaking; and (3) climate change in the courts. American climate policy developed in these three different policy arenas, each contributing to its breadth and complexity.

The International and Federal Arenas

The United States was an early leader in supporting climate research. The Scripps Institute and Geophysical Fluid Dynamics Lab at Princeton University, supported by federal grants, focused sustained attention on the carbon cycle and on modeling the global atmospheric system.[9] Charles Keeling famously produced the earliest measures of carbon in the atmosphere, and as early as 1965 a President's Science Advisory Committee report, *Restoring the Quality of Our Environment*, mentions carbon dioxide as an "invisible pollutant." Thanks in part to this research, global warming was raised as a potential problem (but not addressed in a meaningful way) at the 1972 United Nations Earth Summit.[10] During the 1970s, the US Department of Energy and the American Academy for the Advancement of Science were pursuing climate research with the aim of developing a solid scientific consensus on the greenhouse effect. Federal policies, however, simply aimed at funding scientific investigation of the global climate system. This was the focus of the first federal statute addressing climate change, the 1978 National Climate Program Act.[11]

American environmental activists showed little interest in global warming during the 1970s. The Sierra Club, for example, considered and rejected global warming as a priority in 1977.[12] Climate scientists had little reason to reach out to the environmental advocacy community, since they were having considerable success with social movement theory's insider strategies— that is, relying on cooperative relationships with high-level policymakers to achieve their goals. Those goals at this point were still confined to funding research.

On the international level, the WMO and the International Council of Scientific Unions in the late 1970s started to organize a series of workshops and conferences to consolidate research on global warming. These began with a 1978 meeting in Vienna and the 1979 World Climate Conference in Geneva. The Geneva meeting launched the WMO's World Climate Research Program. These early conferences culminated in the 1985 Villach Conference—the first time the WMO actually called for policy solutions to global warming. By that point, American climate scientists were starting to express more concern about the issue. A 1983 study by the National Academy of Sciences investigated the potential impacts of carbon dioxide on the climate system—although it counseled against restricting fossil fuels. The EPA was similarly concerned but saw no solution to the problem.[13] Thus the only federal statutes addressing the climate problem in the 1980s were the 1987 Global Climate Protection Act[14] and the 1990 Global Change Research Act,[15] both of which were limited to coordinating and funding more research.

If you've never heard of those statutes, you're in good company. These

54 CHAPTER TWO

programs did not attract much public attention, even though they would direct a huge amount of money toward climate research, climbing from $133.9 million in 1989 to over $1.1 billion annually through the 1990s.[16] To be sure, some policymakers were beginning to focus on global warming during the 1980s. Senator Al Gore organized congressional hearings on the issue from 1981 to 1984, and both the Natural Resources Defense Council and the Environmental Defense Fund started studying global warming in the early 1980s as well. But climate policy still did not have a very visible place on the national policy agenda. In contrast, the hole in the stratospheric ozone layer and the international policy response to it—the 1987 Montreal Protocol—received a great deal of media coverage.[17]

At the international level, however, a community of policy practice was taking shape around climate change. That process was institutionalized in the formation, in 1988, of the International Panel on Climate Change. This panel held international conferences from 1988 through 1990, building a constituency for a legal framework—specifically, an international treaty—on global warming. That treaty was a central goal of the United Nations Earth Summit in Rio de Janeiro in 1992.[18] The United States signed the resulting United Nations Framework Convention on Climate Change (1992), which committed it to international negotiations to develop a response to climate change. From that point forward, climate policy has been assured of a place on the US foreign policy agenda, with American diplomats and scientists participating actively in the International Panel on Climate Change and periodic UN conferences.[19]

Many histories of climate policy start in 1992 and focus on international negotiations, which have led to a slowly growing set of international agreements and regulatory mechanisms for climate governance. This emerging international regime had legal implications for American businesses operating in other countries. But the United States did not sign the 1999 Kyoto Protocol, which set out targets for reducing greenhouse gasses, and it did not enact a federal regulatory statute directly addressing climate change. Thus it might appear that climate law didn't really exist in the United States in the 1980s and 1990s. That is a misconception, as the topic of state and local policymaking, discussed in the next section, illuminates.

States and Localities

In reality, there was a growing community of practice around domestic climate policy in the United States by 1990. A 1992 report from University of Maryland's Center for Global Change (titled *Cool Tools*) catalogued the "state and local legislative bills, laws and policy proposals having either direct or incidental effects on greenhouse gas emissions." By this time, several states, including Vermont, Minnesota, and Connecticut, already had policies in place to inventory greenhouse gas emissions. Seventeen states were assigning an explicit value to greenhouse gas emissions when evaluating energy alternatives.[20] California had directed the state energy commission to study the problem in 1988, and it delivered a report, titled "Global Climate Change: Potential Impacts and Policy Recommendations," to the governor and legislature in October 1991. Even Missouri—not usually among the most progressive states—was taking action: "In Missouri, 1989 legislation established a Commission on Global Climate Change and Ozone Depletion and charged it with assessing the state's contribution to greenhouse emissions, the impact of projected growth on emissions, and alternatives to reduce these emissions. The Commission's Report, delivered to the Governor and legislature in September 1991, contained recommendations in nine sectors including options for increasing public awareness."[21] The *Cool Tools* report identified seven categories of policies being considered and adopted by state governments: Create a state energy office; create an energy portfolio plan (mandating increases in the state's reliance on renewable energy); incorporate climate impacts into state procurement policies; regulate utilities to encourage renewable energy use; incorporate climate impacts into transportation policy; integrate climate policy into land use planning; and impose a carbon tax (being debated but not yet adopted by any state). Renewable energy portfolios have now been widely adopted. Transportation and land use planning also emerged as important areas for policy innovation, but it's important to note that states typically devolve considerable authority in these areas to local governments.

Cities were also beginning to develop climate policy, beginning with the nation's first climate action plan in Portland, Oregon, in 1993.[22] City-level climate action planning spread throughout the 1990s, supported by the International Council for Local Environmental Initiatives (ICLEI), founded in 1990 at the World Congress of Local Governments for a Sustainable Future, a meeting at the United Nations in New York. The United States ICLEI website traces its US origins to the initiative of Larry Agran, mayor of Irvine, California, which adopted a "first-of-its-kind local ordinance" restricting the use of ozone-depleting chlorofluorocarbons in 1989. Later that year, Irvine hosted a two-day conference, inviting twenty-four US and Canadian cities to explore how local governments could combat depletion of the ozone layer. This group, the North American Congress of Local Governments for a Stratospheric Protection Accord, attended the 1990 UN conference and decided to take on the issue of climate change.[23] Agran, we should note, graduated from Harvard Law School in 1969 and served as legal counsel in the Committee on Health and Welfare in the California state senate before entering municipal politics. He has been a fixture in Irvine politics from 1976 to the 2020s, serving several terms on the city council and as mayor during those years. His career illustrates the role that lawyers often play in the American policy system, acting as policy entrepreneurs encouraging innovation (in an area of law that barely existed when Agran graduated law school).

Agran was only one of many policy and legal experts involved in ICLEI's Cities for Climate Protection Campaign (CCPC), started in 1993.[24] The program aimed to help cities reduce greenhouse gas emissions by providing tools to inventory emissions and to keep track of reductions. It also began to identify a range of policies needed to manage the climate system, as Gard Lindseth's analysis of the early history of the CCPC points out. The program framed cities as both a cause of and solution to climate change: "CCPC points to the possibilities local governments have because they exercise key power over many activities which create sources and sinks of GHG emissions such as decisions governing urban form; transportation; energy use, production and distribution; waste and waste-water management, and forest protection."[25] ICLEI's broad approach to climate policy was motivated largely by a desire to emphasize the cobenefits of GHG emissions reduction (that is, benefits to policy goals other than mitigating climate change). Indeed, early local climate action consisted mostly of adding climate change as an additional reason to pursue energy efficiency and other familiar policies. As Lindseth argues: "At some stage we are no longer talking about climate change policy per se, but about integrating climate concerns in other sectors of local policy, such as traffic, economic development, urban and land-use planning, housing, tax policy, etc."[26] One might expect that this focus on how a whole range of policies affects the climate system might have led to equally broad coverage of climate policy in law schools. As I will explain later, however, that didn't happen (at least not immediately). ICLEI remained the main resource for municipal policymakers interested in addressing climate change until the Sierra Club's Cool Cities program in 2005 and the Mayors Climate Protection Agreement in 2007 (the work of a subgroup of the US Conference of Mayors).[27]

In short, during the 1990s the American policy community—supported by international organizations like ICLEI—was beginning to produce climate policy. Nevertheless, a lawyer starting practice in 2000 probably would not have needed any special expertise in climate law. A 2008 overview of the policy landscape written by Stephen Wheeler concluded that "almost half of U.S. states have produced nothing even resembling a plan for climate change, and the majority of U.S. municipalities are not members of the Cities for Climate Protection campaign and have not signed the . . . Mayors Climate Protection Agreement."[28] He noted that the plans that had been created were often detailed but either not aggressive enough or not being implemented:

> Officials we interviewed often indicated that the kinds of measures most often being implemented related to greening public vehicle fleets, improving the energy efficiency of public buildings, and establishing renewable portfolio requirements for utilities. They also frequently viewed the creation of emissions inventories and climate change plans as significant achievements in themselves. But interviewees said frankly that many other recommendations were not implemented, and frequently cited politics as a barrier to this.[29]

Thus even a lawyer working in energy law may not have encountered any climate policy per se. Still, it should have been possible for an enterprising environmental law professor to put together at least a unit, if not a full course, on climate law during the 1990s. Indeed, there would even have been a few judicial decisions to consider.

Climate Change in the Courts

Joyeeta Gupta's overview of the history of global climate governance notes that lawyers involved in the international negotiations were focused on developing international law during the 1990s and did not turn their attention to litigation strategies in earnest until 2003, after the United States announced it would not ratify the Kyoto Protocol.[30] However, by 2000 there were already a few reported cases in the United States discussing climate change.[31] These early cases demonstrate that, even without new federal legislation, existing statutes already provided a basis for addressing climate change. They also identify the major legal issues that climate lawyers would have to grapple with. They are worth reviewing here, since they give a sense of how a professor might have addressed climate change in a typical law school course in the 1990s.

The first climate case in US courts appears to be *Los Angeles v. National Highway Traffic Safety Administration (NHTSA)*, which was filed in 1986. Los Angeles, New York City, and several environmental groups, including the NRDC, sued the NHTSA for failing to prepare an environmental impact statement addressing (among other things) global warming before issuing new rules on Corporate Average Fuel Efficiency (CAFE) standards for automobiles made in 1987–1988 and 1989.[32] The legal basis for the lawsuit was the National Environmental Policy Act,[33] which requires government agencies to prepare an environmental impact statement before taking any action that would impact the natural environment. NEPA does not limit the kinds of environmental impacts that agencies must consider; it essentially directs government agencies to constantly update the environmental scientific basis of their decisions. The statute can thereby force agencies to take into account new environmental threats, but judicial interpretations of the statute have limited its usefulness in some key respects, as *Los Angeles v. NHTSA* illustrates.

The petitioners asked the United States Court of Appeals for the District of Columbia Circuit to review the NHTSA's rules, and the case was heard by Chief Judge Patricia Wald, Judge Ruth Bader Ginsburg, and Judge Douglas H. Ginsburg. The court issued its decision in 1990, dismissing the suit. One problem was standing, or the preliminary judicial determination that the party bringing the suit has a direct interest in the result and that the interest is one that can be satisfied by the sort of remedies that courts can order (usually either monetary compensation or an injunction ordering the defendant to do or not do something). Much litigation aimed at changing policy faces standing problems, since advocacy groups bringing these lawsuits often don't have a direct financial interest at stake and the impact of the remedies they want may be speculative. This lawsuit illustrates those problems.

All the judges agreed that the cities had standing to challenge the rules, because the rules made it more difficult for them to fulfill their obligations to protect air quality under the Clean Air Act. But the judges disagreed as to whether the NRDC had standing to challenge the agency's failure to consider global warming. Wald and Ruth Bader Ginsburg held that the

NRDC did have standing to raise the issue; Douglas H. Ginsburg disagreed, because the NRDC failed "to explain how the injury they allege from global warming can be traced causally to the agency's decision setting the [Model Year] 1989 CAFE standard, and how the relief they seek could redress that injury."[34] Specifically, the NRDC argued that the NHTSA, by setting the CAFE standard at 26.5 miles per gallon instead of 27.5 miles per gallon, would contribute to global warming, "causing a rise in sea level and a decrease in snow cover that would damage the shoreline, forests, and agriculture of California," and that "these local consequences of such a global warming would injure the NRDC's members who now use those features of California for recreational and economic purposes."[35] The basic problem with this argument is the speculative nature of those impacts. This issue would plague most climate lawsuits: any given agency decision typically results in only a tiny increase in greenhouse gas emissions, so it's difficult to argue that such a single decision is actually *causing* the harm.

On the substantive question, Chief Judge Wald agreed that the NHTSA had acted arbitrarily in concluding that the 1989 CAFE standard would not have a significant impact on global warming, and she would have remanded the case to the agency to revisit that issue. She was in the minority, however; the two Ginsburgs decided that the agency's decision was adequately supported.

Who has standing to challenge the government's response to climate change? How can courts determine whether the challenged policy will actually cause redressable harm? How much consideration must a government decision maker give to climate impacts in light of the complex and evolving state of the science? These questions were prominent in the four climate lawsuits decided in the 1990s. In 1989, the Foundation on Economic Trends sued the secretaries of the federal Departments of Energy, Agriculture, and the Interior for failing to consider the impacts of 42 separate policy actions on global warming. Again, the basis for the lawsuit was NEPA and also the Administrative Procedure Act,[36] which requires agencies to demonstrate that their decisions have a rational basis. The case was filed in federal district court for the District of Columbia. Judge George Revercomb issued summary judgment in 1992 dismissing the case because the plaintiffs lacked standing. This time the plaintiffs argued that mere failure to provide information (like the impact of the decision on climate change) might serve as an injury requiring legal redress. But recent precedents suggested mere failure to provide some information requested by a member of the public did not

60   CHAPTER TWO

constitute the sort of specific, palpable harm that is constitutionally required in order for a federal court to exercise judicial power.[37]

The other three lawsuits decided in the 1990s did surmount the standing issue, only to run aground because of the courts' unwillingness to second-guess a government agency on the impacts of climate change. In 1992 the Seattle Audubon Society sued the secretaries of agriculture and the Interior on the grounds that their forest management plan for certain northwestern forests was legally inadequate. One of the claims was that the Forest Service's environmental impact statement failed "to disclose adequately the impacts of timber harvest on water quality, air quality, and climate." The judge, William Dwyer, concluded (without discussion) that the EIS did discuss these ecological impacts adequately, if at a very general level, and granted the defendants summary judgment.[38] In *Association of Public Agency Customers, Inc. v. Bonneville Power Administration*, filed in the US Court of Appeals for the Ninth Circuit in 1995, several different groups challenged a complex new business plan by the Bonneville Power Administration (BPA), a federally owned hydroelectric company.[39] One of the challenges concerned BPA's environmental impact statement, which the environmental groups claimed did not discuss global warming implications from the effects of greenhouse gasses released from increased operations by industrial firms using BPA energy, or the transboundary impacts of the plan in Canada, including increased natural gas exploration that the plan (through a chain of economic events) might lead to. The court rejected these arguments, concluding that the plan did sufficiently consider these issues, pointing to sections of the plan specifically addressing CO_2 emissions and transboundary impacts.[40]

The final case, *In re Quantification of Environmental Costs Pursuant to Laws of Minn. 1993*, was based on one of the new state laws enacted to address climate change.[41] In 1991, the Minnesota legislature passed a statute requiring public utilities to pay for environmental costs as a component of the price paid for the purchase of energy.[42] In March 1994, the state's Public Utility Commission (PUC) set cost values for five pollutants, including carbon dioxide, which the court noted "is believed to contribute to global warming, which in turn adversely impacts the global environment."[43] The PUC set the environmental cost values of carbon dioxide at $.30–$3.10 per ton for four "geographic ranges": urban, metropolitan fringe, rural areas, and areas within 200 miles of Minnesota's borders. After some public debate, the PUC reconsidered and removed the costs of carbon dioxide emitted within 200 miles of the state's borders, citing concerns about the practicality of requiring utilities not located in Minnesota to apply the values, the lack of additional analytical benefit in applying the values, and "comity."[44] Several parties then appealed the PUC's decision, some wanting carbon dioxide costs eliminated altogether and others wanting the costs on emissions impacting outside Minnesota to be reinstated.

The state appellate court affirmed the PUC's decision, concluding that, even considering the scientific uncertainties surrounding climate change, the PUC (relying on the record developed by an administrative law judge [ALJ]) had adequate grounds for setting the value of carbon dioxide. The court's opinion illustrates the level of scientific and economic expertise that lawyers and judges would need to deal with climate law:

> The ALJ conducted a careful review of (1) Intergovernmental Panel on Climate Change (IPCC) research and the peer review process; (2) research on $CO[_2]$ values by other scientific review panels; (3) the uncertainties in the scientific reports and how the uncertainties are acknowledged in the scientific community; (4) Dr. Ciborowski's testimony and the basis for his testimony; (5) damage estimates; (6) discount rates; (7); the Minnesota Pollution Control Agency's and the Attorney General's recommended values; and (8) several parties' recommendations that a zero value be used. The ALJ determined that some testimony and suggestions were supported by the evidence and others were not, and explained the bases for his determinations.[45]

The court was satisfied that the PUC had adequately considered the relevant issues in making its decision.

There was one more relevant case filed in 1999 but not decided until 2016: *Harris County Flood Control District v. Kerr.*[46] This case did not directly address climate change; it concerned whether government agencies that engage in flood control efforts are liable to homeowners who suffer flood damage under the Takings Clause of the Fifth Amendment. Climate change was mentioned in the opinion because one of the amicus briefs "ask[s] whether hurricanes allegedly caused by global warming would be a compensable taking under the homeowners' reasoning."[47] After all: "Experts can be hired who will testify that burning fossil fuels raises sea levels and makes storms more intense. Yet governments issue permits allowing exploration and production of fossil fuels, and construction and operation of the power plants that burn them."[48] By 2016, of course, that possibility had become very real.

62   CHAPTER TWO

These cases illustrate the difficulty not only that courts were having with the climate issue but also that law professors might face in teaching this issue in a traditional environmental law class. Given the focus of legal education on mastering doctrine as developed in appellate decisions, any problem that is not amenable to judicial resolution is hard to fit into a law school classroom. Climate change promised to affect everyone on the planet—but that ubiquity was part of the problem. Whose interests should the court be considering? And exactly when and how would those interests be affected? What actions were needed to prevent those harms in an equitable and effective way? Courts are not well equipped to handle problems involving a lot of different interests and mired in scientific uncertainty. And if courts can't handle these problems, the traditional law school classroom might have trouble addressing them as well.

However, climate change might be a useful teaching tool for precisely this reason: it allows professors and students to explore the limits of judicial power and doctrines like standing and to do so in the context of a particularly interesting and important issue. Certainly, just because climate change didn't seem to present a specific, palpable, identified harm to someone's rights doesn't mean it wasn't legally relevant. As this series of cases demonstrates, even in the early 1990s consideration of climate change was already becoming routine in environmental impact statements. At the very least, an environmental law professor in the 1990s could have identified two significant legal issues posed by climate change under the domestic environmental statutes: Who has standing to challenge agency decisions that might affect climate change? and How much consideration must agencies give to the risk of climate change given the scientific uncertainties?

Nevertheless, it's fair to say that there still wasn't very much climate law in the 1980s or even the 1990s. The most concrete policy responses to climate change were, at the federal level, funding research and developing international law; at the state level, developing energy policy, including renewable energy portfolio standards; and at the local level, creating emissions inventories. At all levels, government agencies were beginning to incorporate climate change into their decision-making, as required by existing statutes and the courts. But policy innovation was proceeding only incrementally. None of these policy approaches significantly challenged existing legal frameworks. The most ambitious—state-level renewable energy portfolios—were well within states' traditional authority over the energy system.

By the late 1980s, however, climate policy experts were aware that the climate problem would require much more ambitious and innovative policy action than renewable energy portfolio standards. Even before the fossil fuel industry began its infamous campaign to undermine climate scientists, judges like Ruth Bader Ginsburg were raising questions about the feasibility of regulating carbon dioxide. Dealing with climate change was not going to be as simple as dealing with acid rain or stratospheric ozone had turned out to be.

Climate Change in the Legal Academy

This is the point in the story where legal scholars are supposed to step in. Their role is to clarify the legal dimensions of a novel policy problem, to propose legal strategies and tools for dealing with it, and to develop concrete, well-reasoned policy approaches that make sense within the framework of American law—or concrete, well-reasoned changes to that legal framework. And that is exactly what legal scholars did. But their efforts initially were almost entirely focused on international law.

This international focus was not inevitable, but it is understandable. During the 1980s and 1990s, there was a great deal of highly publicized work being done by the IPCC and the UN Conferences of Parties aimed at developing international climate law.[49] The American state and local policy efforts were less visible, less well organized, and much more limited in scale and ambition. So it's not surprising that, among American legal scholars, global warming initially was framed as an international law issue and received attention primarily from international environmental law experts.

The law review literature supports that generalization. Indeed, it suggests that climate change (or global warming) was barely conceptualized as a subject for legal research in the 1980s. Before proceeding with this discussion, however, it's important to explain the place of law reviews in the law school ecosystem. Unlike most scholarly journals in the United States, law reviews are typically produced not by professors but by law students. They are nevertheless treated as peer-reviewed journals and are the principal forum for legal scholarship in the United States. They usually have a faculty adviser, but students select, review, and edit the articles; usually some of the content is written by students as well. Most law schools have at least one main law review. Working on the main law review is considered an honor (it is not a paid position, though there are sometimes stipends for officers), and students earn their way onto the staff either by virtue of their grades or through a writing competition. (Many schools also produce specialized law

64 CHAPTER TWO

reviews that students can volunteer to work on.) Thus when a topic begins to appear in law reviews, it is good evidence that the topic has entered into the legal education ecosystem; law professors and at least some law students are starting to think about it.

To explore the emergence of climate change in the law review literature, I turned to the *Index to Legal Periodicals*, a series of bound volumes published annually that indexes articles from all the major law reviews in the nation by author and subject. This was the primary legal scholarship research tool in the pre-internet period and was still widely used in the 1980s and 1990s.[50] Computerized databases (LexisNexis and Westlaw) were available to law professors and students in the 1980s, and they included some law review literature. But coverage was incomplete; until the late 1990s, a thorough search of the literature still required use of the *Index*.[51] It is therefore significant that it did not use "global warming" or "greenhouse gasses" or "climate change" as subject headings until the 1990–1991 volume.

Of course, there are now legal databases available that allow natural-language searches of the law review literature from earlier periods. Hein-Online has the best coverage of law reviews published before 1990. To begin, I searched its Law Journal Library using the keywords "global warming," "climate change," or "climatic change" from 1970 to 1979. That search generated 61 mentions. However, some of these were in journals that are not law reviews (*Foreign Affairs*) or in collections of UN documents. Some articles were using terms metaphorically ("political climate change") or referring to local climate changes (like drought). None of the law review articles focused on global climate change or offered anything approaching a legal analysis.

The same search from 1980 to 1989 generated 542 mentions.[52] Again, however, most of these are either in sources that aren't law reviews or are brief references to climate change (in a footnote or in passing). That number suggests that many environmental law scholars were aware of the phenomenon of global warming in the 1980s and were beginning to think about how it might affect the issues that they were interested in. But only a handful of articles actually focused on it, and all those articles address it as a problem of international law.

One of the earliest law review articles focused directly on climate change was Gus Speth's "Global Energy Futures and the Carbon Dioxide Problem," published in the *Boston College Environmental Affairs Law Review* in 1980. The article is an edited version of a report by the President's Council on Environmental Quality, of which Speth was the chair. It focuses on the likely impact of global warming, recommends setting a goal for atmospheric carbon concentration, and suggests several mitigation strategies to reduce vulnerability to climate change. It's a very good introduction to the subject, but it does not include any legal analysis.

I would nominate Edith Brown Weiss's 1981 article "A Resource Management Approach to Carbon Dioxide During the Century of Transition" as the first legal analysis of the climate change problem in American legal scholarship. It appeared as a contribution to a symposium titled "Global Warming: An Introduction" covered in the *Denver Journal of International Law & Policy.* This symposium grew out of a conference sponsored by the Aspen Institute of Humanistic Studies and the International Legal Studies Program of the University of Denver College of Law. In summer 1980, they assembled a group of scientists, international lawyers, and social scientists in Denver to discuss global climate change. The resulting symposium included five articles, including an introduction by Ved Nanda (Distinguished Visiting Professor of International Law, IIT Chicago–Kent College of Law). However, three of the articles focused on weather modification and acid rain—suggesting that American legal scholars were not yet sure how to categorize climate change as a legal problem—and most of the authors seemed somewhat puzzled and unsure what to say about it. Only Edith Brown Weiss's article focused on legal options for managing the problem.

Brown Weiss was unusually well prepared to tackle this subject. She was interested in weather and climate from her youth in the Pacific Northwest. After receiving her JD from Harvard in 1966, she went on to get a PhD in political science at UC Berkeley, focusing on the legal problems posed by weather and climate modification.[53] This topic put her into regular communication with meteorologists, and she followed up that project with a book on governance of global commons, including oceans, weather, and outer space.[54] By 1981 she was an associate professor at Georgetown University Law Center teaching what she believes was the first course on international environmental law in the country.[55] With this foundation, she was able to produce a remarkably perceptive legal analysis of the climate problem.

First, she explained the challenge of the carbon dioxide problem for international law:

How, in the face of serious scientific uncertainties, should states manage the emission and release of carbon dioxide into the atmosphere, when many states contribute to the problem in widely varying degrees, when

66 CHAPTER TWO

all states will be affected by the resulting climate change but in different ways, when the activities contributing to a carbon dioxide buildup are central to the energy and land-use practices of states, and when costly preventive strategies, to be effective, would have to be initiated at least a decade or more before the full effects of CO_2-induced climate change would be felt?[56]

She goes on to explain why we should think about this problem as involving not only emission control but also management of the entire energy system:

> What makes the carbon dioxide problem so uniquely difficult is that it is caused by many point sources of pollution and that the pollutants emerge as byproducts of the use of critical natural resources-the consumption of fossil fuels, and to an extent yet unknown, the harvesting of forests and the misuse of soils. Moreover, the problem develops slowly with no immediate health or environmental effects, making it all the more difficult to convince decisionmakers to take immediate action. Approaching the CO_2 problem as a pollution problem reveals its basic nature: it is a problem in energy management.[57]

The article proceeds to set out the international law principles that apply to carbon dioxide accumulation: a principle of "equitable use," applicable to countries using a shared natural resource (like the climate system); and a principle that makes states responsible for damage caused to the environment of other states in areas beyond their jurisdiction. Brown Weiss identifies the two primary approaches to the problem available in international law: setting a global ambient air quality standard for CO_2, and addressing deforestation. However, she also emphasizes the limitations of international law (which requires voluntary compliance). The article further reviews the domestic policy options available, ranging from impact assessments to restrictions on the use of fossil fuels. Overall it is a masterful analysis, demonstrating a deep understanding of the issue and the legal challenges it presents. But the article also calls for caution in taking policy actions given the scientific uncertainty that still surrounded the problem: "The topic should not be pushed into high-level political debates that would cause countries to adopt premature positions based on inconclusive premises and embedded in national political rhetoric."[58]

No other law review article from the 1980s improves on Brown Weiss's basic analysis. She added to that analysis in a 1983 article forwarding the idea that political institutions have a "planetary trust" obligation to protect the natural and cultural resources of the planet for future generations (making her the first to articulate what has become a central normative pillar of climate policy) and in her 1989 exploration of the implications of climate change for governance of the Arctic.[59] These three articles made Brown Weiss the leading scholar of climate law in the United States in the 1980s. It is true that, as the decade progressed, articles discussing global warming appeared more frequently in law reviews, and in 1986 the *EPA Journal* published an entire issue on global environmental problems, seven of which focus on global warming. These articles discuss the science behind global warming and policy options, but they do not offer any legal analysis.[60] Two student-written articles (by Allene Zanger and Margot Peters) do a good job of presenting the case for an international treaty to regulate greenhouse gasses, but they don't substantially advance the discussion beyond Weiss's analysis.[61]

One other article from this early period does deserve some discussion. In 1986, David Einhorn and R. Alta Charo published "Carbon Dioxide and the Greenhouse Effect: Possibilities for Legislative Action" in a special issue of the *Columbia Journal of Environmental Law* on legal issues arising from the Audubon Energy Plan of 1984. The Audubon Energy Plan was a report written for the Audubon Society by the Columbia University Legislative Drafting Research Fund—the same legislative drafting service established in 1911 and discussed in chapter 1. It's a good example of the kind of applied interdisciplinary work that most law schools were not equipped to undertake in 1984. But the article itself, while showing an excellent grasp of the relevant climate science, continues to sound a very cautious note about regulation: "The problem . . . lies in the nature of our political and legal systems, which demand some degree of immediacy and certainty as a premise to action. Further, the more subtle and distant the problem to be addressed, the more unreasonable will appear the costs of preventive action, thus once again demanding a level of scientific certainty that may not be possible for many years to come."[62] They conclude that "affirmative legislative action on a national scale can only make a small dent in the CO_2 problem," but that it may "help to build the consensus necessary for international cooperative action."[63]

Around 1988, the legal scholarship on climate change started to increase. In 1989, Ved Nanda published a substantial article analyzing the international law principles relevant to addressing climate change, and articles started to appear addressing issues like international responsibility for sea-level rise due to climate change.[64] Then, in 1990, Durwood Zaelke and James Cameron published "Global Warming and Climate Change—An Overview of the International Legal Process" in the *American University International Law Review*.

This widely cited article provides a good snapshot of the state of legal research on climate change in 1990. The authors aim to explain what climate change is and what the international community was doing about it. They frame climate change as a problem in international law, and they draw almost entirely on policy documents and scientific reports rather than on other law review articles. This is quite unusual for American law review articles, which typically begin by summarizing what the law review literature has to say on the subject—a practice that helps to consolidate and advance legal scholarship on a topic. Zaelke and Cameron are British legal experts and possibly unfamiliar with the conventions of American legal scholarship. But law review editors are famous for enforcing American legal citation practices. It is therefore noteworthy that neither Zaelke and Cameron nor Ved Nanda cite the Brown Weiss articles, which are directly relevant to their topic, and Zaelke and Cameron don't cite the Nanda article either. Both articles offer useful, well-informed, and insightful legal analysis; but the fact that each new article proceeded as though it was the first to explain climate change to its audience indicates that by 1990 the law review scholarship on this topic was still underdeveloped.[65]

That changed in the 1990s, however. A search of NexisUni (the successor company to LexisNexis) from January 1, 1990, to December 31, 1999, generated 1,497 mentions of either "global warming" or "climate change," with the frequency increasing steadily throughout the decade. Eighty-nine of those articles contained the keywords in the title. Most of those articles still appear in international environmental law reviews, but there is also a gradual increase in articles devoted to domestic environmental policy, addressing such issues as geoengineering, national policy approaches, how to advise clients on the problem, and implications for property law.[66] The emergence of this body of climate law scholarship suggests that climate change was making its way into law schools, or at least into the parts of law schools devoted to producing law reviews. But at what point in this story did law professors begin teaching students about climate change?

Climate Policy in the Classroom

Climate change is relevant to a number of subjects taught in law schools, including administrative law, international law, corporate law, property, and torts. But in the 1970s, scientists had characterized climate change as a pollution control problem. Accordingly, I focus on how and when climate change began to appear in environmental law courses and in closely related curricular areas, such as natural resource law and energy law.

Introducing Climate into Environmental Law Courses

When I began this project, I expected that serious efforts to address climate change in environmental law courses would have been underway at least by the early 1990s. Joseph Sax's 1989 article "Environmental Law in the Law Schools: What We Teach and How We Feel About It" does mention climate change (briefly) as one the "larger problems that defy traditional legal rules."[67] Surely the 1992 Earth Summit would have provided a good opportunity for law professors to take up this emerging environmental problem? But to a surprising degree it did not. In the introduction I mentioned the 1999 *Harvard Law Review* symposium on trends in environmental law teaching and scholarship. It collected insights by leading scholars in the field: Zygmunt Plater, Richard Lazarus, Daniel Farber, Alison Rieser, and David Wirth. *Only Wirth mentioned climate change*, and he mentioned it as an emerging topic within international environmental law. International environmental law was itself a very new subspeciality within international law. Wirth noted: "At least four new law school texts on international environmental law have been published in the past five years, where previously there had been none." He found that "approximately forty percent of law schools now offer a course on international environmental law," and there were two new law reviews on the subject (at Colorado and Georgetown).[68] Climate change could fit easily into those courses given the ongoing treaty negotiations. But Wirth did not consider whether international climate negotiations might have implications for teaching domestic environmental law.

As for the rest of the contributors to the symposium, Lazarus focused on Harvard's curious dearth of offerings in environmental law (after being an early adopter of environmental law, that school deemphasized the subject in its curriculum and hiring during the 1980s); Farber called for greater attention to environmental compliance; and Rieser discussed the influence of the growing empirical literature on the tragedy of the commons.[69] Plater's contribution voiced the same complaints about teaching environmental law

70 CHAPTER TWO

that Sax had voiced 20 years earlier: The standard survey course focusing on highly technical statutes is difficult to teach; adequate coverage of the field would require 15 to 20 courses; and it isn't suited to the case method. He did note, however, that environmental law professors "have pioneered the academic simulation approach in their law schools, or presented guided reading puzzles for student problem solving, drafting exercises, role playing, or linear tracking of complex and engaging case studies."[70] But he wanted to see more "exploration of a range of fascinating theoretical problems, such as the variety of conceptual bases for designing different modes of environmental regimes (e.g., the ongoing debates between command-and-control traditions and market-based techniques)."[71]

My interviewees for this project confirm overwhelmingly the fact that climate change was largely absent from the environmental law curriculum during the 1980s and most of the 1990s. I asked each of them when they began teaching about climate change, and while some memories were hazy, almost all were certain that they weren't teaching the subject in the 1980s. Consider the experience of Pat Parenteau, who started teaching environmental law in 1977 in various visiting positions and became a regular faculty member at Vermont Law School in 1993. Parenteau was deeply involved in national environmental policy in the late 1970s, and his first introduction to climate change came in 1977, when Rafe Pomerance, president of Friends of the Earth, came into a meeting of major environmental groups (the Big 10) and announced (in Parenteau's words): "It's the climate! That's the thing! It's changing!" Parenteau was also closely associated with Gus Speth and was aware of his work on the Council on Environmental Quality. Climate change, he said, was "on our minds" during this period. "But frankly, there were so many other issues that were crowding it out: There was water and air and superfund and hazardous waste and wildlife and endangered species. . . . It just never really got a high priority . . . all the way through the eighties."[72] He believes he touched on it in some of his early courses, but he didn't begin focusing on it in his teaching until 1998 or 1999. That timeline is consistent with my other interviewees. No one except Edith Brown Weiss remembers studying or teaching about climate change in law school in the 1980s.

Brown Weiss, of course, was the exception. She was teaching a general course on international law during the 1980s, and she devoted a week during that course to environmental issues; climate change was one of the topics she covered. She went on to develop a whole course on international environmental law in the 1980s, and climate change was "a key part of the course."[73] Thanks in large part to her efforts, Georgetown started developing a climate law curriculum very early. That effort was aided by the hiring of Lisa Heinzerling in 1993. Heinzerling had worked on energy issues during a three-year stint in the office of the Massachusetts Attorney General, including its efforts to regulate greenhouse gasses. Drawing on that background, she offered a seminar on energy and the environment during her first year, and climate change came into that course as one of the environmental impacts of energy production.[74]

I didn't find anyone else quite as precocious in integrating climate change into the curriculum. One of the earliest such courses was developed by Vincent Johnson for the summer-abroad program offered by St. Mary's University School of Law at Innsbruck, Austria. Johnson taught "Legal Implications of Global Warming" from 1990 through 1992, and he recruited Edith Brown Weiss to teach it in 1993. He reports that he also taught it once back on campus at St. Mary's. But by the mid-1990s he had given up the course to focus on other projects.[75] Dan Tarlock, like Parenteau, remembers hearing about climate change in the late 1970s, but he didn't think there was much yet to teach. He didn't start teaching about climate change until the mid-1990s, when he began teaching a course in international environmental law (at the Chicago–Kent College of Law).[76] Richard Lazarus first taught about climate change in 1993, in an environmental law survey course at Washington University School of Law. Richard Parker at University of Connecticut and John Dernbach at Widener University Commonwealth Law School also started teaching the topic in their courses on international environmental law around 1997.[77] Dernbach around that time developed an innovative course on sustainable development in which students addressed global issues like climate change, and by 2003 he was offering a seminar on climate law. His sustainable development framework offered a promising approach to address national and subnational climate law, but his early efforts to teach about climate change focused on international law. Bill Funk at Lewis & Clark Law School recalls starting to cover the topic in his survey (introductory) course on environmental law at some point in the 1990s, but he also addressed it as an international law issue.[78] William Buzbee doesn't recall any attention paid to climate change while studying environmental law with Frank Grad at Columbia Law School in the mid-1980s.[79] None of the interviewees who studied at Lewis & Clark in the 1980s or early 1990s remember coverage of climate change in the introductory course.[80] Neither Jeff Civins, who was teaching environmental courses at University of Texas

School of Law starting in 1987, nor Kelly Haragan, who received her JD from that school in 1995, remembers climate change being covered in the curriculum.[81] Neither did Tyler Giannini encounter climate change in any significant way in his coursework while studying environmental law at University of Virginia School of Law in the mid-1990s.[82]

This pattern is reflected in the environmental law casebooks published in the 1980s and 1990s. It's important to bear in mind that professors seldom confine themselves only to the material in the casebook; it's common practice to supplement the text with additional readings. So we won't characterize casebooks as a perfect reflection of what is covered in class. Nevertheless, they are useful for understanding how leading environmental law professors were conceptualizing the field and what topics were most likely to be taught regularly in a typical environmental law course.

It is therefore significant that Anderson, Mandelker, and Tarlock's 1984 casebook, *Environmental Protection: Law and Policy*, did not discuss global warming at all. Neither did Bonine and McGarity's 1984 *The Law of Environmental Protection* or the 1982 edition of Schoenbaum's casebook *Environmental Policy Law*. Philip Weinberg also published a casebook in 1985 titled *Environmental Law: Cases and Materials*, which did not address global warming. Of the casebooks published or updated in the 1980s, I found only two that did discuss global warming. The 1981 casebook by Roger Findley and Daniel Farber covered global warming in the chapter on intergovernmental relations, which included a section on international environmental law. They presented carbon dioxide accumulation along with ozone depletion as two kinds of global atmospheric changes that they expected to become more urgent in the future. To introduce the subject, they relied on excerpts from government reports, including the Council on Environmental Quality report (chaired by Gus Speth) and the then-recent Global 2000 Report (commissioned by President Jimmy Carter in 1980). But they also noted that the projections contained in these reports were very uncertain, and international legal mechanisms for dealing with problems like this were still "very primitive."[83] Richard Stewart and James Krier took the same approach. Their *Cases and Materials on Environmental Law and Policy* was first published in 1975; a second edition came out in 1978. Neither edition mentioned global warming, but an update was issued in 1982 that did include a brief mention. Like Findley and Farber, they brought it up in a discussion of the Global 2000 Report, presenting it as a global problem with uncertain negative effects.[84]

Global warming started to gain more consistent coverage in casebooks in the 1990s. Anderson and colleagues begin to address the subject with a note on global warming in their 1990 edition, and Findley and Farber continued to address it in their discussion of international law in their 1991, 1995, and 1999 editions. Major new casebooks issued during this decade were *Environmental Regulation: Law, Science and Policy* (1992, Robert Percival, Alan Miller, Christopher Schroeder, and James Leape); *Environmental Law and Policy: A Coursebook on Nature, Law and Society* (1992, Zygmunt Plater, Robert Abrams, and William Goldfarb); *Environmental Law: Cases and Materials* (1992, William Murray Tabb and Linda Malon); and *Environmental Law and Policy* (1994, Peter Mennell and Richard Stewart). Plater and colleagues and Tabb and Malone don't discuss climate change at all. However, Percival and colleagues and Mennell and Stewart do address the subject, notably in their discussions of air pollution. Specifically they pose the question of whether carbon dioxide can be regulated under the Clean Air Act.

Some legal context: The Clean Air Act requires the EPA to regulate any air pollutant from a motor vehicle that the EPA Administrator determines may endanger public health or welfare.[85] It goes on to offer a fairly broad definition of "air pollution agent" as "any physical, chemical . . . substance . . . emitted into . . . the ambient air."[86] Climate change thus raises a question: Is carbon dioxide such an agent? That is not hypothetical. On the contrary, the Massachusetts Attorney General office (Heinzerling's previous employer) petitioned the EPA in 1999 to regulate carbon dioxide under the Clean Air Act, starting a litigation process that would ultimately reach the United States Supreme Court. The question also became a common strategy for addressing climate change in introductory environmental courses beginning in the 1990s. Dan Farber (at Minnesota), William Buzbee (Emory in the 1990s), Lisa Heinzerling (Georgetown), and Richard Lazarus (who taught at Washington University and Georgetown in the 1990s, along with some visiting positions) all identified that question as the primary way they introduced the issue into their environmental law survey courses. Lazarus first used it as an exam question in 1998. He explains: "It was such a great exam question, because greenhouse gasses clearly fit the definition of a criterion pollutant [which must be regulated under the CAA] but it was such a disaster if you [regulated them]. . . . It's a great discussion problem: How do you fit this pollutant into a statutory scheme, which isn't based on a global pollutant?"[87] The question raises complex issues of statutory interpretation, judicial review of agency decision-making (Should a court let the agency

74 CHAPTER TWO

decide whether carbon dioxide is a pollutant? Or second-guess the agency decision?), and the proper scope of agencies' rulemaking authority (Doesn't trying to regulate a global pollutant exceed any reasonable understanding of the EPA's mandate?). This makes it an excellent teaching tool. The question itself would be answered eventually (in the affirmative) by the Supreme Court in 2007, in *Massachusetts v. EPA*—making it a little less useful as an exam question.[88] But the opinion quickly became integrated into environmental law casebooks after 2007 and still serves as a useful way to teach a number of issues in environmental and administrative law.

Some interviewees also mentioned learning about climate change in the very late 1980s or early 1990s in connection with cap-and-trade regulation. This was a new approach to emission regulation pioneered in 1990 in amendments to the Clean Air Act program for regulating sulfur dioxide, involving capping total emissions and then setting up a market for tradable emissions permits. It was being discussed in law school classes in the late 1980s (as I recall, it was a prominent topic in my introductory environmental law course at Berkeley). Richard Stewart and James Krier were among the first environmental law professors to explore whether it could be used to regulate carbon dioxide. Lisa Heinzerling remembers Richard Stewart talking a good deal about cap-and-trade in her course with him at University of Chicago, albeit with little discussion of climate change. But Patrick Tolan, who studied environmental law with James Krier at University of Michigan in 1989, does remember discussing climate change in the context of Krier's treatment of cap-and-trade regulation.[89] Farber also mentioned using climate change in his treatment of marketable permits.[90] We can say with some confidence, then, that climate change made its first appearances in domestic environmental law courses as an air pollution control issue, with a focus on regulatory tools for controlling carbon dioxide emissions. This is not to deny that it may have come up in other ways as well. Most obviously, it may have been raised in the context of discussing what needs to be addressed on an environmental impact statement under NEPA. But interviewees didn't recall this becoming a major theme in discussions of NEPA in the early 1990s.[91]

Climate Change in Other Courses

What about other law school courses beyond the basic environmental law course such as natural resources law? Judging from the major natural resources casebooks in the 1980s and 1990s, climate change was not yet a major theme in this subfield. In 2007 Michael Blumm published a useful and detailed overview of the evolution of natural resource casebooks from the original 1951 book by Clyde Martz. He discusses the expansion of natural resources to give greater attention to resource protection (rather than just extraction), but he does not mention climate change as an emerging theme. The major natural resources casebook of this era was *Federal Public Land and Resources Law* (1981, George Coggins, Charles Wilkinson, and John Leshy), which offered a new synthesis of public lands law. But neither this edition nor the next four mention climate—not even the fifth edition, published in 2002.

My interviewees similarly did not recall discussion of climate change in the context of managing public lands or protecting endangered species in the 1980s or 1990s. However, Robin Kundis Craig was studying environmental law at Lewis & Clark from 1990 to 1993, and she does remember some coverage of climate change in her water law course. Indeed, experts on water law seemed to be ahead of the curve in considering how the impacts of climate change might affect the legal system. Climate change wasn't mentioned in the major casebooks on water law in the 1980s: *Cases and Materials on Water Law* (Frank Trelease and George Gould, in its fourth edition in 1986) and *Legal Control of Water Resources* (Joseph Sax and Robert Abrams, the first edition published in 1986 edition and the second, with Barton "Buzz" Thompson, in 1991). Charles Meyer and Dan Tarlock first published their *Water Resource Management* casebook in 1971 but updated it in 1980 and 1988 (with James Corbridge and David Getches added), and none of these editions take up climate. However, Getches did mention the topic in his 1984 *Water Law in a Nutshell* (a study aid aimed primarily at law students). The connection between water law and climate change turned out to be weather modification: it came up briefly in a discussion of intentional efforts to increase rain ("cloud seeding").[92] William Goldfarb also covered weather modification in his 1984 and 1988 editions of *Water Law*, noting that he would not discuss "inadvertent weather changes such as those potentially caused by fossil fuel burning" or "climate modification involving relatively long-term or lasting climatic change."[93] These brief mentions suggest that water experts were at least aware of the issue in the late 1980s (and, like the experts at the Denver conference, were still associating it with weather control). Buzz Thompson remembers that climate change was becoming a major topic in the field of water law between 1995 and 2000. He started to address it in his water law course during that period as something that would affect water supply.[94]

76 CHAPTER TWO

Energy law is another topic in which one might expect climate change to be discussed. But energy law was only beginning to emerge as a field in the 1980s. Before that time, law schools taught courses on oil and gas law as part of their natural resources curriculum, but usually with a focus on how to access these resources. That started to change in the 1970s, with the Mideast oil crisis and growing interest in renewable energy. William Rodgers's 1979 casebook, *Cases and Materials on Natural Resources and Energy*, reflects this interest; he made energy a central theme, approaching individual resources primarily as energy sources—but not highlighting environmental impacts of either resource extraction or use.[95] The field developed in the 1980s to cover the whole energy system, from accessing resources to generating and distributing power to addressing environmental impacts.[96] This broad focus would have made it a good vehicle for addressing climate change, but according to energy law professors interest in the field waned in the 1980s and 1990s. However, the fracking (hydraulic fracturing) boom in the early 2000s generated new interest, and energy law is now well established and thriving, with new journals, casebooks, and programs appearing regularly.[97] Donald Zillman reports that climate change became an important topic in the field in the 1990s.[98] That timeline is reflected in the extensive coverage of climate change—a whole chapter—in the casebook *Energy, Economics, and the Environment* (2000, Fred Bosselman, Jim Rossi, and Jacqueline Weaver). But even many of my interviewees who went on to specialize in energy law—David Spence, Alexandra Klass, Hari Osofsky, Joshua Fershee, Oday Salim, and Samuel Panarella—do not report having taken an energy law course in law school (although Spence does recall having taken a seminar that covered public utilities regulation, and Salim took Energy Law in 2009 while getting his LLM at Lewis & Clark Law School). In short, energy law in the 1980s and 1990s wasn't yet sufficiently developed as a curricular focus to offer substantial coverage of climate change.

Finally, I wondered whether students might have encountered climate issues in experiential courses like the environmental law clinics that were starting to appear in the 1980s. Because clinics take on so many different kinds of cases, and any case can raise multifarious legal issues, it's impossible to know how frequently climate change was coming up in that arena. But Susan Kraham, a veteran legal clinician who worked in the environmental law clinic at Rutgers Law School from 1998 to 2005 and Columbia Law School's environmental law clinic from 2008 on, suggests that environmental law clinics weren't focusing on climate change in the 1990s.[99] That would change in the next decade, as law school clinics began to play a larger role in bringing climate litigation to the courts. Before turning to that story, however, we need to understand why environmental law professors, who were increasingly aware of climate change during these early decades, were not rushing to incorporate it into their courses.

Obstacles to a Climate Curriculum

Understanding the factors impeding the incorporation of climate change into the environmental law curriculum during this early period is important to understanding the evolution of the climate curriculum. There were several interrelated obstacles that interfered with a quick uptake of the climate problem. What follows is not a complete catalog of the challenges of teaching climate change; other difficulties would emerge in later years after professors developed a greater understanding of the problem and began addressing it in more depth. The initial obstacles centered on the awkward fit between the climate problem and the structure of the environmental law field in the 1980s and 1990s.

Crowded Agenda

One obvious obstacle to addressing climate change was eloquently expressed by Pat Parenteau in the passage quoted above: the existing and far-too-crowded agenda. The impossibility of covering all the important topics in the field was the dominant theme in the law review literature on teaching environmental law in the 1980s. But the crowded agenda is a problem only if (1) climate change is best addressed as a separate topic added to the existing list (rather than integrated into the treatment of other topics); (2) there aren't multiple courses available for addressing new topics; and (3) the topic is not clearly urgent enough to prioritize. All of those conditions existed in the 1980s and 1990s.

First, we already noted that law schools tend to change the curriculum by adding courses, and the same additive approach seemed to be at play within the introductory environmental law course. It was reinforced by the fact that professors in the field had by the 1980s become focused on teaching several federal statutes regulating different subjects (air, water, hazardous waste, etc.), so that the most obvious way to add a new topic was to add a new subject of regulation to the list. Indeed, one reason the Findley and Farber casebook discussed global warming in its first edition was because it defied the statute-oriented approach to some extent, devoting a chapter to

78   CHAPTER TWO

intergovernmental relations—a topic that can be explored very effectively through discussion of the climate problem, since policy action was taking place at the international level that would have to be implemented through coordinated federal, state, and local actions.[100] Alternatively, climate change might come up more easily in courses focused on a set of complex real-world problems like the Dwyer/Sax seminar on water pollution. Such problem-based courses are less concerned with covering a standard set of topics and more open to allowing new issues to arise in their real-world context. The federal statute–focused approach, in contrast, makes it difficult to address a new topic without eliminating a subject.

Second, the fact that the introductory course in environmental law was expected to cover so many topics was itself a function of the continuing underdeveloped state of the environmental law curriculum in the 1980s and even 1990s. As discussed in chapter 1, even leading environmental law programs often had only one regular faculty member in the 1980s. William Buzbee noted that in 1993, when he started teaching environmental law at Emory, "I was it. I was the first full-time person teaching environmental law courses." He built that program over the next two decades.[101] That was a common story among interviewees. Environmental law was not a priority at leading law schools. As mentioned in chapter 1, Georgetown Law Center relied on Edith Brown Weiss until it hired Hope Babcock in 1991 to start an environmental law clinic. She also taught a domestic environmental law course, and they were joined by Lisa Heinzerling in 1993, which greatly expanded the program's capacity.[102] But Harvard, which was a leader in environmental law in the 1970s, had no regular faculty teaching the course by the late 1990s.[103] And many of the solo environmental law professors had to teach courses in other areas as well; Dan Farber at Minnesota, for example, taught constitutional law as well as environmental law. Adding content by adding new courses wasn't very practicable given the limited faculty resources devoted to the field.

Of course, climate change might have made its way onto even a crowded agenda if law professors had felt a stronger sense of urgency about the issue. Here the state of climate science, especially with respect to the impacts of climate change, is important to keep in mind. As William Buzbee put it, in the 1980s and early 1990s climate change was "something you read about . . . a scientific phenomenon but not yet a crisis." As the IPCC put out more reports predicting more extreme impacts at higher probabilities, environmental legal scholars increasingly grasped the seriousness of the issue.[104] But in the 1980s and most of the 1990s, climate change was still conceptualized even among scientists as something that would become a crisis only several decades in the future.

Also relevant to this question of priorities is the fact that, at the time of publication of this book, climate law is not a subject covered by bar exams. A couple of interviewees mentioned the pressure to teach subjects that are on the bar as a factor limiting coverage of climate.[105] Importantly, however, the bar was not identified by any interviewee as a *major* restriction on the ability to offer new electives. Joshua Fershee (an expert on energy law and currently dean of Creighton School of Law) has taught at several law schools that were concerned with bar passage rates. He did not find the bar topics to pose many constraints on the curriculum, because specialty courses like energy or environmental law provide the opportunity to review basic legal principles that are essential to the bar exam.[106] It is possible, of course, that how basic legal issues might come up in climate litigation is more obvious today than it was in the 1980s and 1990s, when climate litigation was still in its earliest stages.

Lack of Federal Regulation

A different obstacle to teaching climate change in the 1980s and 1990s was the fact that—in the words of several interviewees—"there was no law to teach."[107] Of course, that's not strictly true; by the 1990s there were state and local policies as well as some judicial decisions. There was also after 1992 a growing body of international law. What was lacking was a federal regulatory program—a coherent body of legal rules applicable to government and private actors that was developed to address this problem. As Doug Kysar put it, describing the situation as late as 2009: "There wasn't nearly as much law there as there would be in a comparable subject like air pollution. . . . We don't have a well-developed legal framework that's equal to the problem . . . a body of law that's coherent and comprehensive and has been designed to address this problem . . . the way we have the law of property or a law of corporations or a law of taxation." These other subjects are "quite mature, and you can map it and teach it in a way as if there was some intelligible design behind it."[108]

So this problem as well had much to do with how the field of environmental law had come to be defined. There were laws and regulations relevant to climate and various policy approaches and conversations going on in the 1980s and 1990s. But there wasn't an independent, coherent body of law for professors to explore using the usual pedagogic strategies of the law school classroom—pedagogies designed for doctrinal analysis, for unearthing underlying principles from a collection of legal decisions. As we will see in chapter 4, the early courses on (domestic) climate law in fact tended to draw heavily on, rather than case law, the kinds of materials and teaching strategies commonly used in the teaching of public policy.

Moreover, to the extent any conventional "environmental law"—a regulatory program designed to address climate change specifically—was developing in the 1990s, it was international law. The division between domestic and international law is quite stark in American law schools, and it persists in the environmental law field. Several interviewees explained simply that they didn't address climate change because their courses focused on domestic law, taking for granted that it was a topic better addressed in an international law course. Even Dan Farber, a coauthor of the first casebook to address climate change, did not cover it in his environmental law courses at the University of Minnesota in the 1980s. He focused instead on "domestic environmental law," suggesting that the relevance of climate change for issues like protecting endangered species or even air pollution weren't particularly salient at that point.[109] Indeed, Hari Osofsky (who started teaching at Whittier Law School in the early 2000s and is now dean of Northwestern Pritzker School of Law), noted that, early in her career as a climate scholar, she was pressed to identify as *either* an international *or* domestic law expert. She was eventually moved to publish an article in 2009 arguing that this division wasn't appropriate to multi-scalar phenomena like climate change.[110] International environmental law was taught at some law schools by the 1990s, but it's fair to say that it was not widely available to most law students.

The same problem prevented coverage of state and local laws addressing climate change. American law schools typically spend little time on state-specific laws, focusing instead on either federal law or legal principles that are widely shared across all the states (leaving it to students to prepare for state-specific bar exam questions on their own). Even today, I found among interviewees a strong federal and international orientation; very few covered state-level climate regulatory programs in any detail. Coverage of local law traditionally has been even more threadbare. Land use planning, for example, is central to environmental management and primarily the responsibility of local governments, but courses in land use and local government law are often hard to find in the standard law school curriculum. True, this seems to be an area of curricular evolution; the legal scholar John Nolon would note in 2002 that "local environmental law" is emerging as a "new field of environmental law."[111] But scholarly discussions of the environmental law curriculum in the 1980s and 1990s didn't highlight local law as an area needing greater attention.

Other Obstacles

Other obstacles to teaching climate change were mentioned by interviewees less consistently than one might expect. One was the lack of teaching materials. Although several interviewees noted that most of the major environmental law casebooks didn't address climate change in the 1980s and 1990s, most law professors I interviewed were comfortable developing their own teaching materials. Many of them don't even like to use casebooks, relying instead on cases, policy documents, and scholarly articles they collect themselves (which is considerably cheaper for students, as several noted).[112] In discussing how they developed their courses, it became clear that the availability of materials on the internet now plays an important role in facilitating this work—but it is also clear that the practice of teaching from self-collected resources was already well established by the time the internet was created. Indeed, at least two of the early casebooks written by my interviewees began as collections of mimeographed or photocopied materials.[113]

Somewhat more problematic for a few professors was the fact that climate law was not yet a recognized practice area. Like many professional schools, some law schools focus on connecting students to specific practice areas where there is strong local demand. And the growth of climate law as a practice area awaited the growth of a client base: businesses seeking legal services to address climate risk and clean energy.[114] That client base is only now (as of 2023) beginning to take shape.[115] Thus Wil Burns taught an early climate law course (in 2009) at Santa Clara University School of Law on the strength of his faith that this *would* become an active practice area in the future.[116] True, climate change is an important issue, and one can teach a good deal of basic environmental law in the context of addressing it.[117] As mentioned above, though, that may not have been as obvious in the 1980s and 1990s, that is, before climate litigation increased attention to the variety of administrative and procedural issues posed by this subject. Perhaps even more important is the fact that, in the absence of a set of lawyers actively practicing climate law, it would be difficult for law schools to add it to the curriculum simply by hiring adjunct professors, which is a common way that law schools (with their relatively small faculties) enrich the curriculum.

Finally, it's worth noting one possible obstacle that was not cited by anyone as a barrier to teaching climate change: political pressure. Given the attention in the scholarly literature to the influence of the movement of climate denialism, I asked most of the interviewees whether they feared or had experienced any serious political resistance to covering climate change. The answer was uniformly "no." While some did note that, at least in the early days, they had to address the fact that some of their students might not believe in climate science, they did not find that task especially troublesome.[118] A very few professors involved in clinics reported that occasionally a law school alum or trustee would complain to the dean about their activities—but those complaints didn't generate any negative consequences, and in any case they weren't prompted by climate litigation.[119]

This lack of concern over the politics of climate change is somewhat striking; in other parts of the academy, climate scholars have experienced public harassment campaigns, lawsuits, and other intimidation tactics as the result of research and teaching about climate change.[120] Law professors' lack of concern about political attacks is undoubtedly due in part to their professional training: lawyers are not afraid of a fight and are pretty secure in their ability to defend their rights. But it is probably also due to their status as a group, as members of the political class in the United States. The professors I interviewed were for the most part very well connected. Of course they are also well paid (compared to the average academic) and have a good career alternative to fall back on if they needed to leave academia. But none of my interviewees even contemplated that teaching about climate change might have such drastic consequences. They all expressed an enviable confidence in their academic freedom.

Politics, then, doesn't explain why the standard environmental law curriculum coming into the twenty-first century was not centered on or even paying much attention to climate change. The explanation for that inattention has more to do with the underdeveloped state of the environmental law curriculum combined with the structure and definition of the field. But even in the 1990s forces were at work that would alter this picture. Climate policy and the climate movement continued to develop, particularly after 2000. The evolution of the law and increasing social interest in the subject inevitably influenced the law school curriculum, which may be insulated from the rest of academia but is very much open to influence from the public policy arena. But even more surprising (given their history of stubborn resistance to innovation), law schools themselves were changing in ways that made the incorporation of subjects like climate change easier. Hiring practices, pedagogical practices, and curricular reform all helped to create a new context for teaching hard-to-teach subjects like climate change. Thus after 2000 the pace of curricular and pedagogical innovation picked up considerably. By 2010 climate change was being addressed in most environmental law casebooks, and the first casebooks focusing specifically on climate law had appeared. To understand this pattern of slow and then rapid transformation, we must begin by examining how the climate policy and law school landscape changed after 1990.

CHAPTER THREE

The Changing Landscape

When I started this project, I began by looking at the websites of several law schools. What I found surprised me, and to be honest it depressed me. Law schools appeared that they were offering a much richer and more interesting set of courses, including a variety of experiential learning opportunities, than had been available to me. Having graduated in 1992, it appeared that I *just missed* the biggest transformation in legal education since Langdell.

That impression was misleading, of course. The transformation I saw did occur, but not all at once. Beginning around 1990, law schools began changing in terms of who they hired, what resources were available to professors, and what pedagogic approaches were being widely used. This transformation is a major part of the story depicted in this book, because such institutional changes helped to support the incorporation of climate change into the law school curriculum. Climate policy was also evolving dramatically during this period. Despite the failure to enact a federal climate regulatory statute, all levels of government increased their promulgation of climate policy. California in particular began a very ambitious program to control carbon emissions that featured a suite of new policy tools. Litigation over climate issues also increased dramatically, encouraging the growth of doctrine in this area. Thus before delving into how the law school climate curriculum developed, it's useful to begin with an overview of the evolution of law schools and climate policy more generally from 1990 to 2020.

Development of Law Schools from 1990 to 2020

A comprehensive history of American law schools from 1990 to 2020 would note some important continuities with earlier decades, including a focus on serving the business community and the struggle to diversify student bodies —a struggle made more difficult by a political campaign to limit schools' ability to use affirmative action in admissions decisions.[1] In addition, it would have to cover three emerging and intertwined stories: the changing financial landscape, shaped by rising law school tuition; the changing competitive landscape, shaped by the *U.S. News & World Report* rankings; and a more vigorous campaign to reform the law school curriculum. I am not attempting such a comprehensive history, so I will focus on the curriculum reform story, which is most relevant to this analysis. But the financial and competitive landscapes provide important context for that reform campaign.

The Financial Story

The main theme of the financial story is the steep increases in law school tuition over this period. The ABA reports that average law school annual tuition (and fees) for a state resident at a public law school has increased steadily—sometimes as much as 12 percent over the previous year. The average tuition at a public law school rose from $4,343 in 1985 to $23,879 in 2013 (adjusting for inflation by using 2013 dollars). At private schools, average tuition has increased from $16,294 to $41,985 (again in 2013 dollars).[2] Moreover, these figures do not cover housing or other living expenses; the overall cost of attending law school is much higher. A chief consequence of the tuition increase is a dramatic increase in student debt. The ABA data show that the average debt from law school (not including debt from undergraduate education) had risen between 2001 and 2012 from $46,499 to $84,600 for public schools and from $70,147 to $122,158 for private schools.[3]

Of course, to put these numbers in perspective we would also have to know how much household incomes increased, the availability of loans, the salaries that new JDs could expect to earn, and many other factors. However, most commentators conclude that increasing law school tuition, while not a new trend, has in recent decades made law school much less affordable than it was in the 1950s or even the 1970s. As Paul Campos reports, in 1956 "median law school tuition represented 9.9% of the median American family's annual income." By 2015, "private law school tuition represented 64.3% of median family income, and public resident tuition was equivalent to 33.3% of that income."[4] There is some evidence that prices are stabilizing and perhaps even declining since 2015 in response to decreases in law school enrollments since 2010.[5] Nevertheless, the increasing price of law school has dominated much of the discourse about legal education from 1985 to 2020.[6]

86   CHAPTER THREE

Law schools are not alone, of course. Skyrocketing tuition at American colleges and universities has been the focus of a wide-ranging social and political discussion about the affordability of higher education in the United States during the period from 1990 to 2020. But colleges and universities can at least claim that much of their increasing tuition revenue is going to improving students' experiences—better facilities, more comprehensive academic, health, and financial support, and more staff in general. Law schools have fewer obvious improvements to point to. Legal education doesn't require expensive laboratories or equipment, and law schools never provided the full complement of support services that colleges do—although law libraries, arguably the most important physical resource at any law school, have been expanding their collections and the services they offer.[7] Law schools may also have added administrative staff, which is one potential source of increased costs.[8] Faculty teaching loads did decrease, and the overall size of the faculty increased at most schools, which (as I discuss below) may have affected the quality of teaching. But the connection between administrative staff and class size on one hand and teaching quality on the other can be opaque. So while colleges and universities could point to demand for more services and better facilities as a justification for tuition increases, law schools are open to the charge that they raised tuition simply because they could.

And that does seem the most common explanation for the tuition increases. To be sure, increasing tuition has some negative consequences for law schools. Most obviously, it makes more challenging efforts to diversify the student body and encourage careers in public service. Law schools, like any other important social institution, must worry about maintaining their social license to operate, a task that is not helped by their reputation as the domain of the privileged class. But increasing tuition did not decrease demand for places in this privileged domain; law schools continued to find students to fill their seats throughout the 1990s. Indeed, applications to law schools increased during this decade, peaking in 2004 at about 100,000 (after which they fell steadily to about 53,000 in 2014 and then started slowly rising again). Matriculation also rose to a high of nearly 53,000 students entering law school in 2010. Those numbers fell to about 37,000 in 2015, rising slowly in subsequent years.[9] But the lesson law schools seem to have taken from the 1990s is that students are at least somewhat insensitive to price.[10] Indeed, Campos argued as late as 2017 that students were likely using tuition price to evaluate the quality of law schools. In the absence of better information, higher tuition may be taken as a signal of a better-quality degree.[11]

As noted above, the shrinking pool of applicants seems to be putting some downward pressure on tuition in recent years. But it is also helping to maintain the second dynamic: increasing competition among law schools for students and prestige.

The Competition Story

Presumably, law schools have always competed with one another. But that competition has been shaped by a new factor, beginning in 1987 when *U.S. News & World Report* introduced its law-schools rankings. The impact of the rankings on institutional priorities has been one of the dominant stories in American higher education for decades.[12] Critics of the Best Law Schools rankings point out that, because they use students' college grades and LSAT[13] scores as measures of institutional quality, schools increasingly compete for students with high undergraduate grade-point averages and test scores. That competition in turn has led to an increase in merit-based scholarships, which schools use to woo high-performing students. Those scholarships account for some of the increased revenue from higher tuition. But attracting more qualified students doesn't actually do anything to improve the quality of instruction. The rankings also measure—and therefore increase the importance of—factors like faculty publications, institutional spending, and reputation. But these factors also seem to have little direct impact on teaching quality. In short, the rankings create a perverse incentive for law schools to focus on competing for the small set of high-performing students and faculty rather than investing in improvements in teaching and learning.

Moreover, the increased focus on grades and test scores seems to be exacerbating the long-standing concern that law schools are inaccessible to many minority populations. As Mary Lu Bilek and her coauthors note in a 2013 ABA report on legal education: "Between 1993 and 2008, law schools added 3,000 seats. Yet, snapshots of those two years show a 7.5% decrease in proportion of enrollment of African Americans and an 11.7% decrease in the enrollment of Mexican Americans. Even in real numbers, there were fewer African-American and Mexican-American matriculants in the 2008 class (4,060 combined) than existed in the fall 1993 class (4,142 combined)."[14] And this was despite the fact that the LSAT scores and GPAs of these minority groups increased during this period, as did their numbers in the US population.

Even worse, the pressure to maintain rankings has led to outright fraud by some law school administrators. Some schools inflated their employment numbers—the number of graduates in full-time jobs within nine months of graduation—by giving their graduates short-term temporary jobs and using various creative data-reporting practices. Others simply started lying about such basic information as the LSAT scores of students. These tactics were revealed in a 2011 exposé in the *New York Times*, leading to a great deal of public attention. US Senators Tom Coburn and Barbara Boxer even called for an investigation of law schools by the Department of Education. In December 2011, the ABA bowed to the pressure and implemented changes to law school reporting guidelines, at least with respect to employment figures.[15] But those changes did not end the annual Best Law Schools rankings report, which continues to influence the decisions of law school administrators.[16]

In short, the above critiques paint a discouraging picture of American legal education in the twenty-first century: law schools seem to be mired in a race for prestige, increasingly out of reach for, and out of touch with, ordinary Americans. But that picture may be too bleak. After all, normally we would expect increased competition combined with more resources to lead to innovation: law schools should be using their wealth to offer new and exciting opportunities to lure the best students (and best faculty). If students were only paying attention to the Best Law Schools rankings, there would be little point in such innovation, since the rankings don't reflect things like curricular richness. But law school administrators clearly do not believe that the Best Law Schools rankings are the only source of information potential students consult (nor is this my experience advising hundreds of prelaw students). Students also look at law school websites. And those websites tell a story of curricular innovation: new courses, programs, clinical, and other experiential opportunities.

This development makes sense according to the model of curricular change I outlined in the introduction. Although faculty members—the primary actors driving teaching innovation—may not care much about competition among law schools, their administrators do. Administrators can influence curriculum development by devoting resources to areas of the curriculum that seem important to prospective students, and environmental law does seem to be one field in which law schools are seeking a comparative advantage. The growth of the environmental law professoriate and the proliferation of environmental law certification programs during this period (discussed below) support that conclusion.

It's harder for administrators to drive pedagogical innovation, and there's little evidence that competition is a main driver here. Law schools don't seem to be trying to attract students by promoting innovative teaching methods (although experiential learning opportunities do appear prominently on law school websites). But the difficulties of teaching environmental law in the traditional way provide ample reason for entrepreneurial faculty members to try different teaching methods when reduced course loads allow them to. And pedagogical innovation is also driven by reform campaigns within the legal academy. These stories of curricular and pedagogical innovation since the 1990s are central to my analysis.

Curricular and Pedagogic Reform

To be sure, there are still plenty of critics of law school pedagogy. Brian Tamanaha argued in his 2012 book *Failing Law Schools* that law schools are doing very little with their increased revenue to improve student education. Rather, they use merit-based scholarships to entice high-performing students to their schools, and they use the rest to inflate faculty salaries. Faculty expenses typically account for about half of a law school's budget, and faculty salaries increased 45 percent from 1998 to 2008, when the median salary for law school faculty was $147,000 (not including benefits)— making them among the best-paid university teachers. He points out that they also receive generous stipends for doing research in the summer.[17] And this increase in compensation is occurring while teaching loads have decreased at many of the top schools. While data on course loads is hard to find, Tamanaha estimates that three courses per semester was the standard for most of the twentieth century. Now the standard load at elite law schools is two courses per semester, and some schools have even gone to three courses per year.[18] Tamanaha concludes from this trend that faculty are being paid more to do less.

Tamanaha was not alone in his criticism. As he notes, the Department of Justice (DOJ) in 1995 went so far as to sue the ABA for violating antitrust laws. The ABA is the only accrediting organization for American law schools, and ABA accreditation teams are dominated by law school professors. It was therefore worrisome to the DOJ that the ABA had written into its accrediting standards protections for faculty, which ended up inflating salaries. These include maximum teaching loads, standards for faculty compensation and tenure, and mandates for sabbaticals and research support (which the ABA has interpreted as paid sabbaticals and stipends for research work).[19] The standards also excluded for-profit law schools from being accredited and restricted students from transferring in from unaccredited schools, both of which protected law schools from competition.

Of course, other accreditation organizations for higher education may have similar requirements. But most colleges and universities have a choice about which accreditation organization to join. There is competition among organizations to keep their standards in line with what college administrators think is reasonable. No such competition exists for the ABA; on the contrary, at least 45 states *require* that lawyers graduate from an ABA-accredited law school in order to be admitted to the bar.[20]

The lawsuit ended with a consent decree ending such practices as restricting transfers and collecting information about faculty salaries as part of the accreditation process. The DOJ also required the ABA accreditation teams to include more people from outside the law school. The consent decree was not entirely successful; in 2005, the ABA had to face another DOJ lawsuit for violating some of its terms.[21] But the ABA's (somewhat begrudging) compliance with these changes since 2005 did not put a stop to the general trends to which Tamanaha was objecting: the dramatic increase in the size, compensation, and credentials of law school faculty and the effect of those changes on what and how law schools were teaching.

More specifically, there were two major structural changes in the law school faculty between 1985 and 2020 that reformers noted with either alarm or satisfaction, depending on their point of view. First, regular faculty (those who teach subject-matter courses, usually focused on legal doctrine) became more focused on research and spent less time in the classroom. As mentioned above, standard course loads for tenured and tenure-track faculty at many schools declined from three to two courses per semester (a change reflected also in the growing size of law school faculty), which allowed these professors to spend more time on scholarly or other professional activities. Law schools encouraged this trend by offering summer research stipends and by focusing on research productivity in hiring and performance reviews. One notable consequence of this focus is that an increasing proportion of new law school faculty have a PhD either in addition to or in place of a JD, which greatly increases their capacity for interdisciplinary research and teaching. Brian Newton reports that the proportion of new law school faculty hires with a PhD rose from 5 percent in the late 1980s to more than 18 percent in 2010.[22] This growth probably reflects competition among law schools for more prestigious and productive faculty.

Importantly, though, that 18 percent figure excludes clinical and legal writing faculty, which is the second important structural change. Law schools are increasingly relying on a growing cadre of clinical faculty and legal writing instructors—people who teach courses focused on skills rather than doctrine. These faculty members are often in temporary appointments, not eligible for tenure, and may not be eligible for other benefits like summer research stipends.[23] They are increasingly important to law schools' educational goals, however, thanks to the most successful law school reform effort during this 1985–2020 period: the campaign by the Clinical Legal Education Association, among others, to require law students to take courses focused on building skills.

The Rise of the Clinicians

As discussed in chapter 2, the campaign for more law school clinics and more legal writing courses is an old one. Law schools began offering clinics in the 1960s, and most required at least one legal writing course by the mid-1980s. The legal writing requirement is now part of the ABA's accreditation standards. But the traditional first-year training, focused on drafting briefs and oral advocacy, hardly lessens the gap between law school education and professional practice. Skills that might be needed by American lawyers are diverse given the variety of different roles that lawyers play. They may include negotiating; conflict resolution; drafting contracts, wills, patents, articles of incorporation, complaints, and other legal documents; examining titles to real property; advising clients; investigating, collecting, and evaluating evidence; or drafting regulations and statutes. Depending on their area of practice, lawyers might find themselves needing further education in forensic accounting, child psychology, computer science, or hydrology. And those subjects compete not only with the need to master legal doctrine but with training in professional ethics. The conversation about "skills-training" is thus shorthand for a complex judgment about how best to use the short, three-year training period that precedes professional practice.

The contemporary version of that conversation kicked off with a 1992 ABA report titled "Legal Education and Professional Development—An Educational Continuum,"[24] commonly known as the MacCrate Report. This widely discussed[25] report advised the ABA to reconceptualize the mission of law school from merely preparing students to pass the bar exam to preparing students "to participate effectively in the profession." It recommended in particular more courses focused on specific skills, including

92   CHAPTER THREE

the opportunity to work with real clients or conduct simulated client interactions. The report gave support to the segment of the legal education establishment concerned with teaching skills, such as the Clinical Legal Education Association (formed in 1992) and the Association of Legal Writing Directors (1996). Their efforts resulted in the adoption in 2005 of a new accreditation standard requiring law schools to offer students "substantial instruction" in the "professional skills generally regarded as necessary for effective and responsible participation in the legal profession," including "live client or other real-life practical experiences."[26]

While the standard encouraged creation of more skills courses, it did not yet *require* students to take clinical courses. But the MacCrate Report was followed by two additional reports in 2007: "Best Practices for Legal Education," by a group led by Roy Stuckey for the Clinical Legal Education Association, and "Educating Lawyers: Preparation for the Profession of Law," by a group led by William Sullivan for the Carnegie Foundation (the Carnegie Report). Again, both reports emphasized the continuing need for more training in the skills needed for professional practice. More specifically, the reports recommended reducing "doctrinal instruction that uses the Socratic dialogue and the case method" and integrating the teaching of skills and values into the courses delivering subject-area knowledge. (The above reference to "values" reflects the continuing concern with instruction in professional ethics.)[27]

These reports, we should note, were not as critical of legal education as they may sound. The Carnegie Report, for example, emphasized that training in a profession is a long-term process that only *begins* in professional school, and it noted that law schools do a very good job of training students in doctrinal analysis, affirming the place of the case method in law school classrooms. Nevertheless, discussion of legal education during this period reflects strong and near-universal consensus that law students could benefit from more training in the skills of professional practice, and a requirement that all students take at least one experiential course (a clinic, field placement, or course involving simulations) was finally adopted by the ABA in 2014.

But have these reform efforts actually affected the law school curriculum? There is at least some evidence that they have. The Curriculum Committee of the ABA Section on Legal Education, under the leadership of Catherine Carpenter, surveyed law school curricula from 1992 to 2002 and again in 2010. The reports on those surveys describe two decades of "dynamism."

The committee saw "experimentation and change at all levels of the curriculum, resulting in new programs and courses, new and enhanced experiential learning, and greater emphasis on various kinds of writing across the curriculum."[28] The major findings in both reports were similar, reflecting some consistent trends over 20 years.

In the first place, while the first-year set of required courses has remained remarkably static over this period, some law schools are allowing first-year students to take an elective, often offering a choice among courses focused on statutory interpretation (such as environmental law) or courses offering broader perspectives on law in society, such as legal history, jurisprudence, or comparative law.[29] However, most of the dynamism that the committee described affects the second- and third-year curricula. Schools continued to address new areas of law by adding elective courses, the most popular areas being intellectual property, business law, international law, and health law. In addition, however, many law schools are now offering certificates in certain areas like intellectual property or environmental law—that is, they support a degree of specialization in those areas, which usually requires more specialized courses as well as additional programming and experiential opportunities like internships in the subject area. The reports also describe an increase in interdisciplinary courses such as bioethics, law and economics, and law and literature—some of which are taught in conjunction with faculty from outside the law school. And at least some respondents reported a deemphasis on the case-dialogue teaching method, with an increase in problem-based learning (a pedagogic technique in which students are given either hypothetical or real-life problems to respond to).[30]

A final piece of evidence about curricular change is the increase in experiential and skills-based courses. The 2002 survey reported that over half the respondents offered students externships at nonprofit organizations, over 50 percent offered courses on legislative or regulatory drafting, and the variety of clinics available was increasing:

> Traditionally clinics would set as a goal for themselves the development of the lawyering skills essential for effective client representation. Now, other skills are emphasized in some clinics, for example, the development of public policy positions and their advocacy. In some instances this latter set of skills is the focus of a separate clinic, while in others it is an aspect to be developed along with the skills necessary for client representation.[31]

For example, Martha Davis has identified the reemergence of law labs, legal innovation clinics aimed at promoting new approaches in law and legal practice.[32] In sum, the entire period from around 1990 to 2020 was described by the committee as one of significant curricular and pedagogical reform in the direction of a richer set of advanced courses and greater attention to practical skills, including some that are directly pertinent to influencing public policy.

It is necessary, however, to qualify this conclusion: judging from my interviews with people who graduated from law school between 2007 and 2022, these curricular and pedagogic reforms are still unevenly distributed. Some students—particularly those at second- or third-tier law schools—reported that most of their courses were in the traditional subjects taught in the traditional way. Students at top-ranked law schools did report some pedagogic innovation, such as the opportunity to take seminars and do research on public policy, and many were able to take one or two advanced courses in environmental law.[33] But the Harvard model has not by any means disappeared from law schools. On the contrary, interviewees report that it is primarily in the emerging fields and newer topics—like climate law and energy law—that they found more creative teaching methods. This suggests that the addition of new topics to the curriculum is an important factor supporting pedagogic innovation. And the enrichment of the curriculum is being driven largely by changes in who is being hired to teach these courses and what they are spending their time on.

The Transformation of Regular Faculty?

As discussed above, the increase in courses devoted to skills was accomplished largely by hiring more clinical faculty. Not surprising, accompanying this change in the composition of the faculty has been a debate about what the regular (nonclinical) faculty should be doing. Most law schools are encouraging regular faculty to do more research, and some are promoting interdisciplinary scholarship, particularly by hiring people with PhDs in addition to JDs. This trend undoubtedly supports the enrichment of the curriculum, but it is not universally applauded. On the contrary, law professors have received a surprising amount of criticism for doing research—particularly "theoretical," "empirical," and "interdisciplinary" research (as opposed to focusing on doctrinal analysis).[34] This is surprising because law professors' focus on doctrine at the expense of more empirical or interdisciplinary scholarship has been a major criticism of the field since law schools' earliest days. But that line of criticism was never uncontested, of course; there have been and apparently still are defenders of the narrow definition of legal scholarship as doctrinal analysis.

Representing the old guard in this debate over faculty research priorities is Judge Harry Edwards, who published a widely read[35] article in the *Michigan Law Review* in 1992 titled "The Growing Disjunction Between Legal Education and Legal Practice." Edwards complained that much of the scholarship occurring in law schools is impractical, of little value to practicing attorneys and judges. While he was willing to tolerate some "scholar-to-scholar" articles focused on theory, he asked law reviews—and presumably law professors—to devote more attention to articles directed at answering the questions commonly faced by practitioners and judges, many of which, he thought, concerned doctrine.[36]

Edwards's critique prompted many defenses of empirical, interdisciplinary, and other types of scholarship as legitimate avenues for law professors to pursue. Importantly, however, those defenders largely agreed with Edwards that the basic goal of legal education was to equip lawyers with practical problem-solving skills that would be useful in their practices. They simply disagreed about the role of nondoctrinal research in doing that. Edward Rubin's 2008 defense of the more innovative kinds of legal research, for example, insisted that, even if such research didn't enhance the doctrine-focused courses very much, it "provide[s] knowledge for its own sake, it sustains our cultural traditions, and it serves as the basis for *pragmatic advances in technology, social services and public governance.*"[37] Indeed, he concluded that if the new, more empirical and interdisciplinary orientation of law school faculty did not fit comfortably with the traditional doctrine-focused curriculum, then perhaps the curriculum should change.[38]

Rubin's reference to interdisciplinary research is of special interest to us because much of the support for more interdisciplinary research and teaching during this period was coming from environmental law professors. A good example is Kim Diana Connolly's article "Elucidating the Elephant: Interdisciplinary Law School Classes" (2003). Connolly at the time was an assistant professor at University of South Carolina School of Law and director of its Environmental Law Clinic, as well as an associate faculty member in the university's School of the Environment and affiliate faculty in the Women's Studies Program. Sounding a common theme in environmental studies generally, she argued that solving environmental problems often

96 CHAPTER THREE

requires looking at them from multiple perspectives and collaborating in multidisciplinary teams.[39] Interdisciplinary courses are thus the preferred approach.

Unfortunately, she found that interdisciplinary research and teaching still faced a daunting list of barriers—most of which, we should note, were *not* addressed or even recognized by the reformers interested in increasing skills training. The interdisciplinary faculty member faced "physical and psychological isolation; faculty marginalization; overly simplistic instruction in a discipline; potential overreaching; views that dual degree or specialized programs offer sufficient interdisciplinary opportunities; different ethical norms between disciplines; bar passage pressure; different student expectations; parochialism; cost; and logistics."[40] More concisely, law faculty often lack the interdisciplinary training to teach such courses effectively by themselves, team-teaching can be difficult and costly to arrange, and students don't always see the value of interdisciplinary training. The first of these problems may be addressed by the increase in law faculty with PhDs and thus at least some training in a second discipline. But we should note that even the long doctoral training period does not produce a fully mature and experienced scholar in any field, and training in one additional field may not equip a faculty member to tackle broadly interdisciplinary subjects like environmental management. Neither does additional training help with such barriers as student expectations, the pressure to prepare students for the bar, and the logistics of interdisciplinary courses.

Thomas Ulen's article "The Impending Train Wreck in Current Legal Education" (2009) illustrates some of these problems. Ulen focused his complaint on the fixed-in-stone character of the first-year curriculum, which he characterized as "seriously out of alignment" with the kinds of problems lawyers currently face. He was not simply rehearsing the argument for more skills training, though. In the tradition of Felix Frankfurter and the Legal Realists, he argued that law schools should understand their subject as "social governance," not merely advising private clients. And such a conceptual change posed serious challenges. To illustrate, he described his own experience teaching the course "The Law and Economics of Global Warming" at the University of Illinois College of Law. This experience is worth examining in some detail.

First, he needed to find readings to assign: "I had to devise a structure for the course and then assemble readings that would help me and the students come to grips with the topic."[41] Ulen has a PhD in economics from

Stanford University (instead of rather than in addition to a JD) and has a distinguished record of scholarship in the interdisciplinary field of law and economics. Moreover, he had actually helped to create a multidisciplinary center on global change at the University of Illinois. But he was not an expert on climate change, and "providing material for a fourteen-week-long course required both filling in lots of gaps in my knowledge and generating a structured presentation of a great deal of material." He soon discovered that

> in order for me and the students to understand the issues of climate change, we would have to inform ourselves about a large number of topics. We would, for instance, need to understand the role that carbon dioxide plays in making the planet habitable and, more generally, the role of greenhouse gases in influencing temperatures at various points on Earth; about the history of the Earth's climate and the causes for the variations in the climate; about the methods for modeling climate change and for evaluating the veracity of those models; about the costs that climate change might impose on the planet and when and where those costs might fall; about acceptable methods for discounting future costs to present value so as to be able to decide what policy changes to address climate change make sense at various points in the next century; about the various policy options available to slow or adapt to global warming (such as the fostering of alternative energy sources (nuclear, tidal, wind-powered, and solar), the prospects for relatively inexpensive carbon-capture-and-sequestration (CCS) systems that would allow continued use of coal-powered utilities, geoengineering, cap-and-trade systems, carbon taxes, private liability actions against those emitting temperature-raising gases, and more); about the various national policies to address climate change and their lack of success; about the United Nations Framework Convention on Climate Change of 1992 and the Kyoto Protocol of 1997 and why the United States did not accede to that Protocol; and about the grave difficulties and daunting prospects of an international agreement addressing global warming.[42]

I apologize for the long block quote, but this list vividly demonstrates the difficulties of designing a course on climate policy even as late as in 2009—some 25 years after the first calls for climate policy. Ulen understood quite well the need to draw on different disciplines to cover this subject. Unfortunately,

98   CHAPTER THREE

the rewards system in the modern research university does not encourage interdisciplinary innovation. A scholar who strays too far beyond the narrow focus of the discipline risks a great deal. The scholar's work is difficult for colleagues to evaluate and may not be welcomed by those into whose domain the scholar may have strayed. Generally speaking, being a productive scholar in one discipline is a far safer route for success than being a productive scholar (or innovator) across disciplines.[43]

Indeed, to offer just one example of this institutional bias, Michal Meyerson noted in a 2015 article that law schools also still discourage coauthorship of articles. Collaborative research is common in most fields, but law schools have a strongly individualistic culture that views legal work "as the result of primarily individual effort and hence a source of solely personal achievement."[44] To be sure, there is evidence that this norm is changing—that there has been (in the words of Andrew Hayashi) an "explosion in coauthorship" since 2000. Hayashi's research shows that a dramatic increase in coauthored articles "has created a connected network of scholars to which more than 50% of legal scholars belong."[45] But just as the increase in faculty with interdisciplinary training does not automatically eliminate barriers to interdisciplinary teaching, neither does the increasingly networked community of legal scholars automatically change the institutional barriers to collaboration.

On the contrary, a 2014 study by Stephen Daniels, Martin Katz, and William Sullivan assessing the impact of the Carnegie Report found that, while curricular innovation was accelerating, only about 24 percent of the respondent law schools actually changed their criteria for tenure, promotion, merit pay, or hiring. "Changing the personnel process," the coauthors point out, "poses the greatest challenge to the legal academy because it changes what it means to be a part of the legal academy."[46] Thus the prolific Edward Rubin in 2014 was still complaining that law schools are "among the most static and rigid institutions in the United States." They needed to change in order to prepare students to face current problems, including "the potential depletion of the Earth's resources and the destruction of its environment." As he put it: "Consider, for example, how much sophisticated legal work will be involved in developing a comprehensive system of carbon accounting that achieves its intended purposes and avoids unintended consequences."[47] Such problems, he argued, required less focus on traditional common law doctrine and more training in crafting regulations, conducting complex transactions, and solving real-world problems—as well as more interdisciplinary courses.[48]

Like pedagogic innovation, the trend toward interdisciplinary scholarship is uneven across law schools. The interviewees who engaged in interdisciplinary teaching or scholarship affirmed the critical importance of institutional support, and some law schools seem particularly open to interdisciplinary collaboration. Kim Diana Connolly, for example, noted the supportive culture at the University of South Carolina's law school. The university had the very good School of the Earth, Ocean & Environment, which served as a strong interdisciplinary center bringing together scholars from around the campus—which, she notes, was a small campus where it was easy to connect with colleagues outside the law school.[49] Informal conversations with outside colleagues are a common theme among the more interdisciplinary legal scholars. Thomas Ulen sounded the same theme: "We're all buried in our disciplinary silos, [unless] you happen to be serving on university committees and happen to become friendly with somebody in another department in these big universities." (In fact, he attributes his initial interest in law and economics to a casual meeting with Dan Farber at a dinner for new professors during Farber's brief tenure at the University of Illinois.)[50] But only a few interviewees reported that their institutional home was particularly supportive of interdisciplinary collaboration. Many of them, however, did identify another useful institutional support for interdisciplinary work: the establishment of environmental centers and institutes.

The Rise of Centers and Institutes

This brings us to a final element of law school curricular reform: the proliferation of centers and institutes within law schools and the increasing participation of law schools in campuswide interdisciplinary centers and institutes since 1990. Although terminology can vary among institutions, centers are usually located within a law school, while institutes are usually separate from the law school and under the administration of the university. However, their purposes and activities can overlap. These organizations can help to create a network of faculty focused on a subject and promote collaboration. They may interact with or even create a broader community outside the law school by conducting formal research programs or organizing conferences and public talks, and they also may contribute to faculty development and offer internships and research opportunities to students.

The rise of interdisciplinary centers and institutes has not received as much attention as other trends in higher education, but it was a prominent theme in my interviews. While universities have been coordinating interdisciplinary research and teaching with these cross-departmental and cross-school administrative units for decades, law schools traditionally did not participate in them very much. As Hari Osofsky explained:

> The most radical thing I was up to [while Dean] at Penn State [Law School] was to say that law schools are traditionally pretty siloed from their universities . . . but what if they're not? What if we took a law school and fully embedded it in a major R1 [research university], what would happen? It turns out all sorts of cool things can happen. But law schools often aren't making that many joint hires with other units, they're often not part of big university-scale research projects where law could be relevant to them.[51]

She went on to explain that the Center for Energy Law and Policy at Penn State intentionally reached out to law professors with the aim of encouraging their participation in policy-oriented research. That theme was echoed by Joseph Macdougald, at the University of Connecticut Law School, who participated in the university's Institute for Resilience and Climate Adaptation on developing a model of climate-induced sea-level rise in order to inform state planning targets. That sort of collaboration between law professors and STEM scholars, he notes, is still unusual.[52]

In addition to this still-nascent trend of including law school faculty in campuswide research centers, law schools are increasingly creating their own centers and institutes to facilitate teaching, scholarship, and especially public policy work. A center is an administrative unit run by a director, usually with at least some administrative support, and is funded either by the law school or by outside donors and grants (or both). They usually focus on a problem or cluster of problems of public policy requiring input from legal scholars; examples include Stanford's Center for Internet and Society and Martin Daniel Gould Center for Conflict Resolution. Centers focusing on environmental problems are becoming increasingly common; my research assistant found 38 such centers focused on environmental issues at American law schools, most of which were founded after 1990 (see appendix B). They engage in a range of activities, including administering certificate and LLM programs; organizing public talks, conferences, and other events for the law school, the university community, policymakers, scholars, or the general public; consulting with policymakers or other stakeholders on policy issues; and publishing scholarship intended to influence outside constituencies. I will discuss how these centers engage with the policy community on climate change in later chapters. Here the main point is that they make it easier for participating faculty to collaborate, or at least interact, with one another and with experts outside the law school, and they support faculty in research directed at influencing public policy—research that can influence classroom teaching as well. They can also enrich students' educational experience through co-curricular activities like public talks and conferences (sometimes organized by students themselves), and they may also provide opportunities for students to participate in the centers' research and policy work.

For example, Joseph Macdougald directs the Center for Energy and Environmental Law at University of Connecticut Law School. That center connects him with local issues that his students can research, as well as stakeholders and policymakers he can bring into his classes. It also helps place students in externships and offers talks and events, such as meetings with the state bar section on energy or the environment. Students participate in organizing on-campus conferences hosted by the center, and it has even funded students to participate in international conferences.[53] Centers can vary quite a lot in how active they are and the degree to which they engage students, but their potential to support more interdisciplinary, problem-based, experiential learning either inside or outside the classroom shouldn't be underestimated. Several student interviewees reported participating in events or organizing conferences hosted by an environmental center; for some, the center offered the principal networking opportunity for students interested in environmental issues.

In sum, during the period from 1990 to 2020—in the broader context of increasing financial resources, increasing competition for high-performing students and faculty, and a growing need to justify the privileged position of law schools in American higher education—law schools were engaged with curricular and pedagogical reform. Judging from the scholarly literature, the legal professoriate has achieved a broad consensus about the basic goal of legal education: preparing students for professional practice, conceived broadly as helping to solve complex social problems by bringing to bear on them a rich set of skills and legal tools. Despite the strangely persistent first-year focus on common law doctrine, law professors seem to have embraced the idea that practicing law includes not only serving private clients but also engaging in policy creation, implementation, and advocacy. This consensus is evident in both the campaign for more clinical, skills-based courses and the debate about faculty research priorities during this period. Of the two campaigns, the movement for more skills-based courses has had the most success, resulting in a new ABA requirement, more varied clinics and other experiential options for students, and more hiring in this area. There is some evidence that faculty research is evolving as well, in the direction of more empirical, interdisciplinary, and theoretical work—an evolution guided (or constrained?) by the demand that it meet the test of enhancing legal professionals' ability to tackle complex, real-world problems and supported by the growth of centers and institutes organized for this purpose. The experience of faculty attempting to do interdisciplinary teaching and research suggests that this evolution is neither easy nor complete. On the contrary, pedagogical and curricular innovation seems to be most prevalent in emerging and rapidly changing fields—fields like environmental law. Thus this evolving institutional context is critical to understanding how law professors tackled the curricular and pedagogical challenges of preparing future legal professionals to grapple with climate change.

Evolution of Climate Policy

Because American climate policy was also evolving, the need for special training in climate law became increasingly more apparent during this period . To be sure, the story of American climate policy from 2000 to 2020 is usually told as a story of failure, beginning with the decisions, in 1999 by President Bill Clinton and again in 2001 by newly elected George W. Bush, not to submit the Kyoto Protocol to the Senate for ratification. There were also several failed efforts to pass a federal regulatory bill addressing carbon emissions between 1999 and 2009: the Byrd–Stevens Climate Change Strategy and Technology Innovation Act was introduced in Congress in 2001, and the McCain–Lieberman Climate Stewardship Act was introduced each session from 2003 to 2009, failing to pass each time. President Barack Obama also failed to achieve a federal climate statute, but he did make climate change a priority in his second administration, issuing new regulations on carbon dioxide emissions under the Clean Air Act (such as the Clean Power Plan) and joining the 2016 Paris Agreement.[54] But this brief overview doesn't do justice to the evolution of US climate policy during these two decades.

Indeed, even as the Bush administration decided not to ratify Kyoto in 2001, it was working on four international side agreements aimed at promoting climate-friendly energy technology: the International Partnership for Hydrogen Economy (2003), the Renewable Energy and Energy Efficiency Partnership (2004), the Global Methane Initiative (2004), and the Asia-Pacific Partnership for Clean Development and Climate (2005). Some of these are still active (as of 2023) and can claim some success in developing solutions to climate change. However, they focus on international cooperation, information-sharing, and funding technological innovation. None of them have significant implications for domestic policy, such as restricting greenhouse gas emissions by regulating private behavior. The Bush administration did approve legislation requiring automakers to improve corporate average fuel efficiency (CAFE) to 35 miles per gallon in 2007, a measure that would help contain carbon emissions from the transportation sector.[55] But it also denied California permission to set a more ambitious CAFE standard, as the state tried to do in 2002.[56] California was not alone in its efforts, though. State and local governments were becoming quite active on climate policy during this period.

State Climate Policy

Stephen Wheeler's 2008 assessment of state and local climate action reported that 29 states had climate action plans by that point, and 22 of them had set specific GHG reduction targets. State-level policies are diverse, including adopting California's fuel efficiency standards for vehicles (which are usually stricter than the national standards required by the Clean Air Act), pursuing energy efficiency in government buildings, electrifying government vehicle fleets, and expanding recycling efforts to reduce methane from landfills. To be sure, Wheeler noted that the state plans were not very aggressive in their goals and were not being widely implemented yet.[57] But by this time, several states were turning away from fossil fuels, at least for electricity generation. As Patrick Parenteau noted in a 2008 review of state-level climate action, Kansas, Florida, Iowa, Oklahoma, and Texas (as well as more progressive states like Oregon, Washington, California, and Maine) were blocking the development of new coal-fired power plants on climate grounds.[58] Moreover, Wheeler's assessment understated the significance of some major developments in new state-level GHG policy.

In 2005, a group of northeastern states (Connecticut, Delaware, Maine, New Hampshire, New Jersey, New York, and Vermont) created the Regional Greenhouse Gas Initiative (RGGI), the first carbon dioxide emissions trading system in the United States. Massachusetts, Maryland, and Rhode Island joined later that year (and Virginia joined in 2021). The RGGI created a regulatory program in which each participating state established a carbon dioxide budget trading program that limits the emissions of carbon dioxide from electric power plants. These major emitters are initially allocated a set of allowances, with some additional allowances auctioned off. They may then trade allowances among themselves, thereby creating a regional market for carbon dioxide emission allowances. The program also allows emitters to offset their emissions by funding projects that lower carbon emissions. Offset projects include initiatives such as methane capture systems, creating forests (to sequester carbon), and increasing energy efficiency technologies. This brief description hardly captures the complexity of the program, of course, which includes sophisticated systems for monitoring the market, emissions accounting, running auctions, evaluating offset projects, and ensuring compliance. The program did not begin operation until 2009, just after Wheeler's paper was published.

Similarly, in 2006 California passed the Global Warming Solutions Act, creating an even more ambitious and wide-ranging set of policies aimed at reducing greenhouse gas emissions, which also took a few years to begin implementing. The centerpiece of this legislation was a state-level cap-and-trade system for carbon dioxide emissions, similar to the RGGI program. By 2009, two other regional voluntary carbon trading programs had been created: the Chicago Climate Exchange, which operated from 2003 to 2010, and the Western Climate Initiative, initiated by Arizona, California, Oregon, Washington, and New Mexico and expanding to include Montana, Utah, and four Canadian provinces. (By 2023, participating jurisdictions had reduced to California, Washington, Quebec, and Nova Scotia.)

We should not underestimate the legal complexity of these new regulatory systems. The creation of a market for emissions allowances was not itself a new idea—the first such regulation in the United States was a federal cap-and-trade system for sulfur dioxide emissions created during George H. W. Bush's administration in 1990. But as the legal scholar Steven Ferrey noted, the idea of auctioning off emissions allowances—requiring emitters to buy permits to emit what they had thus far been allowed to emit for free—was a completely new approach in American environmental law. It presented legal complications. For example, the RGGI and California auctions were challenged by emitters as imposing an unauthorized tax that far exceeded the costs of administering the program and as interfering with the authority of the federal government over energy markets.[59] California's cross-border linkage with Canadian provinces also raised constitutional questions, since states are prohibited from interfering unduly with the federal government's power to conduct foreign affairs.[60] In addition, the California program faced a challenge that it violated constitutional norms by restricting out-of-state producers from selling to California markets (thereby creating a barrier to interstate commerce, which is disfavored under American constitutional doctrine).[61] Another California regulation, the low carbon fuel standard, faced a similar challenge. This standard restricted the sale of fuel in California according to its "carbon intensity," a new regulatory concept defined as "the amount of lifecycle greenhouse gas emissions, per unit of energy of fuel delivered, expressed in grams of carbon dioxide per megajoule."[62] Without delving into the details of these issues, suffice it to say that the new programs represented the intersection of emerging climate science with relatively new, market-based regulatory strategies—posing novel challenges that environmental and energy lawyers would need to grapple with.

These new state-level regulatory regimes pointed toward an emerging need for new legal expertise in climate policy. Indeed, in 2007 Michael Gerrard was already identifying the myriad ways in which lawyers could help fight climate change, from designing and implementing regulatory programs to facilitating construction of "renewable energy plants, district energy systems, and other facilities to generate energy with lower greenhouse gas emissions or to reduce the need for energy" to helping clients in "putting up green buildings [and] retrofitting old buildings to consume less energy" to "helping companies in the industrial, transportation, agricultural, utilities, and other sectors understand and meet their emerging legal obligations[] and developing and carrying out disclosure obligations in real estate transactions." He also pointed out that "[climate] adaptation mechanisms deserve considerably more legal attention than they have received." Possible legal reactions to climate impacts include "flood protection, flood hazard mapping, protecting buildings and infrastructure from rising water tables, sizing of stormwater facilities, sizing of wastewater treatment plants, strengthening structures to withstand higher wind loads, and modifying heating, ventilation, and air conditioning systems to withstand worse heat waves."[63]

To understand how law schools might help meet these legal challenges, consider the Berkeley–UCLA Center for Law, Energy & the Environment (CLEE). UC Berkeley law school and the UCLA Environmental Law Clinic were involved in defending the California climate regulations, among several law clinics and environmental law professors that filed amicus curiae briefs in the California cases mentioned above.[64] But as discussed above, these law school centers often do more than litigation. For example, CLEE has noted the legal challenges of creating programs to encourage projects that sequester carbon and accordingly produced in 2021 a report titled *Seeding Capital* that proposes policy approaches including:

- aligning nature-based investment products with existing international standards and labels;
- leveraging California Environmental Quality Act (CEQA) mitigation to fund projects on natural and working lands;
- standardizing accounting practices for measuring greenhouse gas impacts, environmental impacts, and community impacts; and
- conducting advance planning and permitting for multiple potential projects to create "portfolios" for grantors and investors to finance.[65]

The report was sponsored by Bank of America and drew on experts convened by the two law schools. The report's authors included Ethan Elkind, a lawyer directing CLEE's Climate Change and Business Program, collaborating with Ted Lamm, a lawyer working as a senior research fellow at CLEE, and Katie Segal, a Climate and Ocean Research Fellow at CLEE with a masters in public policy from Harvard Kennedy School. This is the type of collaborative, problem-solving work that evolving state-level climate policy would increasingly require.

Local Climate Policy

Policy and legal innovation was happening at the local level as well. In 2005, Sierra Club's Cool Cities program and the Mayors Climate Protection Agreement joined ICLEI in promoting a flurry of new city-level climate policies. Wheeler found that scores of cities had climate action plans by this time, although many set unambitious targets or weren't being implemented very aggressively. In California, for example, San Diego set the most ambitious short-term carbon emission reduction goal (15 percent below 1990 by 2010), while Los Angeles, Berkeley, and Santa Cruz set more ambitious long-term goals—as much as 80 percent below 1990 or 2000 levels by 2050. Cities more commonly aimed to make their own buildings and fleets carbon neutral. Beyond this obvious step, cities tackled energy efficiency, transportation, and waste reduction (aiming to reduce methane emissions from landfills). Some cities were examining innovative land use policies, attempting to limit urban sprawl and promote urban forestry.[66] Carmen Sirianni reported in 2020 that Portland, Oregon, had updated its climate action plan three times—in 2001, 2009, and 2015—and each time it added more kinds of policies, addressing restoration of watersheds, urban forests, sustainable business, food systems, and green buildings.[67]

Of course, smaller cities often lack the capacity for substantial new policymaking. Larger cities like Chicago and Seattle, with strong tax bases, typically lead the list of climate innovators. Smaller cities were able to take advantage of grants to support climate action planning, such as those offered by the federal Department of Energy as part of the 2009 American Recovery and Reinvestment Act.[68] But that grant program expired in 2012. My own experience with local policymaking with cities, townships, and counties in southeastern Minnesota suggests that cities' institutional capacity is a significant obstacle to climate action. While American localities hold a great deal of authority over land use and some authority in health, safety, and economic development, they are often limited by state law in key ways. In some states, local governments cannot impose energy efficiency mandates on new buildings beyond those required by the state building code. City control of state and federal highways and other transportation infrastructure is also quite limited. Indeed, even creating a fund to support the planting of more trees requires some legal dexterity, since cities may be restricted in how they can receive, handle, and spend donations. Many cities face legal restrictions on the use of city-owned land, which may come into the city's possession with restrictions attached (a common problem with testamentary gifts). In short, innovations in local climate policy, like innovations in state-level policy, suggest the need for more legal support than the average part-time city attorney may be able to provide. Here, too, is a potential field for entrepreneurial law professors to enter.

Climate Change in the Courts

As for the courts, the pace of climate litigation picked up considerably after 2000. The climate litigation database maintained by Columbia Law School's Sabin Center reports that 288 climate-related lawsuits were filed in US state and federal courts from 2000 to 2010.[69] One might expect that most of the litigation would be connected with the new state regulations directed at curbing carbon emissions, but in fact most of it focused on existing federal environmental laws. By far the most important of these lawsuits was *Massachusetts v. EPA*, which began in 1999 as a petition to the EPA, filed by a group

108　CHAPTER THREE

of states and environmental organizations, asking that agency to declare carbon dioxide a pollutant and therefore subject to regulation under the Clean Air Act. The agency took several years to consider the petition and finally rejected it in 2003. At that point, the petitioners launched *Massachusetts v. EPA*, asking the courts to force the EPA to address carbon pollution under the Clean Air Act.

The courts also took their time with the case, but in 2007 the Supreme Court finally issued its decision, holding that carbon dioxide could be considered a pollutant under the CAA and directing the EPA to consider whether it endangered human health. The Bush administration, predictably, did not act on this decision; not until the Obama administration would the EPA issue the first federal regulations directed specifically at regulating carbon dioxide. However, according to David Markell and J. B. Ruhl:

> *Massachusetts v. EPA* forced open the door to agency regulation and triggered a cascade of agency rulemaking and judicial litigation. It is likely for this reason that the case has been deemed exceptional by at least one audience that watches climate change litigation closely—environmental lawyers. Respondents to a 2010 survey of environmental law practitioners and academics asking about the most important environmental law cases overwhelmingly characterized *Massachusetts v. EPA* as the most significant environmental law decision of all time.[70]

But even before that decision was made, the environmental law bar was starting to give more attention to climate law. The ABA's Section on Environment, Energy, and Resources (SEER) started holding annual conferences in 2005 to educate lawyers about climate change, and in 2007 it published a 727-page book titled *Global Climate Change and U.S. Law*. Edited by Michael Gerrard, chair of SEER from 2004 to 2005, the book included contributions by 25 experts in American environmental law.[71] Topics ranged from the Kyoto Protocol and regulating GHGs under the Clean Air Act to state and local initiatives to corporate action (four chapters, including disclosure and fiduciary duties, insurance, and subsidies and incentives), voluntary efforts, emissions trading, and carbon sequestration. Indeed, the book devotes a whole chapter to the impact of the Kyoto Protocol on US businesses, pointing out that, even though the United States didn't join the protocol, US businesses operating in other countries or doing business with foreign companies would have to become familiar with the emerging regulatory strategies for dealing with climate change. In short, by 2008 there was more than enough climate law for a course on the subject.

Markell and Ruhl commented in their 2012 article that

> we anticipate that before long, it will make sense to refer to climate change law for some statutes as being established and reasonably settled through the aggregation of judicial opinions. The courts and agencies have been busy, resolving 110 litigation matters in 2008–10, meaning it is possible for lawyers to research and synthesize bodies of case law. . . . The law of climate change, for long only a prospect, is now on the books in large part due to litigation.[72]

They may have underestimated the pace of climate law innovation. By 2009 two casebooks specifically on climate law had appeared.[73] And in 2014 the ABA published a second edition of *Global Climate Change and U.S. Law*, edited by Michael Gerrard with Jody Freeman. Those events suggest that climate law was earning a place in the law school curriculum. In chapter 4 I explore what that place looked like: How were law schools, in the midst of curricular and pedagogic reform, taking up this complex subject?

CHAPTER FOUR

The Great Transformation, 2000–2010

In 2011, John Dernbach, director of Widener University Law School's Environmental Law Center, summarized what American law schools were doing to further sustainability. His survey (drawing from two major sources[1]) showed significant development of the climate curriculum. He identified a growing number of courses on sustainability and noted that "many law schools (e.g., Duke, NYU, Stanford, and Yale) have well-established programs on greenhouse gas trading markets."[2] Textbooks were increasingly addressing sustainability in general and climate change in particular, and law schools were offering a number of interdisciplinary programs, law clinics, certificate programs, LLM programs, and joint degree programs focused on sustainability or specifically on climate change.[3]

Dernbach noted that resources for teaching about climate change were also increasingly available. He found a dramatic increase in law review articles on climate change, jumping from under 50 in 2006 to over 200 in 2008.[4] The Books In Print database showed that "the number of law-related climate change books also grew rapidly between 2000 (two published) and 2009 (thirteen published)." He pointed as well to law school conferences and new journals on climate change, such as USD (University of San Diego) Law School's *Journal of Climate and Energy Law* and Washington and Lee School of Law's *Journal of Energy, Climate, and the Environment*.[5] Finally, he showed that law school clinics and institutes were beginning to conduct research on climate policy, often in teams including law students.[6]

This summary reflects an impressive growth in the climate curriculum in law schools between 2000 and 2010. How were the early barriers to teaching climate law overcome? And what did the emerging field of climate law look like? In this chapter I contend that some of those barriers were overcome because of factors external to law schools—principally the impacts of climate change itself and the policy community's response to it. But those barriers were also affected by the additional teaching resources devoted to environmental law during this period. Teaching materials were emerging and being disseminated through professional networks focused on climate law, and professors teaching about climate change also benefited when their law schools hired more faculty, expanded clinical opportunities, and gave greater support for interdisciplinary work, such as creating interdisciplinary centers and institutes. These factors supported the emergence of climate law as a distinct field within the law school curriculum, drawing on several areas of law beyond traditional federal environmental law.

To be sure, climate law did not emerge everywhere. Some of my student interviewees attended law schools that barely addressed climate change at all, either because of an underdeveloped environmental law curriculum or because the school focused on training students to work in the oil and gas industry.[7] Where climate law was emerging, it still reflected its roots in environmental law: it focused on top-down regulation, on the rules and policies being fashioned by high-level technocrats. As a teaching area, it focused on training legal advisers to the political and economic global elite. But climate law was proving difficult to teach even from that somewhat limited perspective. By 2010, new obstacles to teaching climate law would appear, as it became clear that climate change posed deep challenges to the traditional curricular and pedagogical approaches of the legal academy.

Emergence of the Climate Curriculum

Climate change itself was responsible for eroding two barriers to teaching the subject: the crowded agenda, and the lack of a practice area. While the early adopters developed climate law on the expectation that it would soon become relevant, most professors took it up in response to either the direct impacts of climate change or the policy actions taken to address it. Climate change became more salient as a pressing social problem and focus of public policy after 2000, and law professors responded to that growing salience.

As I note in chapter 2, Georgetown, Vermont, and Widener law schools were among the early adopters of climate law. John Dernbach was offering a seminar on climate law by 2002. In 2003, students at Vermont could take the seminar "Global Climate Change" from Professor Tseming Yang or a seminar on climate litigation from Pat Parenteau. Georgetown law students would encounter climate change in Edith Brown Weiss's or Lisa Heinzerling's courses.

At most schools, however, climate made its way into the curriculum more gradually. Consider the evolution of William Buzbee's engagement with the topic. Buzbee received his JD from Columbia in 1986 and studied environmental law, including the Clean Air Act with Professor Frank Grad, but he didn't encounter climate change in the curriculum. He worked at the NRDC from 1987 to 1988 and was aware it had a climate initiative, but he didn't work on climate himself. He then took a faculty position at Emory Law School in 1993, teaching the standard environmental law course (among other courses). Buzbee did adopt the Robert Percival and colleagues casebook around 1996 and remembers using the question of whether the Clean Air Act required regulation of carbon dioxide. He also reports addressing climate change to some extent in his coverage of NEPA. But he noted in his interview that, because he prefers to focus on working with statutes, he didn't teach international topics like climate negotiations.

His coverage of climate change did evolve, though, "as I began to understand more about it, as the science became ever clearer, and as it became more and more prevalent in the world of legislation and regulation."[8] But a primary reason he began to focus on it was because he is particularly interested in the division between state and federal authority in environmental regulation. Climate is a good platform for studying that topic, because states like California have taken the lead in addressing the issue. Well-developed state-level programs like California's invite the question of how a federal statute would affect that state regime: Would it preempt state regulation, incorporate it, or accommodate it? Since greenhouse gasses can arise from so many different sources, both sources and carbon sinks fall under different governmental authorities, and climate change affects people in different jurisdictions, climate change necessarily requires attention from different levels of government. So it raises particularly well a question: How does divided power affect the ability to regulate a problem that is global and crosses boundaries? By 2003, Buzbee was publishing on this topic with respect to climate change,[9] and he increasingly focused on it in his course. It is, he pointed out, "a good, challenging problem to think through the limits of law." However, he has not taught an entire course on climate change himself, although there was a course on climate law being taught by visiting faculty by the time he left Emory for Georgetown in 2014.

UC Berkeley was also somewhat slow to develop a climate curriculum, despite having a strong environmental curriculum in the 1990s. Berkeley's story illustrates the consequences of having few faculty covering the environmental field. By 1990, its environmental faculty consisted of Joseph Sax, John Dwyer, and Peter Menell. But during that decade, Sax retired, John Dwyer became dean (and then resigned in 2002), and Peter Menell shifted his focus to intellectual property. So when Daniel Farber left the University of Minnesota for Berkeley in 2002, he was (once again) the primary environmental law professor. With his help, however, the law school built up the program again, hiring Eric Biber in 2006 and Holly Doremus in 2008, along with a series of adjuncts and visiting professors.

Scott Zimmermann, who would end up teaching a course on energy project financing at Berkeley, attended the law school from 2004 to 2007, and he noted that the curriculum was still in flux. The University of California, Berkeley as a whole covered climate change in many different schools and departments, but the law school didn't offer any courses specifically on climate or energy when Zimmermann started his degree. He came to law school after working for 10 years in the oil and gas industry and recalls being "the only student [at the law school] focused on energy." However, he was able to recruit a practicing lawyer to teach a course on financing energy projects—the course he now teaches. And during his second year, the school hired Steven Weissman to teach energy law, which gave considerable attention to climate issues. Moreover, despite the lack of a dedicated course, Zimmermann remembers climate change being very much present in the curriculum. It was covered in the environmental law survey course and in international environmental law, and he remembers *Massachusetts v. EPA* (decided in 2007) being the subject of conversation both in and out of class.[10]

Indeed, several interviewees cited the Supreme Court decision in *Massachusetts v. EPA* as an important event in prompting greater coverage of climate change. But it was not as prominent a theme as I expected. After 2000, climate change impacts were becoming more important in driving curricular development. Kelly Haragan, director of the Environmental Clinic at the University of Texas School of Law, noted that increasingly damaging hurricanes helped to raise awareness about climate change among her students, and Susan Kraham, director of Columbia Law School's environmental law clinic, also pointed to 2005's Hurricane Katrina—which led to massive casualties and the displacement of more than a million New Orleans residents—as an important event in drawing her attention to the issue.[11]

Kraham was one of the few law professors (a small but notable group) who came to the climate issue from a focus on human rights and environmental justice—from the bottom-up perspective of how to deal with climate impacts rather than from the technocratic, top-down perspective of regulating greenhouse gasses. Kraham graduated Columbia Law School in 1992 and did not take any environmental law courses. Like most of my interviewees interested in human rights, she saw environmental law as a fairly dry, statute-based course remote from issues affecting vulnerable communities like affordable housing. But she participated in a human rights clinic that took her to Nairobi to study squatter settlements, which prompted her interest in the burgeoning green movement in Nairobi as it affected rural-urban migration. She went on to do an internship at a small environmental public interest firm led by a number of leading environmental litigators, working on land use and housing. However, she did not think of climate change as directly relevant to her work until the mid-2000s. As she explained: "When I started doing environmental law [in the 1990s], climate change was something else. . . . It wasn't the way that we analyzed issues. Even when I was working on things like fighting an incinerator in Newark, it was about air and toxics, it wasn't about climate change." But Hurricane Katrina changed that. It was a climate-related environmental justice disaster: the hurricane and flooding in New Orleans destroyed over a million houses in the region and led to widespread homelessness, revealing how unprotected the poorer, minority communities in the city were from this sort of weather-related event. The disaster made climate change more salient for Kraham by helping her to see that "there was this area of environmental law and that we really had to make sure we were thinking about what the justice component of it was."[12]

Kraham moved to Columbia Law School in 2009, at which point Michael Gerrard had already started the Sabin Center to focus on climate law. Initially Kraham still saw climate law as very technical and scientific and not focused on civil rights and justice, but at Columbia she found opportunities to collaborate with the Sabin Center, as well as the school's human rights clinic and the Institute for Sustainable Investment. For example, she worked on a project with the United Nations on the global right to food that involved looking at the impacts of climate change on the food system. Specifically, they looked at the effects of extraction contracts on communities around the world, which involved asking what responsibilities the extraction companies had for remediation, which in turn involved thinking about how climate change would affect those remediation efforts. This is the sort of complex interdisciplinary policy work that centers and institutes were making possible. Climate change is now a factor in a variety of projects the clinic addresses, ranging from helping climate refugees to defending climate scientists from charges of fraud.[13]

Similarly, Robert Verchick, who graduated from Harvard Law School in 1989 and started teaching at the University of Missouri in 1993, was also more interested in civil rights and family law than in environmental law early in his career. However, while at Harvard he met the pioneering environmental justice lawyer Luke Cole, who prompted his interest in the intersection of civil rights and environmental law. He brought this environmental justice perspective into his environmental law courses. In 2004, he came to Loyola University New Orleans College of Law to direct its new Center for Environmental Law. From this position, he examines natural disasters (like hurricanes), climate adaptation, and resilience through the lens of environmental justice. Climate change now shows up in all his courses.

Mark Davis, director of the Tulane Institute on Water Resources Law & Policy, also came to the climate issue through an interest in how ordinary people were being affected by climate impacts. When he came to Louisiana in 1991 to serve as general counsel for the Lake Pontchartrain Basin Foundation, he was still largely unaware of how climate change would be relevant to his work. "I tended to believe that if things were that bad, I would have heard about it sooner and top people would be working on it and all the resources that would be necessary would be in the offing, because how could it be otherwise? I since came to learn that it's normally the opposite: the bigger and more systemic the challenge, the less likely it is that we have really adequate responses in play." Climate change impacts introduced him to the civics side of environmental law. Shortly after Hurricane Katrina hit New Orleans, he started teaching at Tulane University School of Law, which had asked him to create a center on water law and policy that would address the problems facing Louisiana, including climate change.

When the institute started in 2007, climate change was not yet covered in Tulane's environmental law curriculum. According to student interviewees, the institute played an important role in bringing attention to the issue at Tulane, and it did so by focusing on its impacts on vulnerable communities. As Davis explained, "I got involved in . . . climate adaptation in dealing with the problem of the disappearing coast and all the things that entailed." The loss of wetlands along the Louisiana coast was one factor leading to the devastating effects of hurricanes like Katrina on coastal communities, since wetlands tend to moderate hurricane impacts. But as Davis discovered, "There was no environmental law in place to deal with [wetland loss]. Even if I could stop new permits from being issued, the monster [of wetland loss] was already on the loose." Davis's interest in environmental law is thus focused on dealing with the "collapse of ecosystems and human communities and, where you can't prevent it, how to adapt as effectively and equitably as possible."[14]

More privileged actors were also beginning to grapple with climate change. For example, Joseph Macdougald was serving on a local zoning board in Connecticut when he first encountered climate-related land use problems like the impact of rising sea levels on coastal development. That experience motivated him to bring those kinds of issues into his teaching at the University of Connecticut Law School, which focuses on land use as well as environmental law.[15]

Alexandra Klass started engaging with climate change through her practice, working with coal companies in Wyoming who were dealing with litigation (or the threat of litigation) addressing the climate impacts of coal. She started teaching at William Mitchell College of Law in 2004 and then at the University of Minnesota Law School in 2006, by which time she was already incorporating climate change into her courses; interestingly, she also addressed the issue in her property and torts courses.[16] Klass noted that, in her experience, a good deal of litigation over climate change was based on public nuisance, which is a property-related tort. Nuisance law, she explained, "is often used [as a basis for litigation] where we don't have strong federal or state regulation," so the absence of federal climate regulation was a key factor in how the issue entered into her teaching. But Klass also noted that coverage of these common law causes of action in the environmental curriculum was (in 2006) quite limited. Recall that environmental law casebooks had largely dropped common law causes of action in the 1980s. That lack of coverage was so striking to her because she used these causes of action frequently in her environmental practice; they offered greater opportunity to receive money damages than did statutory causes of action.[17] Thus her story illustrates how climate change revealed a weakness in the traditional environmental curriculum (lack of coverage of common law causes of action) and provided motivation to address it. Indeed, she notes that, just a few years after she began teaching, environmental law casebooks started to cover public nuisance, in part because of increasing climate litigation based on the theory that greenhouse gas emissions are a public nuisance.[18] But it also illustrates a common theme among interviewees: climate change became salient to them as an important topic to teach when they saw it directly affecting people's lives, as through hurricanes, flooding, sea level rise, or the threat of climate-related lawsuits.

Another force contributing to the evolution of the climate curriculum was the clinical program, which facilitates the influence of the climate policy community of practice on the law school curriculum. As I discussed in chapter 3, law schools were developing their clinical offerings in the 1990s, and by the 2000s environmental law students often had access to more clinics offering more kinds of policy-relevant experiences.

Consider the experiences of Allison LaPlante, now codirector of Lewis & Clark's Earthrise Law Center, an environmental law clinic started in 1996, and Erica Lyman, director of the school's Global Alliance for Animals and the Environment. LaPlante attended law school at Lewis & Clark from 1999 to 2002. At that point, the school did not have its current rich offerings on climate change. It did have an impressive array of environmental courses, and while climate might have been covered in a course on renewable energy, LaPlante didn't take that course. She doesn't recall any coverage of the topic in the introductory environmental law course or in the courses on public lands, trade and the environment, and environmental enforcement or in her clinical experience. Erica Lyman attended Lewis & Clark from 2002 to 2005, and she confirms that climate wasn't covered in the introductory environmental law course. She did study climate change in her course on international environmental law; the Kyoto Protocol came into effect in 2004 and was covered in the course. But that was the extent of the climate curriculum.

After 2005, however, climate change became a prominent issue in the school's justly famous clinical programs. LaPlante came back to Lewis & Clark in 2005 to direct the Northwest Environmental Defense Center (later called the Earthrise Center), and the first case she worked on in that capacity was *Northwest Environmental Defense Center v. Owens Corning Corp.*[19] The lawsuit challenged the construction of a polystyrene foam insulation manufacturing facility in part on the grounds that it would emit greenhouse gasses. The center won the case, in the sense that its complaint survived a motion to dismiss. (The plant was eventually built, after making changes to reduce its greenhouse gas emissions.) The case was an important precedent supporting the right of nonprofit advocacy organizations to challenge permits on climate grounds. LaPlante then turned her attention to a Clean Air Act case against Oregon's only coal-fired plant. *Sierra Club v. Portland General Electric* resulted in a consent decree that required the facility to stop burning coal by 2020.[20] Both cases gave students the opportunity to learn how to conduct climate litigation, as well as setting important precedents.[21]

Meanwhile, Erica Lyman was helping the school's other environmental clinic offer students new opportunities to get involved with climate policy. Lyman went directly from law school to working as a staff attorney for Lewis & Clark's International Environmental Law Project (later called the Global Alliance for Animals and the Environment, the program she currently directs). This clinical program, founded by Chris Wold in 1994, focuses on policy work rather than litigation. However, they do serve clients, and their agenda is therefore driven in large part by the demand for legal services. The program became involved in climate issues shortly after Lyman joined the staff, when it first took students to the Conference of Parties in Copenhagen in 2009 to participate in international climate negotiations. The project then began working with Islands First, an organization that aims to keep Pacific island countries informed about international climate negotiations and to help shape their policy and negotiating positions. Students participating in this clinic learned how international negotiations worked and researched the legal questions that arose. For example, Lyman explained, they might help a small country like Tuvalu maintain its least-developed-country status by clarifying the criteria for that designation and identifying the information that must be submitted, or they might scrutinize proposed language for international agreements and advise country delegations on how that language might affect their interests.[22]

Thus by 2010 environmental law students at Lewis & Clark had multiple opportunities to become involved with the climate policy community of practice. The climate curriculum would be enhanced by the hiring, in 2008, of Melissa Powers, who specializes in climate law and policy, putting the school in a strong position to create climate lawyers over the next decade.

Most of the professors I interviewed started teaching about climate change during this decade. Michael Gerrard taught his first course on climate in 2009; Robin Kundis Craig started teaching it around 2008 at Florida State University College of Law; Thomas Ulen taught his first climate course at the University of Illinois in 2008; Lisa Benjamin, now at Lewis & Clark, first taught climate change around 2008 at the University of the Bahamas; Jeff Civins at the University of Texas began addressing it around 2008; Mark

Davis at Tulane took up climate adaptation as a teaching topic around 2007 (after Hurricane Katrina); and Douglas Kysar reports first teaching a course on climate law around 2009 (although he addressed the subject in a seminar on risk as early as 2001).

It was not only these large and relatively well-resourced schools that addressed climate change, though. Patrick Tolan was teaching at Barry University School of Law in 2005. This law school was fairly new—it received ABA accreditation in 2002—and had only 33 faculty members (for about 750 students). Tolan had extensive practice experience as a member of the Air Force's JAG Corps and came to Barry to teach tax and environmental law. He used the Percival casebook and spent a couple of classes on climate change, but because students wanted a stand-alone climate law course, another faculty member (Eric Hull) started teaching one. However, Tolan moved to Cooley Law School's Florida campus in 2013, and that campus was even smaller—only 11 faculty members at that point. He taught environmental law for a few semesters before being tasked to develop a Florida bar preparation class. Nevertheless, he reports strong student interest in climate law.[23] Similarly, Joshua Fershee was teaching environmental law at the University of North Dakota in 2007 when he started addressing climate change in his energy law course; that law school had only about 225 students and 16 full-time faculty members. The fact that even the small schools offered at least some coverage of climate change suggests that, by the end of the decade, the topic was starting to be integrated into the curriculum.

Contours of Climate Law

As this discussion illustrates, coverage of climate change could come into the curriculum through a number of routes. Most of the interviewees initially addressed the topic in their survey environmental law course, in discussions of air pollution, NEPA, or international environmental issues. Some (like Klass) incorporated climate-related cases into other standard courses they were already teaching. However, a few did develop entirely new courses on climate law. What did these early climate law courses look like?

Of course, in the absence of a federal statute, the early climate law courses could not look much like typical statute-focused environmental law courses. The interviewees who developed these early climate law courses identified three major teaching challenges: the multi-scalar nature of climate law (involving different levels of government); the need to understand climate science; and the rapidly changing nature of the policy area. Addressing these challenges required faculty to develop new teaching strategies and to find different kinds of teaching materials. This is not a trivial task, but it is a task that environmental law professors are well positioned to tackle, particularly since the creation of the internet made it fairly easy to gather resources.

Multi-scalar Policy

Climate law was emerging at the international, national, and subnational levels, which posed the problem of which level to focus on. Most of the early climate law courses included considerable coverage of international law. John Dernbach's seminar, for example, covered the international climate negotiations and used a casebook by David Hunter, James Salzman, and Durwood Zaelke, *International Environmental Law and Policy*.[24] However, he also explored subnational policy strategies. Interestingly, he reports that he didn't spend a lot of time on federal laws such as the Clean Air Act. Instead he focused on international, state, and local law; he drew also on federal laws related to energy efficiency.

That multi-scalar dimension of climate law was one of the challenges of teaching this course—a point made by several interviewees. As Dernbach explained, he had to cover quite a lot of international law in order to provide the appropriate background on the climate treaty process. From a lawyer's point of view, international law is very different from national law; it is merely a set of norms and agreements that nation-states voluntarily follow rather than a binding set of rules authorized by a legitimate sovereign authority. To approach international environmental law, therefore, students have to be introduced to a different concept of law and different institutions for implementing it; they cannot simply draw on their background knowledge of how national law works. The same is true, to a lesser extent, regarding local law. Municipalities in the United States are a division of state government and have a distinctive set of powers and authorizing documents that must be understood before delving into local climate law. So teaching climate law necessarily involves teaching a good deal of background material on how the laws emanating from different levels of government operate and interact.

Complex Science

A second challenge, of course, was deciding how much climate science to cover—a persistent issue when teaching law students whose science background may vary quite a lot. Several interviewees noted that law students often struggle to understand the science.[25] And the science can also be difficult for professors, of course. Robert Infelise emphasized that he does not claim expertise on topics infused with scientific or engineering issues (like solar radiation management strategies), and it can be a struggle to keep those discussions relevant to law students. Adam Babich agreed: "My philosophy is I should teach things that I am actually qualified to teach. By and large, I don't feel comfortable spending a lot of time trying to convince the class that this is an emergency or talking about the number of degrees the world is heating up." Some professors noted that a scientific background isn't essential for teaching climate change given the resources available for learning the basics. Several made reference to the IPCC summary reports and excerpts from cases as useful resources for introducing students to the basic science.[26]

For those with a deeper scientific background, though, teaching the science was one of the things that made climate law interesting. Richard Lazarus —who has an undergraduate degree in chemistry and actually studied the greenhouse effect and global warming in a course on environmental chemistry in 1974[27]—found climate science easy to teach because it raises interesting legal-scientific questions. He described climate science as fairly accessible and a useful case for explaining why and how scientific principles affect lawmaking. For example, the global nature of the climate system raises the problem of spatial mismatch (climate policy is made by governments that don't have full authority over the relevant territory), and the persistent nature of greenhouse gasses raises the problem of temporal mismatch (the actions we take now will affect people in the distant future).[28]

But climate science can also be very depressing, and most people teaching climate change have found it necessary and difficult to address the emotional dimension of the climate problem. Infelise struggles with "not turning it into a 'woe-is-me' fourteen-week session. . . . Given the scale and implications of the problem, it's really hard to keep an objective point of view."[29]

Pace of Change
Finally, Dernbach noted that this is a rapidly changing area, so "it's a different class every time."[30] Barton "Buzz" Thompson at Stanford called it a "fun challenge" that the field hasn't ossified like many other dimensions of environmental law: "The fact that we're still looking for solutions and policies [that] are changing from year to year makes the subject engaging for students." But he admitted that it is challenging for him to stay up to date: "I spent so much time getting prepared for those classes than for anything

else." Babich commented that it was difficult to decide what to teach and how much to teach because of the pace of change in the field.[31] For example, the Obama administration's Clean Power Plan was promptly revoked by the next administration and replaced with another plan that was also revoked shortly thereafter by Joe Biden's administration. These policy shifts are challenging for professors looking to teach law—a fairly stable regulatory scheme designed to address the problem—rather than policy debates and processes. It can also be challenging for students who have been taught to think of law as a fixed order of values. As Holly Doremus put it: "There's a certain number of law students who really want it all to be straightforward and not changing. . . . They just want the algorithmic answer." But she also noted that "this is not a climate change thing. I have always insisted that students need to learn both the current law, something about how it got that way and why, and for sure, the range of ways it might change, the way it might need to change."[32] Climate change requires approaching law in this more dynamic, instrumental way.

Teaching Strategies

To address these challenges, teachers of climate law relied on a broad range of sources beyond legal documents and cases and teaching strategies other than the case-dialogue method. Tseming Yang's syllabus for her 2003 course at Vermont relied on three nonlegal scholarly texts: John Houghton, *Global Warming: The Complete Briefing*; Richard Benedick, *Ozone Diplomacy: New Directions in Safeguarding the Planet*; and Urs Luterbacher and Detlef Sprintz, *International Relations and Climate Change*. Students engaged in a negotiations exercise concerning climate change (as well as writing a term paper), and the course (she advised) focused less on law and more on "general issues of global environmental governance."[33]

Pat Parenteau's early climate law courses were also a departure from the standard law school approach. In fact, he recalls first addressing climate change in an undergraduate course he taught at Dartmouth toward the end of the 1990s. He then developed a course on climate litigation by 2003. Following his standard practice, he didn't use a text but collected articles and other materials (which, he notes, were becoming more easily accessed with the rise of the internet). He reports spending a good deal of time teaching the science of climate change and explaining the models and evidence, drawing on materials from the National Academy of Sciences and the United Nations. In addition to lecturing, he used a number of different teaching strategies, including role-playing and simulations, analyzing a proposed bill, or playing a "carbon wedges" game developed by Stephen Pacala and Robert Socolow (involving high-level strategizing about different policy paths toward carbon reduction).[34] In short, the course looked very much like something that might be offered in a public policy or interdisciplinary environmental studies program.

Michael Gerrard's climate law course at Columbia Law School, first offered in 2009, made use of his new book, *Global Climate Change and U.S. Law*, and it was also a lecture course (assessment consisted of a final exam). Interestingly, he opened up this course to graduate students from other parts of the university and even to undergraduates. Columbia's Earth Institute supported that outreach by providing funds to hire a teaching assistant to work with the undergraduates. The course was thus aimed at a much broader audience than just law students, and the lecture format was probably well suited to this large and diverse body of students. He also developed a smaller seminar for more advanced students.[35]

Joseph Macdougald similarly taught his climate law course more like a public policy seminar than a doctrine-focused law course, bringing in policymakers as guest speakers and having his students write research papers. Research on climate policy, he noted, posed its own set of challenges. Early in its history, the legal database Westlaw was still relying on terms and connectors to do searches, so students could do a targeted search with keywords like "global + warming + coastal" and generate a manageable set of sources. But by the late 2000s, Westlaw had adopted natural-language searching, and students also were increasingly able to find sources on Google. That led to an overwhelming set of sources that students needed additional instruction in using. He therefore started to bring librarians into the course to instruct students in online research strategies for exploring the policy scholarship—the kind of skills training that in an earlier period would not have been part of a subject-matter course.[36] Thus this course, too, looked more like the sort of offering a public policy school would offer.

Wil Burns may have had an advantage in developing a climate law course, in that he did not go to law school. He has a PhD in international law and had worked on climate issues during several years at nonprofit organizations concerned with international environmental policy. In 2006, he was hired by Santa Clara University School of Law to run its international moot court program and teach international environmental law courses. His policy work had already given him a great deal of background on climate change,

124　CHAPTER FOUR

so he added to his teaching duties a course on climate law. It was a lecture-based upper-level course, and he had to invent it from scratch. His two chief challenges were covering the science adequately and showing students how climate law could be relevant to their legal practice. The textbook he used was well designed for those challenges: Michael Gerrard's *Global Climate Change and U.S. Law* (2007) covered the science of climate change pretty well and was oriented toward serving private clients. He also noted, as other professors did, that climate law was a good way to teach basic administrative, property, and environmental law.[37]

To summarize: the early climate law courses required law professors to depart significantly from the standard, doctrine-focused law school pedagogy. These pioneers did note difficulties in developing these courses: the multi-scalar nature of the policy area, the complexity of climate science, and the pace of change in the field. These challenges led them to adopt teaching strategies more common in schools of public policy. But pedagogical innovation doesn't take place in a vacuum. Professors seeking to develop climate courses needed support from their schools and colleagues. Happily, that support was increasingly available.

Facilitating Factors

As discussed in chapter 3, law schools began devoting more money and attention to curricular innovation during the 1990s. Professors interested in developing climate courses benefited from greater resources for professional development: growing professional networks, proliferation of resources for teaching climate change, and institutional support for interdisciplinary scholarship.

Networks

Innovative climate law teachers need to find teaching resources, including ideas and strategies; the existence of professional networks facilitates the circulation of such resources. Environmental law professors were already networked, and during the 2000s a new cluster of environmental law professors interested in climate change emerged. This networking allowed them to share ideas and materials to support teaching this complex subject.

Like other academics, environmental law professors regularly attend conferences that allow them to discuss new developments in the field with colleagues at other schools. This sort of networking has been going on since the field emerged, and interviewees confirmed the importance of networking opportunities to professional development. Arnold Reitze's LLM program at George Washington was mentioned by several interviewees as offering important professional development opportunities for environmental law specialists during the 1970s and 1980s. The Environmental Law Institute and Vermont Law School also have been holding conferences and offering continuing legal education since the 1970s and 1980s, respectively. Other long-standing conferences mentioned by interviewees were the Rocky Mountain Mineral Institute's annual conference, which focuses on issues relevant to natural resources and energy, and the Southeastern Association of Law Schools's annual conference, which has a particularly active environmental law section.[38]

In the 2000s, these resources evolved. The development of the internet was an obvious factor in that evolution, of course. The Environmental Law Prof Blog was mentioned by several interviewees as an important way that professors teaching climate law shared information and ideas. Entries date back to 2005, and examples from its early years include updates on climate science with links to relevant studies,[39] recommended resources for teaching climate change,[40] and updates on climate politics and policy.[41] A number of interviewees also mentioned an environmental law professors listserv administered by John Bonine (University of Oregon School of Law), on which requests for climate law teaching materials began to appear after 2000.[42] Wil Burns was prompted by those requests to partner with Don Anton (then at Australian National University) to create an online database of syllabi on climate law, hosted by the International Union for the Conservation of Nature's Academy of Law. Begun in 2008, the database has syllabi dating back to Tseming Yang's 2003 course, and it is updated regularly.[43]

Professional organizations devoted to environmental law were also important networking spaces. In addition to the Environmental Law Institute, the ABA has the Environment, Energy, and Resources section, created in 1971, in which law professors are quite active. State bar associations also have sections or events (such as the Texas Environmental Superconference held annually since 1988) focused on environmental law, providing law professors the opportunity to connect with practitioners and other academics.[44] In 2007 the American College of Environmental Lawyers joined the institutional landscape, offering membership to environmental lawyers "recognized by their peers as preeminent in their field."[45] Members include practitioners and academics, and the college holds meetings, runs a blog, and sponsors projects, including educational projects.

Finally, by the end of the decade conferences focused on climate law were starting to appear. For example, the University of Colorado Law School in Boulder started hosting the Climate Change Law & Policy Works-in-Progress Symposium in 2009. Begun by Sarah Krakoff and William Boyd, it is a two-day workshop attended by about 15 professors each year, including leading environmental law professors like Jed Purdy, Doug Kysar, Anne Carlson, Buzz Thompson, Mark Squillace, and David Spence. The workshop is focused on sharing scholarship rather than on teaching—participants read and comment on each other's articles being prepared for publication—but this sort of interaction promotes informal discussions that can range over policy innovation, teaching strategies, and conceptual and theoretical developments in the field. Events like this suggest that climate law was now being recognized as a subfield among environmental law professors, and they contributed to the growth of teaching materials in this area.

Teaching Resources

The more entrepreneurial law professors did not report much difficulty in finding resources for teaching about climate change even before 2000. But in the 2000s, even professors with little background in environmental law could find support for teaching about climate change in the proliferating and evolving casebooks. A number of new environmental law casebooks appeared during this decade, including Fred Bosselman, *Energy, Economics, and the Environment* (2000); Robin [Kundis] Craig, *Environmental Law in Context* (2008); David Driesen and Robert Adler, *Environmental Law: A Conceptual and Pragmatic Approach* (2007); Craig Johnston, William Funk, and Victor Flatt, *Legal Protection of the Environment* (2005); James Salzman and Barton Thompson, *Environmental Law and Policy: Concepts and Insights* (2003); and J. B. Ruhl, John Copeland Nagle, and James Salzman, *The Practice and Policy of Environmental Law* (2008). Toward the end of the decade, the first casebooks specifically on climate law appeared: Gerrard's book in 2007, and in 2009 Richard Hildreth, Nicholas Robinson, David Hodas, and James Speth published *Climate Change Law: Mitigation and Adaptation* and Chris Wold, David Hunter, and Melissa Powers published *Climate Change and the Law.*

To contextualize this evolution, it's useful to hear from Louis Higgins, editor in chief of West Academic, and Pamela Chandler, the company's vice president, about how they solicit new casebooks. The process they describe is very organic; they spend a good deal of time talking to law professors about what they need, often at national conferences like AALS or the Southeastern Association of Law Schools annual conference, but professors also propose new books to them. They are not trying to drive the development of curriculum; on the contrary, as Louis Higgins put it: "Textbooks are designed to be used in the classroom, so we don't typically publish a textbook on a topic until that topic is somewhat established. But you don't want to be particularly far behind the curve either. So we have to watch for those things that are trending, things that more people are starting to teach. . . . But we stay away from hot topics, because by the time the book comes out, the hot topic often isn't hot anymore."[46] Thus the proliferation of environmental law casebooks probably reflects healthy demand from professors. Of course, it also may also reflect reduced course loads, which may give professors more time to devote to such activities, as well as the development of law school pedagogy beyond the case method, including more problem-based exercises, policy documents, and practice notes. As Higgins noted, the range of legal materials and approaches in casebooks expanded dramatically after 2000: "There are more problems, more hypotheticals, more experiential exercises, more narrative . . . [and] interstitial materials connecting things to have it feel more like a textbook."[47] As teaching methods changed, professors wanted different kinds of books to teach from.

To be sure, the new environmental law casebooks did not initially depart from the standard approach of treating climate change as an air pollution problem and an international law problem. But that approach was evolving, as we can see in the development of the Percival casebook. There were no fewer than four editions of this venerable book published in the 2000–2010 period, and each one expanded coverage of climate change. The third edition (2000) continued to discuss climate change in the chapter on air pollution (still posing the question of whether carbon dioxide could be regulated under the CAA) and in the chapter on international environmental law. The fourth edition (2003) promised to integrate climate change throughout the book—although most of the discussion still focused on the Clean Air Act and the Kyoto Protocol. However, a final chapter does introduce the idea of sustainable development. The fifth edition (2006) included considerable new material in the chapter on international law: It included discussion of US state–level responses to climate change as well as national-level responses.

This edition also included a new exercise, of the type that Higgins referred to above: the problem invited students to consider the benefits and drawbacks of various legal strategies to force greenhouse gas regulation. Options

128 CHAPTER FOUR

included suing the Export-Import Bank and Overseas Private Investment Corporation to require them to prepare an environmental impact statement on the effect of financing fossil fuel projects; pursuing an action against the United States in the International Court of Justice based on the effects of sea level rise; petitioning the World Trade Organization on behalf of parties to the Kyoto Protocol to impose duties on goods made in the United States because it did not ratify the protocol; and lawsuits by state attorneys general against coal and oil companies to remedy the health and environmental damages caused by their activities. This exercise illustrates the shift from a focus on doctrine to problem-based learning that law schools were beginning to embrace more fully.

The sixth edition of the Percival casebook (2009) now included coverage of the 2007 *Massachusetts v. EPA* decision in the chapter on air pollution and continued its rich discussion of climate policy in the chapter on international law. It also included an excerpt from Percival's 2007 article "Environmental Law in the Twenty-First Century," which identifies "global warming and climate change" as "problems that will pose the greatest challenge to the development of international environmental law."[48] But the treatment of the subject in the casebook makes it clear that the subject was already escaping the confines of international law and requiring greater attention to the multi-scalar dimension of environmental policy.

That problem—the need to address the interaction of climate policy emanating from different levels of government—was tackled somewhat more effectively by the book by Anderson and colleagues. In the third edition (1999), Robert Glicksman was added as an author, and he took over as lead author in the fifth edition (2007), adding new authors David Markell and William Buzbee.[49] This new set of authors reworked the casebook considerably, including a new chapter on environmental federalism that explicitly addressed the interaction of local, state, federal, and international environmental policy, as well as increasing coverage of climate change (which it predicted would "become the defining environmental challenge of our time.")[50] It still focused its coverage on *Massachusetts v. EPA* (in the chapter on air pollution). But as Buzbee explains, the topic was becoming relevant to several chapters, and "at a certain point we realized that it really was getting unwieldy and that it would be helpful for both professors and readers" to add a separate chapter on climate change.[51]

That separate chapter appeared in the sixth edition (2011). By this time, a new challenge had emerged: climate science had evolved to clarify how climate change would affect a range of different environmental phenomena. It was no longer looking like simply an air pollution problem; climate change was working its way through the whole field of environmental law, including water resources, biodiversity protection, and land use planning. Thus the authors had to decide how much discussion of climate change to keep in the other chapters once they had decided to devote an entire chapter to it. Because professors often assign individual chapters from a casebook, confining discussion of climate change to a single chapter might risk leaving it out of critical discussions on protection of water resources, biodiversity, common law claims, and the like. They ended up keeping some discussion of climate throughout the book, but they cross-referenced chapters to alert readers that the issue comes up elsewhere as well. They eventually moved toward using climate change as an integrative framework to organize the whole book—but that was a later development.[52]

Other casebooks tended to follow this pattern. For example, Johnston, Funk, and Flatt included a note on whether carbon dioxide should be regulated under the CAA in their 2005 edition, and in 2007 they expanded coverage of *Massachusetts v. EPA*. They also added a chapter on international law. The third edition (2010) added a new chapter on climate change while keeping the discussion of climate change integrated into the other chapters as well. The new chapter addressed federal laws and common law approaches to addressing climate change and included a long excerpt from an article by Flatt discussing what a federal climate statute might look like.

J. B. Ruhl, John Copeland Nagle, and James Salzman issued the first edition of their casebook in 2008, and this book is notable for several innovations that suggest new directions for development of the field of environmental law as a whole.[53] In addition to the usual topics, it covers a host of new topics: compliance counseling, enforcement, business transactions and organizations (due diligence, drafting environmental contract provisions, and forming and terminating business organizations), ecosystem management, agriculture, urban development, environmental justice, and transboundary pollution. Climate change is integrated throughout, but it receives the most extensive coverage in the chapter on transboundary pollution. In that chapter, the authors discuss climate science, the impacts of climate change, and international law in addition to subnational responses and even corporate policy approaches. The book's index (under the entry for global warming) gives a good snapshot of the variety of topics discussed, including adaptive strategies, California carbon regulation, carbon credits, carbon reservoirs, citizen suits, corporate initiatives, ecosystem management law and global climate change, impacts of climate change, local initiatives, NEPA applicability, and the Regional Greenhouse Gas Initiative.

Casebooks in related fields were edging slowly into the climate issue. The leading casebook on natural resources, *Federal Public Land and Resources* by Coggins, Wilkinson, and Leshy, did not address climate change in either the fourth edition (2001) or the fifth edition (2002) (despite a major reorganization and updating in that edition). In 2005, Christine Klein, Frederico Cheever, and Bret Birdsong published *Natural Resources Law*; in 2006, Jan Laitos, Sandra Zellmer, Mary Wood, and Daniel Cole offered *Natural Resources Law*; and in 2007, Eric Freyfogle published his *Natural Resources Law* casebook. These books reflect trends in casebook writing: more coverage of economics and natural science, applied problem-solving, and new conceptual approaches. But they contain little to no discussion of climate change.

Water law casebooks were starting to address the topic, however. George Gould, Douglas Grant, and Gregory Weber's *Cases and Materials on Water Law*, in its seventh edition (2005), did not mention climate change. But Robert Beck and Amy Kelly's *Water and Water Rights*[54] includes a section on climate change in the second edition (2007). They give a brief overview of the expected impacts of climate change on water resources, state-level initiatives to control greenhouse gasses, and major litigation.[55] They also briefly address the implications of climate change for riparian rights.[56] But perhaps the most successful attempt to incorporate climate change is the fifth edition of *Water Resources Management*, published in 2002 by Dan Tarlock, James Corbridge, and David Getches. They begin by characterizing water rights as a response to water scarcity. The first chapter is therefore devoted to earth systems science and the social and economic dimensions of water scarcity—with climate change introduced in this chapter as a cause of scarcity. Climate change is also discussed in a chapter on transboundary allocation of water.[57] That approach worked well enough that it was still used in the seventh edition (2014), with climate change now appearing in the chapter on pollution as well.[58]

Energy law, as might be expected, took up the climate issue more rapidly and thoroughly. Fred Bosselman and colleagues issued a new casebook on energy law in 2000, and it included a whole chapter on climate change. The second edition (2006) continued that approach, and by the third edition (2010), the authors had put climate change into the introduction and integrated the issue throughout (in chapters on renewable energy and energy efficiency, for example) while keeping the chapter on regulating climate-related emissions.[59]

In reflecting on these trends in casebooks, I need to emphasize that professors often depart from the casebook, supplementing the readings and even organizing the course very differently. These casebooks are nevertheless good bellwethers of broader teaching trends. Overall, they illustrate the growing understanding that climate change could not be treated simply as a separate topic, like water or air pollution, but would have to be integrated throughout the discussion of most environmental issues. Adequate treatment would require restructuring the field to include greater attention to issues like intergovernmental relations and common law causes of action. By the end of the decade, authors like Ruhl, Nagle, and Salzman were heralding emerging issues including corporate policy, management of carbon reservoirs, implications of climate change for the food system, and the host of legal problems raised by adaptation to climate change. Although such topics would not necessarily be incorporated into standard environmental survey casebooks in the coming decade, they do suggest important topics for the climate curriculum to address.

The first three textbooks specifically focused on climate law, published in 2008 and 2009, did not embrace all those topics, but they were still ambitious projects. Casebooks in new areas of law are challenging to craft. As Pamela Chandler put it, in new and emerging areas of law "there just isn't necessarily an established body of law. . . . You end up with lots of different perspectives that aren't necessarily cohesive or conducive to curriculum development." And that, she notes, did happen with the climate law casebook they published (Hildreth et al., *Climate Change Law*): "When we first published the climate change book it was very early, . . . and that was one thing we heard about that book very early on, that there wasn't exactly an established body of law."[60] However, Higgins and Chandler have noticed the emergence of climate change as a subject of interest (although they note that most people still, as of 2021, aren't necessarily looking for an entire casebook on the subject).

Nevertheless, the first books did a decent job of formulating climate law as a coherent field. Michael Gerrard published *Global Climate Change and U.S. Law* in 2007 as much as a practice aid as a teaching resource (although he does use it in his climate law course and reports that several law schools did use it as a textbook). Gerrard initiated the project because "it was just increasingly clear that it was an important issue . . . and nobody had done that kind of analysis."[61] As explained in chapter 3, the 727-page book includes chapters by 25 authors, most of whom were in practice rather than full-time professors when it was written, and the book reflects that practical orientation. In Gerrard's words, it is written for lawyers who will "negotiate and document transactions for the development and transfer of technologies and for the emissions trade. They will advise companies and government on the rapidly changing regulatory scheme. They will litigate the inevitable disputes."[62] This description captures one vision of what a climate lawyer would look like: a technocrat advising high-level policymakers and corporate actors. (And he was right: one student interviewee was doing this sort of work, advising a client on a carbon capture project as early as 2010.) The first chapter offers an overview of the climate problem: the history of climate policy, policy tools, litigation efforts, state and local policies, voluntary programs, relevant policies from the Securities and Exchange Commission, and implications for insurance. The rest of the book ranges widely, discussing traditional environmental law topics such as the implications of climate change for environmental impact review and the Endangered Species Act, in addition to an in-depth coverage of new topics like emissions trading systems, how the insurance industry is responding to climate-related disasters, energy regulation, legal issues involved with carbon sequestration, and corporate disclosure regulations related to climate change. Notably missing is discussion of legal issues related to adaptation. Although there is a very good chapter by Bradford Mank on how private parties could sue government agencies over climate impacts—including some discussion of environmental justice—the book as a whole is focused heavily on top-down regulation of greenhouse gas emissions and how that regulation will affect the business community.

That perspective dominates the other two climate law casebooks as well. Chris Wold, David Hunter, and Melissa Powers published *Climate Change and the Law* in 2009.[63] This book is clearly intended for teaching purposes, and much more than the Gerrard book it reflects the contours of climate law as a subject in the law school curriculum. The preface makes two key points about climate law: it is one of the most dynamic areas of twenty-first century law, and it requires the student to engage with several areas of law: public international law, public administrative law, federal environmental law, state and municipal regulations, and the common law. The authors promise to offer a comprehensive approach.

The first part (about 125 pages) covers the science of climate change and mitigation and adaptation policy responses. This part, which could serve as a textbook in itself, draws on the IPCC reports and public policy scholarship, although it also highlights the work of legal scholars like Douglas Kysar, David Hunter, James Salzman, and Durwood Zaelke. The next section of the book (pages 127–464) focuses on the regulatory regime that has taken shape under the UN Framework Convention on Climate Change, with a chapter on the impact of climate change on other international law regimes such as ozone, biodiversity protection, human rights, international trade, and the law of the sea. The final (and longest) section (pages 492–926) covers US law on climate change. Two chapters cover the justiciability of climate change in the courts (issues like standing) and how federal environmental laws relate to the problem. The rest of the section covers national energy and transportation law and policy, the use of tort law to address climate change, state and municipal responses, and the private sector's response to climate change (addressing issues like corporate policy and green investment). The final chapter offers ideas on legal and policy pathways to a carbon-free future.

This book reflects how law professors were beginning to understand the domain of climate law. It does an impressive job of integrating science, policy, and law, and it covers quite a lot of territory that was not being addressed in most basic environmental law casebooks. For example, there is a whole chapter on the legal issues involved with using forests as carbon sinks, and the coverage of US energy and transportation systems is far more detailed than one would find in most environmental law textbooks. Again, however, the book focuses on top-down regulation, reflecting the perspective of climate policy advisers, litigators, and corporate counsel (as opposed to lawyers interested in using legal tools to help poor communities adapt to climate change).

The other casebook published in 2009 is similar. In *Climate Change Law: Mitigation and Adaptation*, authors Richard Hildreth, Nicholas Robinson, David Hodas, and James Speth describe climate change law as "a new synthesis of several fields,"[64] specifically environmental law, securities and commodities, energy law, and international and municipal law. Promising an interdisciplinary approach, they devote a chapter to climate science and another to "economic fundamentals." And, like Wold and colleagues, they go beyond the standard coverage of the international climate regime and federal environmental law to cover such topics as sustainable energy law and business law. There is also a chapter on adaptation, which covers such topics as adapting to sea level rise, hydrological change, and local land use. The final chapter asks the student to consider "what is needed to move to a carbon-neutral legal system for energy?" Throughout, the authors emphasize policy debate and scholarship more than legal doctrine. The stated goal of the book is to "strengthen a global legal perspective on Earth's changing climate and biosphere" in order to build an "epistemic community" of climate lawyers.[65] Again, climate law is conceptualized as a field for legal advisers to the global economic and political elite.

Notably absent from these textbooks is substantial discussion of environmental justice. Although most of them bring up equity issues, they do not frame climate change as a problem of social inequality but rather treat climate impacts as common hazards shared by everyone. This framing, which is common in the field of environmental law more generally, is somewhat misleading, since the wealthy are usually able to protect themselves from the impacts of environmental hazards. The effects of climate change promise to be most devastating for the poor, for marginalized communities without economic and legal resources. Thus it is possible to conceptualize climate law as part of the field of human rights and environmental justice. As discussed above, some professors, such as Susan Kraham, Robert Verchick, and Mark Davis, have done that. But that perspective was not prominent in the teaching materials and courses that were showing up in law schools by 2010.

Nevertheless, professors wanting to address climate change in their courses had, by the late 2000s, a well-developed set of resources for teaching the basic science and the two basic approaches to controlling emissions: regulation under the CAA, and the international regulatory regime. The more ambitious could attempt to teach about state-level regulatory programs like California's and the RGGI or local initiatives, and they could also include some discussion of the implications of the emerging climate regime for US businesses. By the end of the decade, it was possible to find teaching materials relating to the basics of climate adaptation and some resources for thinking about going beyond emissions control to discuss how the law could support the transition away from fossil fuels.

However, even if one focused on what was emerging as the core of climate law—the international climate regime, treatment of GHGs under federal environmental laws, and climate litigation—actually teaching a course on climate change law might still stretch the capacity of many law professors. Recall Thomas Ulen's 2009 article on his attempt to teach such a course. Even without addressing adaptation, his list of topics to be covered included climate science, economic theory, public policy, energy technology, and international politics. As the Wold and Hildreth textbooks show, and as many of my interviewees confirmed, teaching climate law required developing greater interdisciplinary competence. But there is evidence that the diversification of the law school faculty and the rise of centers and institutes were beginning, in the 2000s, to create more supportive environments for addressing this emerging challenge—at some schools, at least.

Interdisciplinary Support

While some of my interviewees felt comfortable focusing their teaching of climate change on their own areas of legal expertise,[66] several insisted that interdisciplinary competence is critical to this field—and clearly many law schools were still struggling to encourage that sort of competence.[67] Alan Miller has taught in law schools, business schools, and public policy and natural resources programs, and he nicely summed up the persistence of the traditional legal ideology in law schools: "Law schools relative to the other disciplines [are] much more narrow and [view] themselves as owners of a unique body of knowledge that they and they only can endow on their worthy young proponents."[68] Scott Zimmermann, for example, had to look outside the law school at UC Berkeley, finding climate-related courses in the business school and the energy program.[69] Fortunately, the law school is fairly supportive of interdisciplinary work by students and faculty. Dan Farber found it easy to find experts on climate science and economics to bring into his course on climate change,[70] and in 2008 the law school hired Holly Doremus, who has a PhD in plant physiology. That credential in fact helped her land her first permanent teaching job at the University of California, Davis (in 1995) and the position at Berkeley (in 2008). Both schools were explicitly looking for someone with interdisciplinary expertise.[71]

For Douglas Kysar, "interdisciplinary competence" means "competent enough to understand the various disciplines that shape the contours of climate change as a subject of policy." As he noted: "That's a lot—that's the natural sciences, the social sciences, engineering, it goes on and on." His goal, he said, is to have "the basic understanding necessary to define the interests that are at stake in climate change policies." So he "tried very much to form professional relationships with people who can help me." Institutional context mattered here: he taught at Cornell from 2001 to 2008 and at Yale from 2008 on, and he described both institutions as "enthusiastically interdisciplinary." He noted that "every college and university has the problem of the silos of the disciplines. And it seems like we all periodically invest in these huge cross-campus interdisciplinary centers to bring people together."[72] Kysar himself has participated in this sort of interdisciplinary research center (focused on nanotechnology) at Cornell, but he pointed also to opportunities, at both Cornell and Yale, to coteach courses with economists, natural scientists, and even faculty from the divinity school as particularly valuable interdisciplinary experiences.

Similarly, Kim Diana Connolly, as discussed in chapter 3, found it easy to learn from faculty at the School of the Environment during her tenure at University of South Carolina from 1999 to 2010. "That was a very, very formative part [of] causing me to say, 'I need to really start thinking about how I'm going to be creating change in this space.'"[73] However, she left South Carolina for University at Buffalo School of Law in 2010, where her interdisciplinary efforts were more difficult. For example, she ran into some of the common challenges of coteaching courses: different schools often have different calendars and different meeting times for their courses. It can take considerable institutional support to arrange opportunities for coteaching across departments and schools, and not many interviewees cited this sort of collaboration as a common or expected approach to teaching climate change.

Most of the professors who discussed how they expanded their teaching competence cited the existence of an active center or institute on environmental matters at their university as an important factor in promoting their own learning on the subject. Peter Byrne, for example, was teaching at Georgetown in the 1990s but had only recently moved into environmental law when John Echevarria recruited him to become involved in the Environmental Policy Project, aimed at producing policy-relevant research supporting environmental regulators. This was an innovative project for a law school; indeed, the organizers had some trouble figuring out how an advocacy-focused project like this would fit into the law school's mission. But it survived, and its annual conference, Byrne reports, "became a spectacular kind of educational experience for me. I developed relationships with a lot of very impressive people from whom I learned a great deal."[74] The project began in the mid-1990s and ran for about 25 years, and today Georgetown has a multitude of centers and institutes like this. As discussed in chapter 3, Joseph Macdougald and Hari Osofsky also underscored the value of these kinds of centers and institutes for supporting interdisciplinary work.[75] Most of these environment-focused centers, institutes and programs were founded after 2000.

To summarize: between 2000 and 2010 professors seeking to teach climate law had access to a growing network of peers and a body of teaching resources. Some universities also provided access to a multidisciplinary community of scholars focused on climate change, often organized by means of a center or institute. But the challenges of teaching climate law were far from resolved.

Emerging Challenges

Innovative law professors were largely successful during the 2000–2010 period in overcoming the initial barriers to teaching climate change. They tackled the science by making use of the ever-improving explanations of climate science written for policymakers, especially in UN documents (or leaving it to their students to educate themselves); they addressed the multiscalar nature of climate policy by dividing the topic between international, federal, and subnational regulations and explicitly taking up the issue of intergovernmental relations in environmental policy; and they coped with the pace of change, the need to integrate climate throughout the field, and the need for greater interdisciplinary competence, largely by spending more time developing their own understanding of the subject.

But as the climate curriculum developed, the deeper challenges of teaching climate law were starting to become clear. First, the complexity of climate law was of a different nature than the complexity of traditional environmental law. As Robin Kundis Craig explained, climate change has added complexity because we are addressing it with statutes that weren't designed for this problem (the Clean Air Act and Endangered Species Act, for example) and because it's starting to become clear that mitigation and adaptation strategies can conflict. Should the Endangered Species Act be interpreted to allow for species to migrate north as the climate changes? Should public land conservation regimes be relaxed to allow for more solar and wind energy projects? How should water rights be reconciled with protection of the environment as water resources diminish? As Craig summed it up: "Environmental law is not an easy subject to begin with. But climate change is starting to raise some real 'many many many parts in motion at the same time' [problems] with statutes that aren't designed to work together necessarily."[76] A student cannot master this area by mastering a statutory scheme. Students of climate law have to be unusually creative, comfortable with uncertainty, and willing to tolerate ambiguity and deal with questions that have no clear answers. These are not attributes that law school traditionally emphasizes.

138 CHAPTER FOUR

A second emerging issue is field definition: professors were increasingly questioning whether climate law is or should be considered part of environmental law. The Stanford law lecturer Kate Gordon, for example, describes climate law as different from environmental law, which is focused on local pollutants and their local impacts:

> Carbon emissions aren't [local pollutants]. . . . Immediately you get . . . boundary and jurisdiction issues because carbon emissions are everywhere and everything. You get attribution issues . . . and most of the impacts are not impacts on the environment per se. They're impacts on the economy, on people's livelihoods, on resource management, on labor, on human health . . . and the policy implications are very global. . . . Environmental law is too narrow to get at all these things.[77]

Buzz Thompson also asked whether we can say there is a "law of climate change." "Is climate change simply an application of environmental law? Or is it a unique subject in itself that has its own special and unique attributes?" He pointed out that "climate is unlike virtually any other thing that we have dealt with, because of both the complexities of the issue, the fact that it is both a mitigation and an adaptation issue, and those relate, and that it involves application of so many other areas. So it's not just statutes, not just litigation."[78] The new climate law casebooks confirm this understanding that climate law has to incorporate a different set of legal fields, and engage more deeply with public policy, than is common in environmental law courses. It may not be a subject that fits neatly into the environmental curriculum.

Or perhaps it is the traditional understanding of environmental law as a field that needs to change. Climate change is forcing those teaching environmental law to return to the earliest days of the field and reintegrate energy law, local land use law, and common law causes of action. It is also requiring greater attention to corporate and international law (which is becoming harder to treat as a separate subfield). More generally, it is forcing environmental law professors to teach environmental policy—to focus more attention on how to use one's legal training to contribute to developing innovative and effective policy.

In sum, teaching climate law requires law professors to shift away from traditional legal pedagogy and focus on preparing students for their role in helping the twenty-first century state cope with challenges like global climate change. This shift does not mean abandoning the teaching of law, of course. Clearly, environmental law professors are still teaching traditional topics such as standing, jurisdiction, and the interpretation of statutes. Indeed, several student interviewees reported that their introductory environmental law course still focused on the major federal statutes and doctrinal analysis and was still taught in the traditional case-dialogue manner (although they also report doing papers and presentations in addition to the final exam). Indeed, as noted previously, climate change is well suited to teaching some standard subjects such as standing. But environmental law professors are also using climate change to explore new and more theoretical subjects, such as intergovernmental legal interactions and how scientific principles relate to legal principles. And to address climate change in any depth requires one to teach law as an evolving set of rules and policies rather than as a fixed order of values. The complexities of climate law therefore put it in position to help drive the transformation of legal education during the next ten-year period, which I address in chapter 5.

CHAPTER FIVE

Making Climate Lawyers, 2011–2020

By 2010, the early barriers to teaching climate change had been overcome, at least at the top-tier law schools. The issue was now highly salient and clearly relevant to legal practice in a number of ways. The growth of law school faculty meant that more resources could be devoted to the environmental curriculum. Teaching practices had evolved to be more conducive to teaching about emerging policy issues. Law schools were more welcoming of interdisciplinary scholars and courses. Accordingly, the climate curriculum evolved during this period—but not necessarily in the traditional way: adding new units or courses on climate. Some such courses did appear, but the transformation of the environmental law curriculum was more complex. Climate change was increasingly integrated throughout the existing environmental and natural resources law courses, while most of the new courses focused on energy law. Indeed, during this period environmental and energy law largely merged, reflecting the understanding that climate change is not best understood as a pollution problem; it is (as Edith Brown Weiss put it back in 1981) a "resource management problem" requiring a transformation of our energy system.

As the climate curriculum evolves, however, professors are grappling with new teaching challenges stemming from the complex nature of the climate problem. In this chapter I begin by describing the growing body of climate law coming from legislatures, agencies, and courts. I then explore how climate change is being incorporated into environmental law and how it is affecting pedagogy. Finally, I turn to what law professors are learning about the disruptive potential of climate change on environmental law and on the legal system more generally.

Living with Climate Change

By 2010, climate change was no longer a distant threat but the source of a constant stream of new crises in the United States: torrential rains and extreme flooding, droughts, more powerful hurricanes, and increasing wildfires. Not all of these events were yet connected in public discourse to climate change, but changing weather patterns—tornadoes and wildfires in the middle of winter, for example—have made climate change real and present rather than theoretical and distant for a substantial number of Americans. By 2020, the Pew Foundation reported that 67 percent of Americans not only believed in climate change but also thought the government was doing too little to address it.[1]

In fact, American governments have been addressing climate change. Most notably, under the Obama administration (2009–2017) and the Biden administration (beginning in 2021), the EPA has promulgated new standards addressing greenhouse gas emissions from new motor vehicles, the electricity sector, the oil and gas industry, civilian aircraft, and solid waste landfills. The most controversial of these are fuel efficiency standards for automobiles and carbon dioxide limits on power plants; both were subject to policy reversals and litigation under the Trump administration (2017–2021), and their future under the Biden administration was unclear at the time of publication. But Joe Biden was the first president to highlight climate change as an urgent issue in his campaign, and he has proposed a wide range of policies—some of which have been adopted but many encountering political resistance. His administration has used its regulatory authority vigorously, however. The Columbia Law School Sabin Center's database of federal climate regulatory actions listed 97 such actions between January 20, 2021 (when Biden took office) and January 31, 2022.[2]

States and localities have also continued to address climate change with policies promoting renewable energy and energy efficiency. For example, a 2016 study comparing renewable energy policy from 2000 to 2016 in the United States, Argentina, Mexico, Canada, and Brazil found that the United States used the most policies and instruments: a total of 147 instruments were used in the 51 renewable energy policies at the federal and state levels —far ahead of second-place Canada's 27 policies and 67 instruments.[3] But policymakers are also starting to understand better that mitigating climate change is not simply a matter of curbing GHG emissions; what is needed is a transition in energy and food systems. Restrictions on emissions may prove less important than policies that promote technological innovation

142 CHAPTER FIVE

and redirect investment toward renewable energy. Accordingly, the federal government is increasingly using energy policy to achieve environmental goals, primarily by subsidizing renewable energy and electrification. Substantial federal investments in both came via the 2005 Energy Policy Act (subsidizing solar energy); the 2007 Energy Security and Independence Act (subsidizing electric vehicles); and the 2009 American Reinvestment and Recovery Act (which supported a range of clean energy activities from renewable power to mass transit to upgrading the electricity grid).[4] The Biden administration also followed this path of promoting clean energy through spending. The major infrastructure spending bill, passed early in Biden's first year in office, included policies aimed at supporting public transit, building out electric vehicle infrastructure, improving the grid, and generally promoting the shift to electrification.[5] In 2022, Congress passed Biden's ambitious Inflation Reduction Act, which (while possibly doing little to reduce inflation) directed over $370 billion to climate solutions.

In addition to these policies focusing on mitigating greenhouse gas emissions, we are seeing the growth of policies aimed at adapting to climate change. Indeed, only after 2010 did the policy community come to terms with the complexity of climate impacts. A substantial body of climate science scholarship is now documenting the effects of climate change on the energy system,[6] agriculture yields,[7] fisheries,[8] flooding,[9] wildfire,[10] sea level rise,[11] and demographic changes.[12] These impacts are far-ranging. To take just one example: the impacts of climate change on human health include a rise in vector-, water-, and food-borne diseases and an increase in acute and chronic respiratory conditions (including asthma and allergies) and heat-related and extreme weather–related morbidity and mortality. Indirect health implications include illness related to food and water safety, poor nutrition related to food insecurity, malignant melanoma from UV exposure, chronic kidney disease from dehydration, and mental health impacts.[13]

We clearly need a diverse suite of policies to reduce vulnerabilities to climate change, but tackling emissions reduction and adaptation at the same time is proving difficult. Shifting the energy system away from fossil fuels is complicated by the fact that climate change is creating weather events that disrupt the system while also increasing the demand for energy. More severe storms might impact one part of the electricity grid while a heat wave elsewhere further strains its capacity.[14] Similarly, climate change threatens food security, but measures to reduce greenhouse gas emissions—such as raising the price of gasoline—could have economic impacts that would also impair food security.[15] Carefully crafted, nuanced policies are needed to cope with these complexities.

Skilled lawyering is also increasingly needed to deal with the growth of climate-related litigation: the Sabin Center climate litigation database includes 1,362 cases from the United States, based on laws ranging from the 1851 Fort Laramie Treaty (challenging an oil pipeline) to the Biggert–Waters Flood Insurance Reform and Modernization Act of 2012 (concerning rate increases in the National Flood Insurance Program in response to climate-related flood risks) to the Securities and Exchange Act of 1934 (alleging misleading or fraudulent statements by publicly traded companies about the impacts of climate change on their profits or the sustainability of their products). Indeed, the database lists over 200 statutory, common law, and constitutional bases for climate litigation, making climate change an area of legal risk for most businesses.

To gain a picture of the challenge that climate change poses to practicing lawyers and policymakers, consider the 2019 publication by Michael Gerrard and John Dernbach, *Legal Pathways to Deep Decarbonization in the United States*.[16] This collection provides over a thousand specific policy options for encouraging the shift away from fossil fuels at the federal, state, or local level, covering 35 different policy areas including electricity generation, biofuels, energy efficiency, transportation, carbon capture and storage, international trade, materials management, agriculture, and reducing other greenhouse gasses, to name just a few. Attention is given not only to regulation and tax policy (e.g., a carbon tax) but also to other policy approaches such as information disclosure and promoting innovation. There are two chapters specifically on financing projects: large-scale projects, and "grid edge" technologies (furthering a decentralized, distributed, transactional energy grid). And Gerrard and Dernbach focus on mitigation only; they don't address the policies that will be needed to adapt to climate change. Whether they are creating policy, advising business clients on new climate policies, or helping those affected by climate change, legal professionals emerging from US law schools in the 2020s will be facing an extremely dynamic regulatory environment.

How well are law schools responding to this challenge? In 2014, Daniel Farber reported that his survey of American law schools found that 53 schools had a course on climate law.[17] A snapshot of that year shows that conferences and symposia on climate change were becoming common: the USD (University of San Diego) Law School was holding an annual Climate

& Energy Law Symposium; the University of Minnesota had started an interdisciplinary environmental and energy law workshop; the University of Utah S. J. Quinney College of Law, which was already hosting conferences like the 2012 Electric Power in a Carbon Constrained World, announced that its flagship publication, the *Utah Law Review*, would be publishing an annual special issue on environmental, natural resources, and energy law.

For environmental law professors, climate change was now firmly on the agenda, and for many it was at the center of their teaching practice. Robin Kundis Craig wrote in 2013 that "climate change is the environmental and natural resources problem of the 21st century."[18] By 2021, Holly Doremus suggested that it would be educational malpractice not to teach climate change throughout the environmental curriculum. In her interview, she explained the implications of the climate problem for entire regulatory systems: "In California, climate change and water law are 100% linked. . . . Climate change creates drought; coastal lands are affected by sea level rise." That necessitates changes in both water law and ocean and coastal law. "For example, fish ranges are changing, and the institutions we have don't take that change into account." Understanding these implications is essential "both for the lawyers that we're training and for the ability of these institutions to respond" because "lawyers and the law have such an important role in defining these institutions and cabining these institutions" as well as affecting "the interplay among institutions."[19]

But even as climate change was becoming central to the environmental law curriculum, energy law professor Inara Scott wondered in the provocatively titled "Is It Time to Say Goodbye to Environmental Law?": "The Anthropocene—and more specifically, climate change—offer existential challenges to the survival of humanity and life on this planet. Many instinctively turn to environmental law to solve these challenges. Unfortunately, I don't think the challenges we face will be solved by items on the environmental law shelf. No, I believe we need to start fresh, create a new genre, and leave environmental law firmly in the past."[20] Scott wrote that "environmental law does not focus on human-to-human interactions or economic transactions. Matters having to do with corporate law, tax, and business are generally not included. It is only recently that energy law—including fossil fuel extraction and electric utility regulation—has been considered alongside or even linked to environmental law."[21] Environmental law, she argued, addresses narrow problems with narrow solutions (e.g., protecting an endangered species as opposed to protecting biodiversity). And the constituency for environmental law is too narrow as well; it appeals (she claimed) primarily to liberal white activists. She proposed that we need a new interdisciplinary, intersectional field focused on the governance of common pool resources.

These perspectives reflect the dual impact of climate change on the law school curriculum: It is driving much-needed curricular and pedagogic transformation, but it is also a disruptive force that threatens to destabilize the foundations of environmental law.

The Climate Curriculum Takes Shape

After 2010, the environmental law curriculum at many schools developed dramatically, with courses on more specialized subjects like environmental issues in business transactions, environmental negotiation, international project finance, food law, and corporate environmental and social governance. The climate curriculum also expanded—but not necessarily by adding new courses specifically on climate. As discussed in chapter 1, this additive approach was traditionally the most common way to bring new topics into the law school curriculum, but the proliferation of new specialized courses is now running into resistance by at least some environmental law professors. As Richard Lazarus put it: "If you have someone who's just thinking about climate change law, they aren't going to be a good lawyer. . . . I'm not a big believer in [specialty classes] like an advanced class in clean air [or an] advanced class in hazardous waste."[22] The aim of law education, he contended, should be to develop the broad range of skills needed to deal with an issue like climate change as it comes up in any area of practice. (Nevertheless, Lazarus is now teaching a course titled "Climate Lawyering.") As Farber documented, climate law does show up among course offerings at many schools. But the more significant trends are the integration of climate change into the standard environmental law courses and the integration of the energy and environmental law curriculum.

Integrating Climate into Environmental Law

Most interviewees who teach environmental law report that climate change permeates their courses. For example, Barton "Buzz" Thompson teaches an introductory environmental law course that has 18 sessions overall, four of them devoted to climate change: on international negotiations, the Clean Air Act, state-level regulation, and litigation. Such expansive coverage isn't unusual. Kim Diana Connolly echoed a common theme when she explained in her interview that she tries to use climate change as an overarching

146 CHAPTER FIVE

framework in her courses so that climate is woven through her courses on natural resources and on environmental law.[23] The topic is making its way into natural resource law as well; Michael Blumm, Holly Doremus, and Buzz Thompson all brought up the impact of climate change on water resources, a central topic in natural resource law.[24]

We can see the trends in teaching climate change in the environmental law casebooks published during this period. At least some of the trends in these casebooks are likely tied to the rise of climate change. Most notable is the addition of topics that are important to addressing climate change: common law causes of action (which had disappeared from casebooks in the 1980s); international law; renewable energy; and local environmental regulation and land use. All of these are critical foundations for climate law, which helps explain their reappearance in the environmental curriculum. Another trend—probably not driven by climate change—is the greater attention paid to the practice context, with many casebooks including a chapter on enforcement and more notes on practical matters appearing throughout. That trend may in fact work against greater coverage of climate policy, since it takes up scarce class time.

A review of the introductory environmental law casebooks published during the 2010s illustrates the basic challenge facing professors attempting to bring climate change into the introductory environmental course: as discussed in chapter 4, casebook authors have to decide whether to contain climate policy in one chapter, address it throughout the book, or do both. The containment approach was taken by Ruhl, Nagle, and Salzman, who added Alexandra Klass to the second edition (2010) of *The Practice and Policy of Environmental Law*.[25] This second edition shifted away from the expansive approach taken in the first. The authors moved most of the discussion of climate policy to a stand-alone chapter, and while retaining coverage of the practical dimensions of environmental law, they eliminated the chapters on ecosystem management, agriculture, urban development, environmental justice, and transboundary pollution. The third (2014) and fourth (2016) editions follow the same streamlined strategy. Thus instead of offering separate chapters on energy or international law, they address renewable energy and international law in the chapter on climate policy and discuss its implications for the Clean Air Act, the Endangered Species Act, and NEPA.[26]

The integrative approach is illustrated by Dan Farber's basic environmental law casebook, *Cases and Materials on Environmental Law*. This book is now in its 10th edition, with Ann Carlson and William Boyd replacing Roger Findley. Its structure demonstrates a great deal of continuity with the past; there are chapters on endangered species, air pollution, water pollution, hazardous waste, and toxic substances, along with administrative law and a chapter on constitutional principles that addresses federalism, a long-standing theme in Farber's book. The authors' thinking on climate change is reflected in the preface:

> Climate change is an increasingly central area of environmental law. Although there now seems little immediate prospect of congressional action, litigation under the Clean Air Act continues, and states such as California remain active. In the meantime, each new issue of Science and Nature seems to demonstrate that climate change is happening earlier and more rapidly than scientific models have predicted. The future of climate change is now, and we are at a delicate, interesting and crucial moment in addressing the problem.[27]

But the treatment of climate change isn't particularly innovative. The text contains no separate treatment of energy, international law, or land use regulation. Climate change is covered in greatest detail in the chapter on air pollution, where the focus is on domestic regulatory approaches. It shows up as well in discussions of cost-benefit analysis, the Endangered Species Act, NEPA, standing, and regulatory takings. Notably, a chapter on approaches to risk regulation includes a discussion of climate justice, a topic that still gets fairly minimal coverage in most casebooks.[28] But—and this is an important qualification—the preface recommends that students consult the blog LegalPlanet for current developments in climate law. LegalPlanet, which is supported by the Berkeley and UCLA law schools, reports much of the research produced by Berkeley's Center for Law, Energy & the Environment. Thus that recommendation reflects the limits of focusing on casebooks (which are now commonly supplemented by other materials online) as well as how centers can contribute to student education.

To understand how climate change is being integrated into the field, it's useful to look at the book's chapter on air pollution in detail. This 179-page chapter is a tour de force—as it should be, since environmental law professors have been teaching the CAA for over 50 years (and Farber himself for over 40 years). The chapter illustrates a number of trends in casebooks over decades. For example, in addition to excerpts from cases, it contains a

148 CHAPTER FIVE

good deal of exposition explaining the history and political context in which federal air pollution regulation has evolved. There are also several excerpts from scholarly sources explaining further the policy debates informing the regulatory scheme, such as the role of cost-benefit analysis. The chapter begins with discussion of common law regulation of air pollution and the continuing relevance of nuisance actions, then begins a long and detailed explanation of the Clean Air Act, covering the basic structure of the statute and its central concepts. It next offers sections devoted to major topics that raise important legal and policy questions: how to define central terms like "pollutant," how to set standards, and so on. There are helpful notes in each section. Some raise questions about the impact of the regulatory approach on vulnerable populations, but most provide updates to the evolution of policies, invite the student to consider other regulatory approaches, or offer practical points (such as how damages were calculated in a particular case or what a state implementation plan actually looks like). There are no detailed hypotheticals, however.

Climate change arises quite naturally in several places in the chapter, as the authors explain how the regulatory system creates or limits opportunities for regulating greenhouse gas emissions. There is also a 29-page subsection on regulating carbon dioxide, which gives the reader a good overview of the federal efforts and California's approach (but with no discussion of the international regulatory regime or of climate science). The chapter as a whole is a remarkably useful tour of federal air pollution protection for an aspiring policymaker or someone who hopes to advise businesses on compliance. And it certainly provides a useful, if incomplete, introduction to climate policy.

Of course, the traditional approach to environmental law means there are notable omissions. The student won't find in this book any discussion of how one might actually bring a lawsuit against an oil refinery whose air pollution is affecting a community on its fence line. It doesn't cover the practical dimensions of finding inspection reports, figuring out which corporation actually owns the refinery, identifying the relevant state laws, and the like. The casebook as a whole doesn't address corporate policy, which is becoming an important arena of environmental governance. To be sure, no casebook can cover everything, and one might expect that these skills are better addressed in a clinic or in a course on corporate law. I don't dispute that judgment; my point is simply that the authors had certain practice contexts in mind, and they are the traditional contexts: advising the business community on how to comply with federal law, or actually making federal law. They focus on the material that is relevant to those contexts, which material they know (very well) how to teach.

All the casebooks I reviewed shared that perspective, although they take different approaches to addressing climate change. For example, Driesen, Adler, and Kirsten Engel published the second edition of *Environmental Law: A Conceptual and Pragmatic Approach* in 2011. This text focuses less on statutory schemes and more on the basic regulatory approaches in the policy area (standard setting, economic incentives, information disclosure, citizen enforcement, etc.) It thus has no chapter on climate change; instead it uses "climate disruption" as a continuing case study throughout the book, with discussions appearing in the chapters on common law, administrative law, toxins, cost-benefit analysis, market-based regulation, federalism, and enforcement.[29] This approach centers climate change as a particularly important issue without changing the authors' basic approach to explaining the field.

Many of the more recent casebooks, however, devote a chapter to climate policy specifically or global environmental problems generally while also integrating it into discussion of other topics. For example, Zygmunt Plater and his coauthors issued the fifth edition of *Environmental Law and Policy: Nature, Law and Society* in 2016. They cover climate policy in a fairly short section (17 pages) in the final chapter on international and comparative law, where the focus is on international negotiations. But climate change also shows up throughout the book in discussions of broad themes in environmental law,[30] tort law,[31] NEPA,[32] land use planning and management,[33] the Endangered Species Act,[34] the CAA,[35] and market-based regulation.[36]

We find a more ambitious attempt at integration in *Environmental Regulation* by Percival and others. The coauthors put out a seventh edition in 2013, an eighth in 2018, and a ninth in 2021. Each edition includes a chapter on protecting the global environment, including extensive discussion of climate policy, but they also incorporate discussion of climate change into other topics such as common law causes of action, standing, and land use. Their discussion of climate policy has evolved as well; the 2013 edition, for example, devotes five pages to climate adaptation and two to geoengineering. But in addition to this additive approach, Percival and his coauthors use climate change as a general framework for understanding environmental law. In the 2021 edition, climate change is introduced in the first chapter as informing the authors' approach of the whole book:

Environmental law faces two simultaneous problems. One involves reforming the tools at hand to make them stronger and more effective. The other involves building structures, institutions and rules sufficient for the more transformative demands of the climate crises. This casebook explores the current regulatory instruments of environmental law. . . . It also examines the possibility that these instruments, while essential, have to be supplemented in significant ways if we are to meet the environmental demands of the twenty-first century.[37]

The casebook by Glicksman and others, which issued an eighth edition in 2019, takes a similar integrative approach, devoting a lengthy chapter (over 100 pages) to climate policy but also discussing climate change as it affects the Clean Air Act, the Endangered Species Act, nuisance, standing, federalism, NEPA, protection of water resources, and international law.[38] It also covers climate change and trade, human rights, and national security; adaptation to climate change gets three pages of discussion (and is addressed briefly in other discussions). Environmental justice does receive some discussion, most notably in the chapter on constitutional remedies for environmental harms. And like most other environmental law casebooks, it neglects corporate policy (no doubt reflecting the structure of the law school curriculum, which treats corporate law as a different subfield requiring its own courses).

In sum, we see in all these casebooks the trend noted in chapter 4 of addressing climate change from a top-down, mitigation-focused perspective. They give the greatest attention to the international regulatory regime and control of carbon dioxide under the Clean Air Act. None of them spend much time on adaptation, and even the growing attention to environmental justice does not lead to a focus on the special problems that climate change poses for vulnerable communities. Such perspectives are more likely to appear in clinical courses—as we will see—but even in experiential education there is a trend toward policy labs focused on working with policymakers rather than serving communities impacted by climate change. Moreover, that focus on mitigation over adaptation reinforces and is reinforced by the other major curricular impact of climate change: it is eroding the traditional distinction between environmental and energy law.

Integrating Environmental and Energy Law
In 2011, Law Professor Amy Wildermuth of the University of Utah issued a call for the integration of energy and environmental law:

For many years, the law has largely ignored the obvious connection between energy production and consumption and nature. . . . The primary focus of energy law is to ensure that energy is supplied without disruption at an affordable price. The primary focus of environmental laws is to be sure that the process of creating anything, including energy, does not create "too much" pollution, however we might define that phrase. . . . I contend that, acknowledging the realities of how energy is created and the critical and pressing question of climate change, . . . we need to reimagine energy policy in a way that draws on much of the best thinking in both energy law and environmental law circles, but that creates an integrated energy and environmental law.[39]

That integration may not yet be fully reflected in public policy, but it is a prominent trend in the law school curriculum.

The dynamic is clear at the University of Minnesota. Climate change was already well integrated into the standard environmental law courses by 2010, but it was clear to Hari Osofsky that addressing the issue adequately required greater understanding of the energy system. Unfortunately, she noted, "our legal system doesn't just fragment by scale and by geography but by substance, so we regulate environmental and energy law separately in the United States."[40] The 2015 casebook *Energy Law and Policy* addresses that problem. Osofsky coauthored this book with Minnesota colleagues Alexandra Klass and Elizabeth Wilson, along with Lincoln Davies and Joseph Tomain. The authors work to bridge the environmental/energy divide by addressing a range of issues at the interface of the two subfields, including subjects like decarbonization and environmental justice. Klass also started teaching an energy law course at Minnesota around that time. Although Klass and Osofsky have moved on to different schools, the University of Minnesota's law school now offers an integrated environmental and energy law program, including an energy and utility law seminar and an environmental and energy law clinic, as well as access to interdisciplinary energy policy courses at the Hubert H. Humphrey School of Public Affairs.[41]

We see a similar pattern at other law schools. A student interviewee who graduated from George Washington University Law School in 2007 reported having taken two environmental law courses—the environmental law survey course and Environmental Issues in Energy Law—as well as an externship at the NRDC. Coverage of climate change, he reports, was spotty. Today, George Washington's law school has an integrated environment and energy

152 CHAPTER FIVE

program, including a foundational course in energy law and regulation, an energy law seminar, and courses on oil and gas law, regulated industries, and international project finance. The school also highlights a course on local government law, which includes land use planning, and specialized courses like Trade and Sustainable Development. However, it still offers only one course specifically on climate law: International Climate Change Law.[42]

Georgetown University Law Center, which remains a leader in climate law with a dedicated center on climate change, offers a few specialized courses focusing specifically on climate change, such as Advanced Environmental Law: Climate Change; Energy Problems Seminar: Climate Change and Other Energy Issues; and World Health Assembly Simulation: Negotiation Regarding Climate Change Impacts on Health. Also like George Washington, it has expanded its environmental curriculum and integrated energy law thoroughly into its environmental law program, with multiple courses on energy law and policy, regulation of energy markets, and international energy arbitration.

Berkeley has followed a similar path. Robert Infelise has taught at Berkeley since 1994, and he recalls the faculty discussions that led to development of the school's climate curriculum. He's been teaching about climate change in his environmental policy seminar since at least 2010. But the environmental law faculty began to discuss offering a course on climate change in 2014. By that time, Dan Farber was working on a book on climate law (with Cinnamon Carlarne), and Infelise—with that book in hand—volunteered to teach the course. He's been offering Climate Change and the Law since 2016, and he planned to coteach a course with Farber on carbon neutrality in the future. At the same time, the law school was developing its energy law curriculum. It now has integrated energy law so thoroughly into the environmental curriculum that energy law seems to be a subfield of environmental law. Indeed, it announces on the website section on energy law that the focus of the energy curriculum is "transitioning to a sustainable energy and environmental path."[43]

The integration of environmental and energy law is still in process at many law schools. Tulane has a strong environmental program, but the energy law curriculum traditionally was not well developed, and (despite the creation of the Institute on Water Resources Law & Policy in 2007) climate change was not well represented in the curriculum until the hiring of Sirja-Leena Penttinen in 2018. However, the school founded the Center for Energy Law in 2018, directed by Kim Talus, whose goal is to bring environmental and experts in oil and gas together. He finds that the division between these groups is still too wide, both in academia and in "the real world": "Those two groups never meet, and that's a big problem. . . . The oil and gas side needs to understand that things are moving and we need to change, and the . . . climate side needs to understand that that change will not happen tomorrow." The mission of the center is to look at energy in a holistic, integrative way, including how climate change factors into energy regulation.[44]

There are late adopters as well, even among leading schools. For example, Yale has the Center for Environmental Law & Policy, yet only five faculty members in environmental law and a thin curriculum, lacking basic courses on natural resources and air and water pollution. It does not seem to have a well-developed energy program. The University of Michigan boasts that it has a robust environmental curriculum (and it does), but it offers little on energy beyond a seminar on clean energy and climate change law (taught by the adjunct professor Howard Learner in 2022). Nevertheless, the trend toward the complete integration of environmental and energy law is clear, and so far this represents the most significant impact of the topic of climate change on the law school curriculum.

Other Fields

The integration of climate change is progressing more slowly in other fields of law. As mentioned in earlier chapters, Alexandra Klass brings it up in her property and torts courses, and both Michael Blumm and Peter Byrne reported addressing climate change in their property courses during discussions of topics like externalities, public trust doctrine, ownership of the atmosphere, and standing.[45] Douglas Kysar also brings climate change into his torts course,[46] and Richard Parker brings up climate change in his administrative law course.[47] But my interviewees report that casebooks in these fields typically don't offer much discussion of climate change; whether one encounters the topic in these basic courses probably depends primarily on whether the instructor is particularly interested in environmental law. Most of the student interviewees also reported that they didn't encounter climate change in their nonenvironmental courses. This is not to say, however, that climate change hasn't influenced the larger curriculum. The teaching of climate change has certainly supported, if not driven, the trend toward new pedagogical approaches: the study of public policy, applied problem-solving, and (to some extent) interdisciplinary courses.

Teaching Climate Change

Despite the growth of climate policy in the United States and a growing body of case law, the nation still does not have a federal climate protection regulatory regime. There is no single statute, like the Clean Air Act or the Clean Water Act, that could form the core of a traditional environmental law course. There are quite a lot of cases that address climate change in some way, but they cover a bewildering array of different causes of action and legal questions. So how do environmental law professors cover climate change today?

My interviews suggest a great deal of continuity with the approaches pioneered in the early climate courses: Professors draw heavily on resources beyond casebooks, especially policy documents; some (but not all) continue to aim for basic climate science literacy; they center policy, aiming less at mastery of doctrine than understanding of the policy issue and options; and they turn to experiential learning, often supported by centers and institutes. Some professors try to offer interdisciplinary experiences, either by co-teaching or bringing in guest speakers, but interdisciplinary work still faces substantial barriers.

Teaching Science and Policy

Kelly Haragan at the University of Texas described in detail how she addresses climate change in her environmental law clinic. The clinic does environmental litigation, mostly for low-income communities suffering from pollution, as well as policy work such as commenting on administrative rules and assisting groups lobbying for environmental policies. She has been devoting class time to climate change at least since 2010. Most of her students, she notes, have not taken the environmental law survey course, so she instructs them in relevant areas of environmental law as they go along. The climate change class comes later in the term, and it is oriented toward climate literacy. She gives students a list of websites that have information about the impacts of climate change. They must pick one website and spend 30–45 minutes looking at it and send her a memo about what they learned about climate change. In class, they discuss what they learned, including what their family and peer group think about climate change and their thoughts about how climate change impacts their daily lives. This is clearly a class designed to introduce students with varied backgrounds to the issue and to deal with potential climate skepticism. To be sure, she notes, the students who apply to the clinic are already interested in environmental law, but some are interested in working for the oil and gas industry, and she doesn't want to alienate those students. She wants them to understand that there is factual information on climate change available, that it is possible to educate oneself, and that is a phenomenon directly relevant to their lives.[48]

Joshua Fershee echoed the continuing importance of addressing climate skepticism. He has taught in several conservative communities and reports: "I always would say at the beginning of class, 'I'll be transparent with you. I believe in climate change, I believe it's happening. . . . You're entitled to your opinion on that, but I don't think the science is subject to debate. I think we should have a very serious debate about what we should do about it.'" He focuses discussion on what policy approaches make sense, given the seriousness of climate change impacts, on one hand, and the fact that millions of people in the world still don't have access to energy on the other. "I think that helps frames the conversation in a way that I haven't gotten a lot of pushback."[49]

Kim Talus at Tulane doesn't feel the need to teach climate science at all. His approach doesn't reflect a narrow focus on doctrine, however. Talus was educated in Finland and has a degree in law and a PhD, and his multidisciplinary training influences his teaching style. When he addresses climate change in the context of his course Introduction to International and Comparative Energy Law, he "take[s] for granted that they know what it is. . . . I focus on how does climate change factor into energy, . . . talking about energy efficiency, emission reductions, renewables, and so on and so forth." Moreover, in addition to his introductory course on energy law, he teaches Energy Investment Protection and a seminar on large-scale energy projects. His courses combine law and policy, and his students are likely to investigate actual contracts along with regulations, cases, and policy documents.[50] Talus observed that, in the energy field, law and policy are deeply integrated. In his course on international and comparative energy law, for example, his aim is to give his students an understanding of the whole range of issues that may come up in an international energy law: "The whole value chain from production to energy conservation, how the upstream market works, how transportation works, how the downstream markets works, what does climate change or sustainability bring into the mixture, what does international investment protection bring into the mixture, how does [the World Trade Organization] law play [into the mix]."[51] He sees himself as training students in both policy and law, since both policy and law play into his own practice: "In energy . . . if you are a practicing lawyer in a law firm, you

156 CHAPTER FIVE

have to understand policy. If you are a policymaker and you've never seen a contract and don't understand the contracts that underlie everything—then that's a bit of a problem." The difference between policymakers and law, in practice, doesn't really exist: "We don't focus on details of law. . . . Instead, we focus on why that law exists, what are the problems that underlie the law, and what is the policy around it."[52]

Michael Gerrard's course on climate law similarly draws heavily on policy documents and debates along with more traditional legal materials. He points out that, while there are a lot of cases that address some aspect of climate change, there aren't a lot that address the topics he wants to focus on. Neither does he aim to teach the nuts and bolts of a specific policy, which might require reading statutes and regulations. Rather, he aims to explain the overall concepts and legal tools available to address the problem—for example, spending a class comparing the cap-and-trade approach to a carbon tax. (However, his syllabus does include the memorandum of understanding that created the Regional Greenhouse Gas Initiative; the California Global Warming Solutions Act of 2006; and some case law.)[53]

In sum, much of the teaching about climate change is focused on the climate problem and policy approaches rather than doctrine, and it proceeds in much the same way that the subject would be taught in a public policy school. Legal doctrine is less central to these courses than the policy debates. And even though these are not traditional, doctrine-focused courses, the professors I interviewed did not report any serious resistance from students (or from other faculty members). On the contrary, this kind of teaching seems to fit reasonably well into contemporary law schools, even if it is still not the dominant approach.

Experiential Learning

Beyond addressing policy in the classroom, some courses attempt to engage students more directly with making policy or other experiential exercises. Traditionally, law schools operate clinics as a way to engage students with real-world problems, and environmental law clinics are one area where students can engage with climate law. Indeed, this seems to be the primary area in which students will encounter the impacts of climate law on vulnerable communities. For example, Kim Diana Connolly teaches primarily in a clinical setting. Recent cases concerned the siting of a facility, NEPA work, and a case seeking early intervention for children affected by lead poisoning. Despite the varied topics, climate change is a major theme in her courses:

"That is something that I train on in the first two weeks. We have readings and discussion . . . and . . . they have a big reflective exercise." She also brings up this theme during class discussions by finding readings or other resources that relate to what the students are doing (easily discovered by means of the listservs she uses). She collects a diverse set of resources, including TED Talks and other online resources, because her goal is to familiarize them with the kinds of arguments that will work in different settings—the courtroom, the legislature, administrative settings, and so on. She also invites students to bring in material, making use of the diverse educational backgrounds of a typical law school cohort. In contrast to Haragan, Connolly reports that covering climate change has gotten easier, in part because media coverage has improved and in part because her students typically don't question the basic science of climate change.[54]

Matthew Sanders, a senior clinical supervising attorney and lecturer at the Mills Legal Clinic at Stanford Law School, echoed this theme. He explained that climate change can come up in different contexts: they might handle a case involving an endangered species where the primary threat to the species is climate change, or a case involving environmental impact review under NEPA where impacts include (or will be affected by) climate change. But he also described a more complicated situation that lawyers will increasingly face: a case about pump storage for a hydropower project, raising ethical questions about the tradeoff between renewable energy and the long-term depletion of water resources threatened by the project.[55]

Some clinics take up climate litigation directly, like the Lewis & Clark clinical program discussed in chapter 4. Another noteworthy example is Harvard's International Human Rights Clinic, founded in 2004 (part of a dramatic growth of clinics at the school during that period). The clinic does both litigation and policy projects and has several areas of focus, one of which is human rights and the environment. Indeed, this is a special interest of director Tyler Giannini, who founded and directed EarthRights International, one of the first NGOs to focus on environmental human rights. The clinic website highlights its climate work:

> We have also undertaken initiatives to advance work at the intersection of climate change and human rights, including hosting events on refugees fleeing the effects of climate change. Bonnie Docherty, Associate Director of Armed Conflict and Civilian Protection participated in the drafting of principles for helping people internally displaced from climate change.

Docherty and Tyler Giannini, HRP Co-Director, proposed a convention on climate change refugees. Likewise, Aminta Ossom, Clinical Instructor in the International Human Rights Clinic, has led student teams to examine how human rights law could be used to combat the social and economic inequality that contributes to, and is driven by, climate change.[56]

According to Giannini, students in the clinic learn how to use a variety of tools to protect human rights, from litigation to norm development to treaty negotiations to reporting on and documentation of rights violations. He describes the goals of the clinic as training students in standard skills (such as research, writing briefs, and media advocacy) but also helping them to develop careers through "deep mentoring" and connecting them with practitioner networks.[57] That experiential education is supplemented by seminar courses taught by clinic staff. For example, Giannini teaches a seminar on business and human rights, in which students work on live problems such as addressing the problem of corporations contributing to climate change and the implications for human rights.

Notably, like Talus in the energy law field, Giannini sees the teaching of both human rights and climate law as necessarily involving training in policy and governance. In these areas: "You can't actually separate [law and governance]. . . . The legal issues that are relevant here [are], how does law influence governance? . . . What's your legislative framework, what's your tax code, what are your incentive structures?"[58] Human rights, he notes, has traditionally been approached in a reactionary way: identify a harm and respond to it. His approach also aims to prevent harm by developing governance systems and by training his students to think about those systems. So his courses might focus on corporate accountability practices that reduce human rights violations or on corporate structures that allow corporations to respond better to climate change. He does note that the law school setting may not be the right place to introduce the theoretical literature on regime governance that he encountered in his own graduate program (he has a masters degree in foreign affairs). Rather, he trains students by showing them what governance looks like in practice.[59]

In addition to clinics, many law schools are promoting other kinds of experiential learning, and several interviewees reported these pedagogies being used in environmental law. For example, Peter Byrne at Georgetown has taught a course titled "Urban Laboratory" (cotaught with an urban planning professor) aimed at law students and urban planning students. The course looks at real-world problems in a specific community. For example, one class studied how designating an area as a flood zone would affect a low-income minority community; another worked with a community development organization, researching topics like how to develop affordable housing or parkland and presenting them to the organization and community.[60] Mark Davis at Tulane has students participate in a mock legislative hearing, writing and presenting testimony for a proposed change in water law.[61] Robert Verchick, at Loyola New Orleans's Center for Environmental Law, developed a policy lab focused on standing up NGOs and community advocacy programs. The lab offers instruction on such skills as grant-writing, fundraising, how to work with communities, how to write white papers, and how to do public presentations at local hearings.[62] And Richard Parker at the University of Connecticut developed a semester in Washington, DC, focusing on how government works; such off-campus programs are still unusual at American law schools.[63] Not all of these courses address climate change directly, but they feature pedagogies that are well suited to addressing climate-related legal problems.

Centers and Institutes

How do centers and institutes fit into this story of policy-oriented coursework? The creation of centers and institutes, many of which have an explicit mission of contributing to public policy, seems aimed in part at supporting the more policy-oriented pedagogies in law school classrooms. As discussed in chapter 3, law schools began putting more resources into centers and institutes in the late 2000s, and many are now fairly mature, with strong track records of contributing to the development of public policy. But the connection between the work of the center and student learning can be opaque. In order better to understand what these organizations do, my research assistant Moses Jehng analyzed the activities of three such centers: the Sabin Center for Climate Change Law at Columbia; the Center for Law, Energy & the Environment at Berkeley; and the Environmental Law & Sustainability Center at Widener.

Using annual reports and newsletters, Moses identified two categories of activities aimed at engagement with the public policy community of practice. First, a good deal of this policy work results in publications intended to influence policymakers. Examples include white papers issued by the Widener center on matters of Pennsylvania law and policy, blog posts on the Sabin Center's Climate Law Blog and the LegalPlanet Blog (supported

160   CHAPTER FIVE

by CLEE with UCLA), and more substantial research reports and scholarly articles. Recent reports published by the Sabin Center, for example, cover such topics as municipal climate law; the legal challenges of sequestering carbon through seaweed cultivation; legal impediments to carbon storage; how to adapt securities law to promote disclosure of climate risk; and similar policy-relevant subjects.[64]

Second, these centers undertake projects involving direct interaction with policymakers. For example, the Sabin Center and CLEE have filed amicus briefs in environmental litigation, such as the Sabin Center's brief in litigation over the Obama administration's Clean Power Plan.[65] CLEE convened experts from automakers, electric vehicle charging companies, government agencies, and nonprofits to develop a scenario in which 100 percent of new vehicle sales are zero-emission.[66] The Sabin Center has conducted workshops with communities threatened by rising sea levels and has helped communities develop adaptation strategic plans.[67] The Widener center also works with local governments, drafting sustainability ordinances for policymakers.[68]

So there are direct connections between these centers and institutes and public policy, and there is some evidence that this policy activity makes its way into at least some courses. To be sure, the centers are often staffed by research fellows who may not teach any courses. But usually some of the staff and almost always the director will have appointments in the law school, and these staff members usually offer courses connected to the policy work they are undertaking.[69] Examples include Kim Talus, discussed above, and John Dernbach, who directs the Widener center. Dernbach puts law students directly to work on drafting ordinances, putting out a newsletter for the state bar association, and taking them to environmental law conferences.[70] As discussed in chapter 4, Joseph Macdougald, who directs the Center for Energy and Environmental Law at Connecticut, is also focused largely on students. He has created courses using the city of Hartford as a lab, and he involves students in organizing interdisciplinary conferences, drafting research policy papers, and connecting with internships.[71]

To understand how centers and practice-oriented courses they support are or are not fitting into the law school curriculum, it's worthwhile to take a deeper look at Stanford. Stanford Law School benefited from the flood of wealth that poured into Silicon Valley in the 1990s, and the university as a whole has embraced innovation as a key element of its institutional identity. The law school describes the education it offers as "immersive, interdisciplinary, collaborative, future-focused."[72] In addition to a traditional legal clinic, it advertises a legal design lab, which is a collaboration with the design school to develop new legal products and services; a policy lab, in which students work with government agencies and similar clients to develop policy; and community engagement projects like the Afghanistan Legal Education Project, which produces textbooks about Afghan law for Afghan audiences.

But this innovative attitude did not make Stanford Law School an early adopter of climate law. Matthew Sanders received his JD from Stanford in 2002, and he reports having taken natural resources law, working at the environmental law clinic, and taking some specialized environmental law courses. No climate change course was offered at that time. The topic was covered in his courses—for example, in discussion of NEPA review—but it was just one issue among many, not a cross-cutting or overarching issue.[73] Today, Stanford Law's Environmental and Natural Resources Law & Policy Program offers a richer environmental law curriculum. In addition to standard courses on environmental law, natural resources, public lands, land use, local government law, and water law, it also offers some less common courses like environmental justice. The clinic focuses on litigation but also does some policy work like evaluating proposed legislation.[74] And students interested in climate change can take courses on climate law and policy and energy law—but these are recent additions and as of 2021 were taught by adjuncts.

However, Stanford Law also addresses climate change at the Steyer–Taylor Center for Energy Policy and Finance, which was founded in 2011 to direct attention to developing policy and finance approaches that support the transition to a carbon-free energy system. The center hosts a collection of fellows who conduct research on energy law and policy, and the managing director, Alicia Seiger, teaches a course on climate politics, finance, and infrastructure. Although she teaches at the law school, Seiger is not a lawyer. She received an MBA from Stanford in 2002 and forged a career developing climate and energy strategies for businesses, foundations, investors, and NGOs. She became managing director of the Steyer–Taylor Center in 2018, after an unsuccessful campaign to persuade the business school to create a course on climate risk and opportunity. She aims to build a bridge between academics and business practice through her work at the center, but much of her focus is on the business school. She meets regularly with business

162   CHAPTER FIVE

school students, helping them find internships and inviting them to center activities.

The law school was willing to allow her to teach her course on climate finance and infrastructure as long as she had a coteacher with a JD, which is a common requirement at many law schools. Fortunately, she found a law school professor, Thomas Heller, who was interested in helping her develop the course. She then recruited Kate Gordon (with a JD and masters degree in urban planning from Berkeley) as coteacher. Seiger describes the course as interdisciplinary, with very little law. Indeed, about half the students come from outside the law school, mostly from the business school. They cover such topics as the fundamentals of climate science and the impacts of climate change on systems; climate risk and disclosure; international negotiations; scenario analysis; climate liability; future innovative possibilities; and transition pathways. The course features guest speakers from a variety of fields including finance, climate science, and law. The students are asked to work in teams to develop a technology or policy solution; the course is more like a learning lab, with an experimental atmosphere "where people really feel like they can take risks and be open to new information and not compete with each other."[75] Overall, it is much more like a business school course than a law school course.

The fact that the law school was willing to host the course speaks to its openness to innovative teaching. But not everyone finds Stanford Law a friendly environment for this sort of practice-oriented teaching. Danny Cullenward was a lecturer at Stanford Law who was hired to teach courses on energy and climate law. Cullenward has a JD from Stanford and a PhD from the Emmett Interdisciplinary Program in Environment and Resources at Stanford University and considerable experience as a climate policy professional. Describing himself as a practitioner at heart, he finds academia uncomfortable. He does not have a home in any specific discipline, and he finds that the law school doesn't really respect the practical skills that he uses in his policy work:

Law school faculty culture is totally irrelevant to the world as it exists particularly in technically complex areas like the environment, let alone climate change, where the practical function of day-to-day activities and lobbying and regulatory efforts [are ignored]. . . . In the real world you write materials, you write regulatory oversight reports, you get involved in advisory commissions, you liaise with political coalitions, you interact with the media, you need to know how technical developments are going to affect law and policy strategy. And none of those things are respected as areas of study in the law school world, especially in elite law schools.[76]

He acknowledges that, as a student, he found Stanford's clinics very strong, offering varied practical experiences for many kinds of lawyering. But even the clinics had trouble making use of his scientific and policy background. Stanford Law has a policy against allowing adjunct professors to run policy labs, but Cullenward focuses his courses more on policy than on legal doctrine. And like Seiger and Gordon, he reports that about half his students come from outside the law school.

The Stanford case suggests that a university can create innovative centers and the law school can hire people with practical policy skills and offer a truly different kind of course focused on applied problem-solving—but there is no guarantee that the new pedagogical approach will win the instructor prestige within the legal academy. The tradition of autonomy for law professors may help support such innovative teaching (none of my interviewees reported any pressure from the administration to be more conventional), but it also may prevent the innovator from having a strong influence on other professors. And overcoming the barriers to interdisciplinary teaching also remains challenging.

Interdisciplinary Courses

Although experiential learning opportunities are increasing and some law schools allow students to take courses from outside the law school, truly interdisciplinary courses on climate change are still hard to find, even among the more innovative law schools. This should not be surprising, as research confirms that interdisciplinary scholarship continues to face substantial barriers in the legal academy. True, as discussed in chapters 3 and 4, law schools are showing greater support for interdisciplinary approaches, either by hiring professors with dual degrees or by allowing faculty in other parts of the university to teach courses at the law school. Interdisciplinary courses were already appearing in the environmental law curriculum before 2010, but support for interdisciplinary teaching and scholarship has always been uneven.

Chapters 3 and 4 reported the difficulties that environmental law professors faced in developing interdisciplinary courses, and those difficulties persist. A 2015 survey by Dave Owen and Caroline Noblet found that, "at least within the environmental law subfield, interdisciplinary work remains a relatively minor part of professors' work."[77] While 60 percent of respondents expressed interest in doing more interdisciplinary work, and 50 percent reported doing more such work over the course of their careers, "almost three quarters of the respondents reported devoting less than 25 percent of their research activity to such collaborations, and 45 percent of respondents reported doing no collaborative work at all in the last five years."[78] The barriers they report are much the same as those mentioned by my interviewees: lack of time; institutional factors that isolate law faculty from the rest of the university; lack of formal support for or recognition of interdisciplinary work; and the difficulty of getting such research published. They report as well that these barriers were more significant for junior professors—those seeking tenure.[79] They conclude that law schools could do a great deal more to cultivate interdisciplinary work, including fostering collaboration between law professors and the rest of the university (e.g., with centers and institutes), supporting and recognizing interdisciplinary scholarship, and opening law school courses to students in other disciplines.[80]

As discussed above, the more innovative programs like Stanford's do offer courses that take an interdisciplinary approach, and many of these are open to students from outside the law school. But Seiger echoed Cullenward's complaint about law school. On one hand, not having a PhD gives her "the freedom of the nonexpert." She doesn't claim to have deep domain expertise; rather, she operates more as a "curator," with a broader perspective than either a legal or business scholar might be expected to demonstrate. But she noted that the academic world still treats people without PhDs very poorly. That law school culture is still very discipline-focused was suggested as well by Anna Mance, a lecturer and Thomas C. Grey fellow at Stanford Law. Mance received her JD from the University of Miami (2008) and a masters degree in international development from UC Berkeley (2016), where she developed her expertise on climate policy. She found the masters degree in an interdisciplinary field less helpful on the job market compared to a PhD in a more narrow specialization (with more emphasis on research skills). Research skills are of course valuable, but Mance would like to see law schools offer more experiential learning, where people with a more general, interdisciplinary degree might have an advantage. "Policy labs, where you're working on an actual project for someone, or envisioning 'how can we deal with this problem?' from multiple different angles, I think that work is where you get innovation and multidisciplinary crossover learning." But she found that, "on the market, you are asked about your core courses that you want to teach and what types of research projects you want to do and what methods you'll use. I was never asked in an interview about what policy labs or centers I might like to develop."[81] The challenges faced by Seiger, Cullenward, and Mance support Owen and Noblet's conclusions that law schools remain somewhat unwelcoming environments for interdisciplinary scholars.

Nevertheless, the larger picture suggests that teaching climate change is supporting and is supported by the evolution of curriculum and pedagogy in law schools since the 1990s. There is more room for courses centered on climate and energy, more scope for practical, problem-based learning, and more opportunities to engage emerging policy innovations and to offer interdisciplinary learning experiences. From another perspective, however, bringing climate change more fully into the environmental law curriculum may be destabilizing that curriculum, raising questions about whether environmental law will remain a viable field.

Climate Change as a Disruptive Force

As I explain in chapter 1, when the field of environmental law first emerged, it lacked clear boundaries and determinate form, which made it hard to teach. Focusing on the major federal statutes helped to define the field, clarify its focus, and (not incidentally) support its importance and legitimacy as a field of law. Moreover, the statutes, while not easy to teach, were amenable to traditional, doctrine-focused pedagogies. Climate law is not like that—and it's not clear whether it ever will be like that. Even if a federal climate statute does appear, it may be too late to define the field as focused on a single statute. As Adam Buzbee put it, carbon dioxide simply isn't a normal pollutant: "It's so pervasive and comes from so many sources. . . . . Environmental law has tended to focus on the particular causative agents . . . but here you have something that ranges from land use pattern to urban design to factories to transportation to highway use to investment in mass transit to methane to mining practices. . . . So the challenge of teaching it is fitting it into the usual silos of law."[82] If we add to that description the larger task of transitioning global energy systems, it's clear that the traditional approach to environmental law won't work. Once we add adaptation to climate change to the mix, the problem becomes even more complex and dynamic. Climate change is disrupting environmental law as a field in the law school curriculum by

166 CHAPTER FIVE

challenging the definition of the field and by making traditional pedagogies less effective.

Field Destabilization

Environmental law as a curricular field is changing rapidly. I've discussed the need to integrate environmental and energy law and touched on the importance of local and international law (and intergovernmental relations). The next area of integration is likely to be corporate law, as climate activism aimed at corporate governance continues, with public health and insurance law on the horizon. We may be returning to the earliest period of environmental law, where it seemed to be expanding with every new scientific advance.

Several interviewees discussed this dynamic. As mentioned in chapter 4, Kate Gordon noted that carbon emissions aren't localized, so they raise issues of international law, jurisdiction, and attribution. And their impacts are quite broad and varied, affecting the economy and labor in addition to resource management and human health. The way that environmental law is taught is too narrow to get to all these different facets of the problem. Climate change, she suggests, is like globalization or inequality: it's a far-reaching phenomenon that affects everything. That makes it hard to teach as a stand-alone subject.[83]

Dan Farber agrees. Having published a textbook on climate law with Cinnamon Carlarne in 2016,[84] he explains the difficulty of conceptualizing the subfield:

> To some extent [climate change] is clearly permeating . . . [and] we're incorporating it into different parts of our introductory casebook. Environmental law and energy law have merged and obviously climate change law [is] important in energy law. . . . So I think we're clearly going to see some permeation there. But on the other hand because this stuff covers such a broad range of topics I think it may be hard for students to pull it all together in their mind . . . to get some kind of comprehensive idea of what's happening in the area. So I think there's still going to be room for several courses [on climate law].[85]

Alicia Seiger goes further, suggesting that "climate is not environmental law": "Climate is tax law, it's corporate law, . . . it's corporate form. . . . [So] if we're really going to tackle this crisis we've got to . . . reimagine capitalism, to get those revised rules of the road right, we need good legal minds who are imaginative." More generally, it's imperative that legal professionals integrate the climate problem into their understanding of the ends of law, because, she commented, "I don't know what justice is without that understanding."[86] Doug Kysar echoed that idea, pointing out:

> Those of us who are in the field, even before climate change became such an obvious and omnipresent problem, we've always had the sense that environmental law shouldn't be an elective that some students take, it should be permeated throughout the curriculum, so when you teach property, you can't teach property without thinking ecologically, when you teach corporations, you can't teach corporations without also talking about how the ability to amass capital is tied up intrinsically with an extractive, unsustainable economy. . . . For most [law schools], it's a specialty that's for some people and not for others. I think that reinforces the blinkered approach to climate that we've taken for the last 30 years.[87]

He goes on to state that we need a curriculum that helps people "understand that everything they do . . . will be affected one way or another by climate change."[88]

Of course, integrating climate change throughout the curriculum may not be the best way to do that. It's a well-known phenomenon in curriculum development that the more ubiquitous a phenomenon is in society, the less visible it is in a curriculum. It's hard to know how to teach broad, cross-cutting phenomena like racial inequality, globalization, and environmental justice. They often seem to require special expertise to address, but they're too big to be contained in a single course or set of courses. As a result, they often end up being addressed (if at all) only superficially across a number of different courses. Even worse, they tend to fade into the background knowledge that we (teachers) assume "everyone knows"—but that we never actually teach. There's some evidence that this is happening with climate change in the legal curriculum. My interviews showed that some professors are already bypassing teaching climate science—assuming this is something students either know or can find out on their own. Therefore they miss the opportunity to address, for example, the complexity and dynamism of socio-ecological systems, which has important implications for law.

Indeed, without a dedicated course or courses, a topic may disappear

168   CHAPTER FIVE

altogether. The treatment of climate change in the human rights curriculum illustrates the point. As Tyler Giannini explained, "Climate doesn't squarely fit into human rights and doesn't squarely fit into environment. The climate lawyer fuses the two. And that fusion means, I think, it's not being taught."[89] A student interviewee interested in human rights echoed that point. Climate change appeared in her human rights courses only as a background issue; they didn't delve into climate science or the international climate treaties. This dynamic points toward either expanding the field of environmental law dramatically, to encompass climate change in its multifaceted complexity, or creating a climate program that includes contributions from a number of curricular fields. In reality, both approaches may be necessary in order to satisfy the need for specialists in climate policy along with environmental lawyers prepared to help clients navigate a regulatory world shaped by climate change. The transformation of environmental law is therefore likely to continue, even if separate climate programs also become common.

Pedagogical Destabilization
Environmental law courses may also look very different from the statute-based lecture course that dominated the field in the 1980s. Traditional law pedagogy works best when basic legal rules are fairly stable, changing incrementally through judicial interpretation. Emerging and rapidly changing legal regimes, like climate and energy, challenge these methods.

Of course, it is possible to use doctrinal analysis even where doctrine is changing rapidly, as long as the underlying logic of the doctrine is fairly stable. Indeed, the whole point of doctrinal analysis is to understand the deeper logic driving doctrinal change. In environmental law, that logic has to do with ensuring that the current and future generations can access natural resources in a fair and rational manner: balancing social costs and benefits of regulation while protecting natural values and common pool resources and ensuring stakeholder input on policy. But what if the underlying logic and the standard model of nature it is based on are changing?

According to some of my interviewees, that is the situation created by climate change. By transforming the physical world so quickly, it is destabilizing the legal regime governing natural resources. For example, Robin Kundis Craig contended in a 2013 article that learning about climate change teaches us to think differently about the natural world, to see the world as dynamic complex systems. That conceptualization disrupts traditional assumptions in environmental law: that natural systems are relatively stable, that they can be isolated from one another, that they are predictable. Climate science teaches us that "uncertainty and unpredictability are inherent limitations on the legal system's ability to perfectly control and regulate its subjects, whether those subjects be social systems, ecological systems, or . . . socio-ecological systems."[90] This is most obvious to those who teach water law. As Mark Davis put it:

> Water law . . . was not generally informed by hydrology; it was an adjunct of property. . . . But it was based on all sorts of assumptions we know are not true, that surface water is different from groundwater, that there will always be enough water available for important things. Most of water law has not created any sense of a water budget, or emerging needs, or, specifically, a changing climate. . . . So I always try to remind my students that everything I teach them will be wrong somewhere on the day I teach it, and a lot of other things I teach them will be wrong at some point in the future in most places. The law is a rulebook for a game that will no longer be played. . . . I'm preparing them more for water law as a dynamic field rather than "here are a set of doctrines, go use them." And climate is fundamental to that.[91]

Robert Verchick, from his perspective in teaching disaster law, makes a similar point:

> Climate change is going to change law in many, many fields, and the reason is . . . one of the things we expect from law as a society is stability and . . . allocating entitlements and making sure that they're always the same. So it's easy to think of it in terms of property: you buy a piece of land, what can you do on it, what can't you do on it. . . . The process is supposed to be pretty stable. And the whole recording system and everything is all designed to make things stable. . . . The problem with climate change is that it has thrown a monkey wrench into expectations, so the future is becoming much harder to figure out. So you may not even know . . . what the legal boundaries of a piece of property [are].[92]

Indeed, experts on marine law are already confronting the fact that rising sea levels are submerging the landmarks used to delineate the boundaries of territorial waters, leading to perplexing problems in how to stabilize or manage those legal boundaries.[93]

To be sure, for some environmental law professors this is exactly why climate change is good to teach with. Buzbee, for example, reports that he is teaching "how law moves . . . law not as a static thing with an answer but what are the mechanisms through which it keeps changing, evolving, addressing new problems, not addressing them, how do institutions and people learn. And so I guess in some sense climate change was friendly to my way of thinking and teaching about the law." Holly Doremus echoed that theme when she said (as reported in chapter 4), "I have always insisted that students need to learn both the current law, something about how it got that way and why, and for sure, the range of ways it might change, the way it might need to change." But what if "the range of ways it might change" are themselves changing?

Douglas Kysar suggests that "whether law can achieve its aspiration of stabilizing social order is now in grave question because of climate change. For law school not to have as its mission to engage with that question, it means we're shuffling deck chairs [on the Titanic]."[94] That is, law schools have to embrace the more instrumental view of law—law as a tool for doing things rather than a fixed order of values. But perhaps even more, they need to conceptualize policy itself in less law-like terms: as provisional management strategies subject to rapid change rather than as a stable and predictable set of rules. Climate change may require expanding the regulatory territory subject to discretionary actions made by government agents constrained by only the vaguest of standards, while contracting the territory subject to traditional understandings of the phrase "rule of law." What that means for the teaching of law—for law itself as an academic discipline—is also open to question. Is it possible that, in making climate lawyers, we will end up unmaking the American law school?

That conclusion is premature, to be sure. After all, most law school courses still feature doctrinal analysis and the case-dialogue method. And there is still plenty of demand for lawyers trained in traditional legal skills even in environmental law. Several of the students I interviewed are practicing in environmental law or related fields, and most of them are not (yet) encountering climate change as a destabilizing force. They are aware of the changing climate; it affects what their clients—farmers, foresters, and energy businesses—are doing. But it isn't affecting the lawyer's daily work of drafting wills and trusts, doing title inspections, and ensuring compliance with regulations.

In the legal academy, however, phenomena like climate change seem to be eroding the traditional disciplinary distinction between law and public policy. Most climate law (and much energy law as well) is taught using the methods common in public policy schools: Policy documents and debates are foregrounded; students conduct policy analyses and write policy papers; and the more ambitious courses provide opportunities for students to work with stakeholders on real-world policy problems. These courses seem to fit reasonably well into the curriculum and encounter no opposition from law students or law faculty—which raises the question: Why not merge the training of legal and policy professionals, or at least incorporate policy studies, more directly into the legal curriculum? The developments in legal education since the 1990s make plausible a return to the vision of Frank-furter and Reed of the law school as training students to participate in a public profession—of legal practice as part of the state's governing mecha-nism. With problems like climate change challenging state and society in the twenty-first century, a new kind of law school may, at last, be imaginable.

Conclusion

The question is, "What law was there to teach?"
   —Adam Babich

Climate change is important not only for litigation and rule making but businesses are embracing being green generally and focusing on climate change in particular. So as a law student and a lawyer you need to be aware of these movements. . . . It's how people do business, what their corporate policies are, how they deal with supply chains, how they deal with customers, it spans everything.
   —Jeff Civins

The first quote above is from Adam Babich, describing the situation as he saw it when he first started thinking about teaching climate law. The second quote is from Jeff Civins, explaining the importance of climate law to his students today. They demonstrate the evolution of climate law as a domain of legal knowledge, from not existing at all in the 1990s and early 2000s to a field that today spans an enormous legal territory. Environmental law professors can not only conceptualize climate law as a field; they can explain how climate change and climate policy are likely to affect such fields as insurance law, real estate transactions, energy law, corporate governance, human rights, agricultural regulation, food policy, and a host of other areas of legal practice.

That part of the story is undoubtedly a success story. Environmental law professors are doing what they are supposed to do: diving deeply into a new policy problem and creating the legal knowledge—concepts, tools, theories—needed to address it. Indeed, environmental law has been one of the most dynamic and exciting fields of legal scholarship for decades for precisely this reason. But how successful are law schools at transmitting this knowledge to their students? This part of the story—the transformation of legal education—is more complicated.

The Success Story

The reasons why environmental law professors did not start incorporating climate change into the law school curriculum during the 1980s are clear: despite the modest reforms of previous decades, law school pedagogy by the 1980s was still very doctrine-focused, geared toward training students to master relatively stable areas of settled law. This was particularly true of the environmental law curriculum. Even though it was a newer area of law, the flurry of federal statutes in the 1970s had given environmental law professors a very clear mission that was well suited to traditional pedagogy: help future litigators, advisers, and regulators master the federal pollution control regime. Unfortunately, that mission did not leave much room for addressing climate change. There was no lack of awareness about climate change that I could discover—environmental law scholars were certainly discussing it in the 1980s—and no political pressure to avoid the subject. The problem for law professors was that climate change didn't fit neatly into the pollution control framework that they knew how to teach. It had a distinctive global dimension, involved emerging complex science, and—most problematic— there was no federal regulatory regime to focus on.

But for precisely that reason the early climate law courses were very innovative. The absence of a federal statute encouraged creative approaches to the subject by the more entrepreneurial professors. Led by these innovators, the institution adapted. The story told in this book demonstrates that early adopters started addressing climate change in the late 1990s, and then the wave of innovation grew from 2000 to 2010, resulting in a dramatic increase in the amount of climate-focused courses after 2005. This growth was spurred in part by such events as Hurricane Katrina and *Massachusetts v. EPA*.[1] Indeed, the legal question posed in *Massachusetts v. EPA*—focused as it was on the Clean Air Act, the centerpiece of the environmental law curriculum—was such a good teaching tool that the case was probably destined to become a classic. It is now taught in courses on environmental law, administrative law, and probably other courses as well.

But the innovations of the 2000s also owe a good deal to broader institutional changes that started in the 1990s: the growth of the faculty, which

174 CONCLUSION

gave them more time to learn and teach about climate change; a trend in favor of more innovative pedagogies, such as applied, problem-based learning, that proved appropriate for emerging legal problems; and support for more interdisciplinary teaching (including the creation of centers and institutes). These changes led to an increase in the number of courses addressing climate change and also made a difference in *how* climate change was taught. Without these institutional changes, climate change would likely have been largely confined to courses on international environmental law and the Clean Air Act. The transformation of law schools made it possible to offer more courses focused on different aspects of climate policy and the energy transition more generally, to devote more clinical programs to climate litigation, and to develop more interdisciplinary instruction on the topic.

Thus the expansion of the climate curriculum between 2010 and 2020 was multifaceted. Climate change became a central theme in introductory environmental law courses and became more prominent in courses on natural resources. Climate law courses began to appear in several programs, and law schools began to merge their energy and environmental law programs in order to provide better coverage of climate change. There are indications that climate is now starting to migrate to other fields including human rights, torts, property, and corporate law, although those trends are still tentative. Thus Peter Byrne is surely correct:

> We do so much better a job [of preparing students for issues like climate change] than when I was in law school, helping them consider what their professional life can contribute to society. . . . We also show them how to go about it and get exposure to pathways both in and out of class. Most law schools now fund summer internships with nonprofit organizations; we have a whole office that helps students find public interest jobs. Those things are really making more prominent in the awareness of every law student social and ecological needs and the pathways to address them. We do a lot better . . . than we used to.[2]

The impact of this development is evident in interviews with students who graduated from law school recently. Some examples from my interviews illustrate some possible career paths for climate lawyers in the 2020s:

- One 2016 graduate reported having taken five environmental law courses, including two at an associated public policy school and one on energy law, as well as the environmental law clinic. The courses offered considerable coverage of climate change. This student is now working for an environmental NGO that pursues litigation directly against polluters, including coal-fired power plants.

- A 2021 graduate reported taking four courses on environmental law, all of which had a strong focus on climate law, as well as doing four terms at the environmental law clinic. This student is now at a large law firm doing work connected to corporate compliance, including advising European clients who have to navigate European Union climate laws. In fact, this was one of several recent graduates who are working at corporate law firms helping clients develop solar and wind energy projects.
- Another 2021 graduate took three environmental law courses, including one on climate policy, and a course on human rights that also addressed climate change. This student now works for an NGO on environmental human rights.
- Finally, one interviewee (a 2007 graduate who took two environmental law courses and environment-focused internships) is making climate policy as an elected official.

Importantly, all of these students cited experiential learning—clinics and internships—as having a major impact on their educational experience, giving them the opportunity to work on issues like emissions control, pipeline litigation, and climate adaptation policies. Most of them also participated in co-curricular activities like environmental law journals, moot court competitions, and student organizations focused on environmental issues. Their three years of law school were rich in climate education opportunities.

Continuing Challenges

The task of incorporating climate change is far from complete. To begin with, it is still largely confined to the environmental law curriculum. Not all law schools offer environmental law regularly, and it's not a required course at most law schools. Most of my interviewees agreed that law schools were doing a fairly good job of training those law students who were interested in climate change and were at schools with well-developed environmental law programs. As Robin Kundis Craig put it: "I think most of the ones with environmental law programs are [preparing students adequately], at least for the students who go into those programs. I am not at all confident that even students at law schools with those programs, if they're not in the program, come out with any real understanding of what climate change is or how it might affect their practice over time."[3] Dan Farber agreed, suggesting that "there are things law schools could do. For example, it seems to me that this is a topic that should get significant attention in property law. . . . It seems to me the business law curriculum should be giving more attention to how climate change will impact businesses and how climate policy will impact businesses."[4] Doug Kysar summarized the complaint: "At most places, [environmental law] is a specialty that's for some people and not for others, and I think [it] reinforces the same kind of blinkered approach to climate that we've taken for the last 30 years. . . . If you're teaching lawyers, 'Oh and by the way, there's this thing called the environment and if you're worried about it you can go take this other class.' That doesn't help people understand that everything they do . . . will be affected one way or another by climate change."[5]

Even the most pessimistic interviewees could envision ways that law schools could change to better prepare students—but they did not see that change happening fast enough. As Holly Doremus said, "I think the answer to [whether law schools are adequately preparing students] is probably no, but I'm not sure the answer ever could be yes." She continues: "Are the drivers [of change] adequately connected to what people are going to need in practice? . . . I think generally the answer to that is no. . . . What drives change in the academic setting is the interests of the academics. And change is slow."[6]

Peter Byrne is undoubtedly right that law schools are doing much better at addressing climate change than they were in 1990, and they are likely to continue to improve. The interest of academics has been captured by climate change. But Doremus is also right that "change is slow." The work needed to develop a climate curriculum started about 20 years later than it (ideally) might have, and there are still significant barriers to addressing climate change in all its complexity in law school. Until climate change is integrated throughout the curriculum, many students will graduate without having any instruction in how it may affect their practice. As Farber suggested, addressing climate change in property law (usually a required first-year course) and corporate law (an important elective) would go a long way toward expanding climate education to a broader group.

A deeper issue is that climate law is still being treated more as a pollution-control problem, requiring top-down regulation of emissions, rather than a problem requiring transformation of our energy and land use systems. This narrow focus on controlling emissions may not lead to the most effective policies, and students at schools without a well-developed energy law curriculum may not fully understand the industrial transformation we need. As Lazarus puts it in his new course on climate lawyering: "To meet that lawmaking challenge [of addressing climate change] will require far more than the enactment of traditional pollution control laws that impose emissions limitations on the largest immediate domestic sources of greenhouse gases such as motor vehicles, power plants, and other industrial activities that burn fossil fuels to produce energy. No less than a wholesale transformation of how we produce and distribute energy will be required." Further: "To meet that lawmaking challenge will . . . require far more than traditional environmental lawyers working with environmental protection laws."[7] Expansion of the environmental curriculum aimed at preparing students to facilitate the energy transition is one obvious opportunity for improvement.

Even where the environmental and energy curriculum is well developed, certain important topics are still not well covered. Some gaps, like geoengineering, are likely to be filled fairly quickly, since they fit the standard model of top-down policymaking. But other topics are more challenging. Food and agriculture law, which are also important areas for climate policy, are still only occasionally taught at most law schools. It will require some effort to incorporate climate change into this field, which is currently focused on federal agriculture policy and food safety regulations. But perhaps the most important area requiring attention is adaptation to climate change. This topic poses considerable challenges given the variety of climate-related threats and adaptive responses. As we've discussed, traditional law school courses are best adapted to teaching cohesive regulatory regimes. Helping communities develop bottom-up strategies for dealing with climate change—which is what a good deal of adaptation will probably look like—is the sort of thing best done by clinics. Thus experiential courses like clinics are where we may expect climate adaptation to be taught most effectively.

Even more problematically, law schools still struggle with supporting interdisciplinary teaching and scholarship, and this seems to be a barrier to more effective instruction in environmental law generally. The problem is particularly acute for climate law. To begin with, climate law seems to require at least a basic understanding of climate science—and climate science is hard to teach in a law school. Law professors typically don't have a deep background in this science, students come to law school with wildly different levels of scientific knowledge, and the curriculum as a whole doesn't support scientific training. Indeed, there is evidence in my interviews that climate science is starting to recede from the curriculum, as professors assume students either know what climate change is or can learn about it on their own. Neither is climate science the only kind of interdisciplinary connection needed to address climate change. People teaching climate law may need to develop expertise to address its implications for several areas of practice, such as corporate law, human rights, and insurance law. Connections between the climate law faculty and the public policy community beyond the law school are also valuable—perhaps essential—to addressing climate policy adequately. Increasingly, the training of climate lawyers is drawing on the business school—or at least on people with the ability to teach business school–type courses focused on developing renewable energy projects. Thus several kinds of interdisciplinary connections are needed to create climate lawyers.

Unfortunately, supporting interdisciplinary work is challenging for most academic institutions. The discipline is the primary organizing principle in higher education, structuring hiring, promotion, scholarly research and publication, curriculum, and everything that supports those core institutional functions. Organization by discipline makes it difficult for law professors to collaborate with scholars outside the law school or even to cross into other fields of law within the law school. But judging from my interviews, some universities and law schools support interdisciplinary work better than others. The creation of centers and institutes, either within or outside the law school, seems to help that effort. Explicit attention to hiring and promoting criteria that favor (or at least don't penalize) interdisciplinary scholarship could also be embraced more widely.

Ultimately, of course, law school professors alone cannot teach students everything they need to know about climate change. Law professors in the United States rely on their students' four years of undergraduate education to provide the foundation necessary to understand the social (and ecological) context in which law is practiced. That points to the wisdom of teaching climate change across the undergraduate curriculum—for the benefit not only of professional training in law but also of professional training in just about any field. Law professors can help to promote that broad approach to climate education. Simply identifying a background in climate science as a plus in law school admissions decisions could have a significant impact on the undergraduate curriculum.

A final issue—not raised by my interviewees but apparent in interviews

CONCLUSION 179

with students—is the risk that the curricular and pedagogic innovations I've discussed will fuel inequality among law schools. I did not do many interviews at lower-ranked law schools, so my thoughts here are tentative at best. But I was struck by comments from two student interviews who responded, when I ask them whether they enjoyed law school, as follows:

INTERVIEWEE A: "On the whole, no. I did not enjoy law school. . . . I loved my liberal arts college experience. Law school is nothing like that. You're asked to read case law, memorize black and white legal rules, and regurgitate them on an exam. There's no discussion, no debate. . . . None of it made any sense to me. It's not preparing you to practice law in the real world . . . I found law school on the whole very frustrating, except . . . I did enjoy the clinics and externships."[8]

INTERVIEWEE B: "No. I did not [enjoy law school]. . . . Just the competitiveness of everything. . . . The ranking system is really dehumanizing. And I think it does encourage you to give up some of your values especially when career-searching."[9]

Most of the students I interviewed enjoyed law school, reporting that their courses (even those featuring case-dialogue pedagogy) were generally interesting and engaging, that their clinics and internships were valuable, and that there was a good deal of energy and activity around environmental issues. But the students quoted above attended schools without a well-developed environmental law curriculum. Clearly the changes in law school curriculum and pedagogy I've discussed in this book are not evenly distributed. Some features of traditional law school culture persist: it is expensive and competitive, and too many courses are taught by uninspiring professors in the traditional manner. Moreover, some law schools still struggle to regularly offer even the standard survey environmental law course.

To be sure, even these students at least had the chance to take a couple of policy-oriented and experiential courses, which probably would not have been the case had they attended law school in 1985. But to the extent that the innovations I've discussed depend on a law school's resources and law professors' professional networks, they may not penetrate to the smaller and poorer schools—the schools that are educating most of the lawyers that climate-stressed communities will need.

In sum, providing all legal professionals with climate education—reaching all law students and all law schools—still poses challenges. But at least many law schools are providing models of what climate law education should look like, and many schools do have significant opportunities to make progress delivering it. Maintaining and building on this progress is not a foregone conclusion, of course. If law schools tighten their budgets, they may end up eliminating some of the more innovative courses and subjects, increase teaching loads, and provide less support for experiential learning. I would have more confidence that these trends I've discussed will persist if the legal academy were naming, claiming, and celebrating them more than they currently do. In all the recent commentary on legal education in general and environmental legal education in particular, I've seen little recognition that the traditional model is starting to lose ground to more problem-based, interdisciplinary, and engaged approaches—and that this is the right direction for the twenty-first century law school.

Law Schools and the State

Finally, we should return to the question I started with: Will law schools be able to train enough climate professionals to staff the American state—to provide legal advice, policy innovation, and social mobilization to support effective climate governance at all levels, from the international sphere to the local city hall? On that point, I think the answer is probably "yes." While we may not yet have enough schools working toward that goal—the American state is, after all, enormous—many have already developed the necessary curriculum and are implementing it quite successfully. Given the developments we've seen at the law schools represented in this study, it is imaginable and even likely that American law schools will be able to satisfy the need for climate policy professionals in the near future. That bodes well for twenty-first century state development.

As I discuss in the introduction, the twenty-first century state will need to develop considerable new capacity to deal with emerging problems like climate change. But the experience of law schools gives us some reason to be optimistic that such development can happen. Creating climate legal professionals requires a deep transformation of legal education away from the traditional Harvard model: a shift toward more experiential learning, a deeper commitment to training in public policy, and a broader engagement with multiple communities beyond the law school. Many law schools, and particularly the well-resourced ones, are demonstrating the ability to make this transformation—to become centers for training policy innovators who can help the twenty-first century state deal with complex, global challenges

CONCLUSION 181

like climate change. To be sure, accomplishing that transformation while also tackling the problems of access to, inclusion in, and affordability of legal education isn't easy. But the pressure to deal with climate change has provided the impetus for law professors to work toward that transformation, and that work is making a real difference in how lawyers are trained.

This conclusion, tentative though it may be, points toward an important insight: climate change may be threatening human civilization, but it may also be a progressive force, motivating us to develop better institutions and practices. We are going to need smarter, more flexible, more effective, and more powerful systems for governing the global commons. American law schools are starting to meet that challenge.

APPENDIX A

List of People Interviewed

Faculty (institutional affiliation when interviewed)
Babcock, Hope. Georgetown University Law Center
Babich, Adam. Tulane University Law School
Benjamin, Lisa. Lewis & Clark Law School
Blumm, Michael. Lewis & Clark Law School
Brown Weiss, Edith. Georgetown University Law Center
Burns, Wil. School of International Service, American University
Buzbee, Adam. Georgetown University Law Center
Byrne, Peter. Georgetown University Law Center
Chandler, Pamela. Vice President and Publisher, West Academic
Civins, Jeff. University of Texas School of Law
Connolly, Kim Diana. University at Buffalo School of Law
Craig, Robin Kundis. University of Southern California Gould School of Law
Cullenward, Daniel. Stanford Law School
Davis, Mark. Tulane University Law School
Dernbach, John. Widener University Commonwealth Law School
Doremus, Holly. Berkeley Law School
Farber, Daniel. Berkeley Law School
Fershee, Joshua. Creighton School of Law
Funk, William. Lewis & Clark Law School
Gerrard, Michael. Columbia Law School
Giannini, Tyler. Harvard Law School
Gordon, Kate. Stanford Law School
Haragan, Kelly. University of Texas School of Law
Heinzerling, Lisa. Georgetown University Law Center
Higgins, Louis. Editor in Chief, West Academic
Howland, Joan. University of Minnesota Law School

183

Infelise, Robert. Berkeley Law School

Johnson, Vincent. St. Mary's University School of Law

Kagan, Robert. Center of the Study of Law and Society, University of California-Berkeley

Klass, Alexandra. University of Minnesota Law School

Kraham, Susan. Columbia Law School

Kysar, Douglas. Yale Law School

LaPlante, Allison. Lewis & Clark Law School

Lazarus, Richard. Harvard Law School

Lyman, Erica. Lewis & Clark Law School

Macdougald, Joseph. University of Connecticut Law School

Mance, Anna. Stanford Law School

Miller, Alan. Private consultant

Osofsky, Hari. Northwestern Pritzker School of Law

Panarella, Samuel. Alexander Blewett III School of Law at the University of Montana

Parenteau, Pat. Vermont Law School

Parker, Richard. University of Connecticut Law School

Percival, Robert. University of Maryland Francis King Carey School of Law

Ruhl, J. B. Vanderbilt University Law School

Salim, Oday. University of Michigan Law School

Sanders, Matthew. Stanford Law School

Seiger, Alicia. Stanford Law School

Spence, David. University of Texas School of Law

Talus, Kim. Tulane University Law School

Tarlock, A. Dan. Chicago-Kent College of Law

Thompson, Barton. Stanford Law School

Tolan, Patrick. WMU-Cooley Law School

Ulen, Thomas. University of Illinois at Urbana-Champaign

Verchick, Robert. Loyola University New Orleans College of Law

Zimmerman, Scott. Berkeley Law School

Students

The student interviewees graduated between 2007 and 2022. They attended the following law schools:

Columbia Law School

George Washington University Law School

Harvard Law School

Lewis & Clark Law School

New York University School of Law

Tulane University Law School

University of Connecticut Law School
University of Michigan Law School
University of Minnesota Law School
University of Texas School of Law
University of Wyoming College of Law
William Mitchell College of Law

APPENDIX B

Law School Environment-Focused Centers[1]

Law School	Center/Institute	Year Founded[2]
Barry University School of Law	Center for Advanced Study of Environmental & Earth Law	unknown[3]
Barry University School of Law	Center for Earth Jurisprudence	2006
Berkeley Law School	Center for Law, Energy & the Environment	2007
Columbia Law School	Sabin Center for Climate Change Law	2009
Georgetown University Law Center	Georgetown Climate Center	2009
Golden Gate University School of Law	Center on Urban Environmental Law	2011
Lewis & Clark Law School	Global Law Alliance for Animals and the Environment	1994/2020
Paul M. Hebert Law Center, Louisiana State University	John P. Laborde Energy Law Center	2012
Loyola University New Orleans College of Law	Center on Environment, Land, and Law	2006
New York University School of Law	Guarini Center on Environmental, Energy, and Land Use Law	2009
New York University School of Law	State Energy & Environmental Impact Center	2017
Pace Law School	Energy and Climate Center	1988
Pace Law School	Global Center for Environmental Legal Studies	unknown
Pace Law School	Land Use Law Center for Sustainable Development	1993
Penn State Law	Center for Agricultural and Shale Law	unknown

continued

187

Law School	Center/Institute	Year Founded[2]
Stanford Law School	Steyer-Taylor Center for Energy Policy and Finance	2010
Texas Tech University School of Law	Center for Water Law &Policy	unknown
Tulane University Law School	Center for Environmental Law	2019
Touro University Jacob D. Fuchsberg Law Center	Land Use and Sustainable Development Law Institute	unknown
University of California, Davis School of Law	California Environmental Law & Policy Center	2010
University of California, Irvine School of Law	Center for Land, Environment, and Natural Resources	2012
University of California, Los Angeles School of Law	Emmett Institute on Climate Change & the Environment	2008
University of Colorado Law School	Getches-Wilkinson Center for Natural Resources, Energy, and the Environment	2013
Sturm College of Law, University of Denver	Rocky Mountain Land Use Institute	1992
University of Houston Law Center	The Environment, Energy & Natural Resources Center	2007
University of Mississippi School of Law	National Sea Grant Law Center	2002
University of North Carolina School of Law	Center for Climate, Energy, Environment & Economics	2008/2016
University of Oregon School of Law	Environmental and Natural Resources Law Center	2003
University of San Diego School of Law	Energy Policy Initiatives Center	2005
University of Texas School of Law	Kay Bailey Hutchison Energy Center for Business, Law, and Policy	2015
University of Utah S. J. Quinney College of Law	Wallace Stegner Center for Land, Resources & the Environment	1995
University of Washington School of Law	Arctic Law and Policy Institute	unknown
University of Wyoming College of Law	Gina Guy Center for Law and Energy Resources in the Rockies	2012
Vermont Law School	Environmental Law Center	1978
Widener University Commonwealth Law School	Environmental Law and Sustainability Center	2009
Widener University Delaware Law School	Global Environmental Rights Institute	2015
William & Mary Law School	Virginia Coastal Policy Center	2012
Yale Law School	Yale Center for Environmental Law & Policy	1994

Notes

Introduction

1. Katherine Hayhoe, "Here's How Long We've Known About Climate Change," *Ecowatch*, November 25, 2016, www.ecowatch.com/katharine-hayhoe-climate-change-2103671842.html.

2. David Wirth, "Teaching and Research in International Environmental Law," *Harvard Environmental Law Review* 23 (1999): 423–440.

3. Richard Hildreth et al., *Climate Change Law: Mitigation and Adaptation* (St. Paul, MN: West, 2009); Chris Wold, David Hunter, and Melissa Powers, *Climate Change and the Law* (New York: Matthew Bender/Lexis Nexis, 2009); Michael Gerrard, *Global Climate Change and U.S. Law*, 1st ed. (Chicago: American Bar Association, 2007).

4. Robert Fischman, "What Is Natural Resources Law?" *University of Colorado Law Review* 78 (Spring 2007): 717–749.

5. Michael Robinson-Dorn, "Teaching Environmental Law in the Era of Climate Change: A Few Whats, Whys, and Hows," *Washington Law Review* 82 (2007): 619–648.

6. David M. Hart and David G. Victor, "Scientific Elites and the Making of US Policy for Climate Change Research, 1957–74," *Social Studies of Science* 23, no. 4 (1993): 643–680; Joshua Howe, *Behind the Curve: Science and the Politics of Global Warming* (Seattle: University of Washington Press, 2014); Dana Fisher, *National Governance and the Global Climate Change Regime* (Lanham, MD: Rowman & Littlefield, 2004); S. R. Weart, *The Discovery of Global Warming* (Cambridge, MA: Harvard University Press, 2003); Loren R. Cass, *The Failures of American and European Climate Policy: International Norms, Domestic Politics, and Unachievable Commitments* (Albany, NY: SUNY Press, 2012).

7. Danny Cullenward and David G. Victor, *Making Climate Policy Work* (Cambridge, MA: Polity, 2020), xv.

8. John Nolon, "Shifting Paradigms Transform Environmental and Land Use Law: The Emergence of the Law of Sustainable Development," *Fordham Environmental Law Rev.* 24 (2013): 242–274.

9. John Dernbach, *Acting as If Tomorrow Matters: Accelerating the Transition to Sustainability* (Washington, DC: Environmental Law Institute, 2012); Michael

Gerrard and Jody Freeman *Global Climate Change and U.S. Law*, 2nd ed. (Chicago: American Bar Association, 2014).

10. Stephen Skowronek, *Building a New American State* (Cambridge, UK: Cambridge University Press, 1982); Theda Skocpol, *Protecting Soldiers and Mothers* (Cambridge, MA: Belknap Press, 1992); Daniel Carpenter, *The Forging of Bureaucratic Autonomy* (Princeton, NJ: Princeton University Press, 2001).

11. Adam Bonica, "Why Are There So Many Lawyers in Congress?" *Legislative Studies Quarterly* 45, no. 2 (May 2020): 253–289; Neil Hamilton, "Ethical Leadership in Professional Life," *University of St. Thomas Law Journal* 6 (2009): 358–396.

12. The Social Learning Group, *Learning to Manage Global Environmental Risk*, vol. 1 (Cambridge, MA: MIT Press, 2001), 14.

13. Paul N. Edwards, *A Vast Machine: Computer Models, Climate Data, and the Politics of Global Warming* (Cambridge, MA: MIT Press, 2010).

14. Edwards, *A Vast Machine*, 10; Joyeeta Gupta, *The History of Global Climate Governance* (Cambridge, UK: Cambridge University Press, 2014), xiv, 204–205.

15. Bentley B. Allan, "Producing the Climate: States, Scientists, and the Constitution of Global Governance Objects," *International Organization* 71, no. 1 (2017): 131–162; Fisher, *National Governance and the Global Climate Change Regime*; Hart and Victor, "Scientific Elites."

16. E. M. Rogers, *Diffusion of Innovations*, 5th ed. (New York: Free Press, 2003).

17. Etienne Wenger, *Communities of Practice: Learning, Meaning, and Identity*, 6th ed. (Cambridge, UK: Cambridge University Press, 1999).

Chapter 1. Making Environmental Lawyers

1. Mark Miller, *The High Priests of American Politics: The Role of Lawyers in American Political Institutions* (Knoxville: University of Tennessee Press, 1995), 36–37.

2. Miller, *High Priests of American Politics*, 50–52.

3. Adam Bonica, "Why Are There So Many Lawyers in Congress?" *Legislative Studies Quarterly* 45, no. 2 (May 2020): 253–289.

4. Bonica, "Why Are There So Many Lawyers in Congress?" 5.

5. Miller, *High Priests of American Politics*, 41.

6. Michael Pertschuk, *When the Senate Worked for Us: The Invisible Role of Staffers in Countering Corporate Lobbies* (Nashville, TN: Vanderbilt University Press, 2017).

7. Neil Hamilton, "Ethical Leadership in Professional Life," *University of St. Thomas Law Journal* 6 (2009): 358–396, 362.

8. Margaret H. Lemos, "Aggregate Litigation Goes Public: Representative Suits by State Attorneys General," *Harvard Law Review* 126, no. 2 (2012): 486–549.

9. Miller, *High Priests of American Politics*, 40.

10. "Environmental Protection Agency," FederalPay.org, n.d., www.federalpay

.org/employees/environmental-protection-agency; Miller, *High Priests of American Politics*, 36.

11. Office of General Counsel, EPA.gov, n.d., www.epa.gov/aboutepa/about-off ice-general-counsel-ogc.

12. Miller, *High Priests of American Politics*, 37.

13. Michael Gerrard, *Global Climate Change and U.S. Law*, 1st ed. (American Bar Association, 2007), 137–138.

14. FederalPay.Org, "Department of the Interior," n.d., www.federalpay.org/de partments/departmentofinterior.

15. FederalPay.Org, "Department of Agriculture," n.d., www.federalpay.org/de partments/departmentofagriculture.

16. Miller, *High Priests of American Politics*, 43–46.

17. Miller, 46.

18. Austin Sarat and Stuart A. Scheingold, *Cause Lawyering: Political Commitments and Professional Responsibilities* (New York: Oxford University Press, 1998).

19. Douglas NeJaime, "Cause Lawyers Inside the State," *Fordham Law Review* 81 (2012): 649–704, 654.

20. Miller, *High Priests of American Politics*, 13.

21. Miller, 23–24.

22. At the time of publication, there are 199 ABA-accredited law schools in the United States.

23. William Sullivan at al., *Educating Lawyers: Preparation for the Profession of Law* (Stanford, CA: Carnegie Foundation for the Advancement of Teaching, 2007); Robert Gordon, "The Case for (and Against) Harvard," *Michigan Law Review* 93, no. 6 (1995): 1231–1260; Robert Gordon, "The Geologic Strata of the Law School Curriculum," *Vanderbilt Law Review* 60 (2007): 339–360; Alfred S. Konefsky and John Henry Schlegel, "Mirror, Mirror on the Wall: Histories of American Law Schools," *Harvard Law Review* 95, no. 4 (1982): 833–851; Robert Bocking Stevens, *Law School: Legal Education in America from the 1850s to the 1980s* (Chapel Hill: University of North Carolina Press, 1983); Christopher Tomlins, "Framing the Field of Law's Disciplinary Encounters: A Historical Narrative," *Law & Society Review* 34, no. 4 (2000): 911–972; Stephen Feldman, "The Transformation of an Academic Discipline: Law Professors in the Past and Future (or *Toy Story Too*)," *Journal of Legal Education* 54 (2004): 471–498; Christopher Edley Jr., "Fiat Flux: Evolving Purposes and Ideals of the Great American Public Law School," *California Law Review* 100 (2012): 313–330; Laura Kalman, *Legal Realism at Yale, 1927–1960* (Chapel Hill: University of North Carolina Press, 1986); Joel Seligman, *The High Citadel: The Influence of Harvard Law School* (Boston: Houghton Mifflin, 1978); Steve Sheppard, *The History of Legal Education in the United States: Commentaries and Primary Sources* (Pasadena, CA: Salem Press, 1999); Bruce Kimball, *The Inception of Modern*

Professional Education: C. C. Langdell, 1826–1906 (Chapel Hill: University of North Carolina Press, 2009); Daniel Coquillette, *On the Battlefield of Merit: Harvard Law School, the First Century* (Cambridge, MA: Harvard University Press, 2015).

24. Michael Ariens, "Modern Legal Times: Making a Professional Legal Culture," *Journal of American Culture* 15, no. 1 (1992): 25–35.

25. Seligman, *The High Citadel*, 33–42; Gordon, *The Geologic Strata of the Law School Curriculum*; Sullivan et al., *Educating Lawyers*.

26. Kalman, *Legal Realism at Yale, 1927–1960*, 12.

27. Tomlins, *Framing the Field*.

28. Stevens, *Law School*; William P. LaPiana, *Logic and Experience the Origin of Modern American Legal Education* (New York: Oxford University Press, 1994); Bruce Kimball, "Before the Paper Chase: Student Culture at Harvard Law School, 1895–1915," *Journal of Legal Education* 61, no. 1 (August 1, 2011): 30–67; Tomlins, *Framing the Field*.

29. Ariens, "Modern Legal Times."

30. American Bar Association, "Accreditation: Frequently Asked Questions," n.d., www.americanbar.org/groups/legal_education/resources/frequently_asked _questions; Ariens, "Modern Legal Times," 31–32.

31. Stevens, *Law School*, 177.

32. I've left out the Law School Admission Council, which administers the Law School Admission Test, first administered in 1948. The LSAT looms large in admissions decisions, but the LSAC has less importance for curriculum than other organizations discussed here.

33. Tomlins, *Framing the Field*, 927.

34. Jerold S. Auerbach, *Unequal Justice: Lawyers and Social Change in Modern America* (New York: Oxford University Press, 1976), 77.

35. Alfred Reed, *Training for the Public Profession of Law* (Boston: Merrymount Press, 1921), 442; Stevens, *Law School*, 113.

36. Auerbach, *Unequal Justice*, 84, 140.

37. Auerbach, 149.

38. Stevens, *Law School*, 118.

39. Daniel R. Ernst, "Common Laborers? Industrial Pluralists, Legal Realists, and the Law of Industrial Disputes, 1915–1943," *Law and History Review* 11, no. 1 (1993): 59–100, 74.

40. Stevens, *Law School*, 139.

41. Hendrik Hartog, "Snakes in Ireland: A Conversation with Willard Hurst," *Law and History Review* 12, no. 2 (1994): 370–390, 373.

42. Hartog, "Snakes in Ireland," 372. The case was *Home Building and Loan Association v. Blaisdell*, 290 U.S. 398 (1934).

43. Kalman, *Legal Realism at Yale*, 46, 55–66; Gordon, "The Case For (and Against) Harvard," 1246.

44. Gordon, 1257.

45. Ernst, "Common Laborers?" 76–77.

46. John Henry Schlegel, *American Legal Realism and Empirical Social Science* (Chapel Hill: University of North Carolina Press, 1995), 16–17.

47. Gerald Fetner, "The Law Teacher as Legal Reformer: 1900–1945," *Journal of Legal Education* 28, no. 4 (1977): 508–529, 524; Brainerd Currie, "The Materials of Law Study," *Journal of Legal Education* 8, no. 1 (1955): 1–78, 64.

48. Stevens, *Law School*, 138; Schlegel, *American Legal Realism*, 15–17.

49. Schlegel, 17, 212–213.

50. Kalman, *Legal Realism at Yale*, 75.

51. Schlegel, *American Legal Realism*, 147–209.

52. Kalman, *Legal Realism at Yale*, 187.

53. Tomlins, *Framing the Field*, 932.

54. Tomlins.

55. Hartog, "Snakes in Ireland," 378.

56. Hartog, 378–379.

57. Hartog, 385, 390.

58. Stevens, *Law School*, 136–138, 158.

59. Stevens, 157–158.

60. Kalman, *Legal Realism at Yale*, 218–219.

61. Tomlins, *Framing the Field*; Hartog, "Snakes in Ireland."

62. Stephen Wizner, "The Law School Clinic: Legal Education in the Interests of Justice," *Fordham Law Review* 70 (2002): 1929–1937.

63. Stevens, *Law School*, 216.

64. The ABA began requiring six credit-hours in experiential education (a law clinic, simulation, field placement, or skills courses such as Negotiation and Alternative Dispute Resolution) in its 2014–2015 accreditation standards. American Bar Association, *2014–2015 ABA Standards and Rules of Procedure for Approval of Law Schools* (Chicago: American Bar Association, 2014), 16.

65. A tort is an act or omission that causes an injury to someone, including damage to one's property. Tort law concerns the principles by which private individuals can seek compensation for such injuries.

66. Kimberly Smith, *The Conservation Constitution* (Lawrence: University Press of Kansas, 2019); Noga Morag-Levine, *Chasing the Wind* (Princeton, NJ: Princeton University Press, 2003).

67. Smith, *The Conservation Constitution*.

68. *Hunt v. United States*, 278 U.S. 96 (1928); Smith, *The Conservation Constitution*.

69. "Judge William Dead: Was Noted Conservationist," Department of Interior Information Service, September 24, 1940.

70. Smith, *The Conservation Constitution*.

71. "Judge William Dead."

72. Paul Sabin, "Environmental Law and the End of the New Deal Order," *Law and History Review* 33, no. 4 (November 2015): 965–1003.

73. Richard Oliver Brooks, *Law and Ecology: The Rise of the Ecosystem Regime* (Aldershot, Hants, UK: Ashgate, 2002), 40–60; Richard J. Lazarus, *The Making of Environmental Law* (Chicago: University of Chicago Press, 2004).

74. Brooks, *Law and Ecology.*

75. Lazarus, *The Making of Environmental Law*, 47; Dan Tarlock, "The Airlie House Conference and the Dawn of Environmental Law," in *Pioneers of Environmental Law*, ed. Jan Laitos and John Copeland Nagle, 83–102 (Northport, NY: Twelve Tables Press, 2020); Tarlock interview.

76. Lazarus, *The Making of Environmental Law*, 48.

77. 1 *ELR* 10001–10058 (1971).

78. Marshall Robinson, "The Ford Foundation: Sowing the Seeds of a Revolution," *Environment* 35, no. 3 (April 1993): 10–41.

79. These organizations are still influential members of the public policy communities of practice, although CLASP now focuses more on social inequality than on environmental issues.

80. Joseph L. Sax, *Defending the Environment* (New York: Alfred A. Knopf, 1971).

81. Joseph L. Sax, "The Public Trust Doctrine in Natural Resource Law: Effective Judicial Intervention," *Michigan Law Review* 68 (1970): 471–554.

82. Nino Antadze, "The Role of Leadership in Depleting Institutional Ethos: The Case of Scott Pruitt and the Environmental Protection Agency," *Journal of Environmental Studies and Sciences* 9, no. 2 (June 1, 2019): 187–195.

83. Miller interview.

84. Frances Irwin, "The Law School and the Environment," *Natural Resources Journal* 12 (1972): 278–285.

85. Michael Blumm and David Becker, "From Martz to the Twenty-First Century: A Half-Century of Natural Resource Law Casebooks and Pedagogy," *University of Colorado Law Review* 78 (2007): 647–694.

86. Stevens, *Law School*, 213.

87. The official name is the Northwestern Law School of the Lewis & Clark College, but I will follow common practice and refer to it as the Lewis & Clark Law School.

88. Lewis & Clark Law School, "Environmental Law," n.d., https://law.lclark.edu/law_reviews/environmental_law; Ecology Law Quarterly, "About Us," n.d., www.ecologylawquarterly.org/about.

89. Masters of Law, an advanced degree in law.

90. Parenteau interview; Blumm interview.

91. Irwin, "The Law School and the Environment," 281.

92. Irwin, 279.

93. Irwin, 280.

94. Cyril M. Harris, and Albert J. Rosenthal, "The Interdisciplinary Course in the Legal Aspects of Noise Pollution at Columbia University," *Journal of Legal Education* 31, no. 1/2 (1981): 128–133.

95. Irwin, "The Law School and the Environment," 284–285.

96. I consulted the HeinOnline Bibliography of American Casebooks, the scholarly literature, interviews, and library catalogs. Some professors made their own collections of readings, which can sometimes be found in law school libraries but are not commercially available. Although today there are only a few major publishers of casebooks, the publishing industry was more diverse in the 1970s with many small publishers, which makes it hard to get complete information on casebooks.

97. Robert Fischman, "What Is Natural Resources Law?" *University of Colorado Law Review* 78 (Spring 2007): 717–749.

98. Lazarus, *The Making of Environmental Law*; Donna Attanasio, "Energy Law Education in the U.S.: An Overview and Recommendations," *Energy Law Journal* 36 (2015): 217–259.

99. Fred Anderson, Daniel Mandelker, and Dan Tarlock, *Environmental Protection: Law and Policy*, 1st ed. (Boston: Little, Brown & Co., 1984), xxvi.

100. Anderson, Mandelker, and Tarlock, xxvi.

101. Anderson, Mandelker, and Tarlock, xxvi.

102. Anderson, Mandelker, and Tarlock, xxv.

103. Robert Findley and Daniel Farber, *Cases and Materials on Environmental Law*, 1st ed. (St. Paul, MN: West, 1981); Roger Findley and Daniel Farber, *Cases and Materials on Environmental Law*, 5th ed. (St. Paul, MN: West, 1999).

104. John Bonine and Thomas McGarity, *The Law of Environment and Pollution: Cases, Statutes, and Materials*, 2nd ed. (St Paul, MN: West, 1984).

105. Joel A. Mintz, "Teaching Environmental Law: Some Observations on Curriculum and Materials," *Journal of Legal Education* 33, no. 1 (1983): 94–110, 96.

106. Mintz, "Teaching Environmental Law," 96.

107. William Funk, "Recent Environmental Law Casebooks: Searching for a Pedagogical Principle," *Environmental Law* 15 (1984): 201–216, 203.

108. Funk, "Recent Environmental Law Casebooks," 203–204.

109. Funk, 208.

110. Heidi Robertson, "Methods for Teaching Environmental Law: Some Thoughts on Providing Access to the Environmental Law System," *Columbia Journal of Environmental Law* 23 (1998): 237–278.

111. Joseph Sax, "Environmental Law in the Law Schools: What We Teach and How We Feel About It," *ELR* 19 (1989): 10251–10253, 10251.

112. See also Robert V. Percival, "Green Briefs and Toxic Torts: Educating Lawyers with Environmental Savvy," *Environment* 35, no. 3 (April 1993): 6–37.

113. Commonly called "Berkeley Law School," this is the name I often use throughout the book.

114. Heinzerling interview.

115. Tolan interview.

116. Sax, "Environmental Law in the Law Schools"; Robertson, "Methods for Teaching Environmental Law," 254–255.

117. Sax, "Environmental Law in the Law Schools," 10252.

118. Sax, 10252–10253.

119. Sax, 10253.

120. Blumm Interview.

121. Brown Weiss interview; Babcock interview.

Chapter 2. The Birth of Climate Law

1. Kimberly Smith, *The Conservation Constitution* (Lawrence: University Press of Kansas, 2019).

2. Richard Oliver Brooks, *Law and Ecology: The Rise of the Ecosystem Regime* (Aldershot, Hants, UK: Ashgate, 2002). On the rise of the ecosystemic view in American ecology, see William Robbins, *A Place for Inquiry, A Place for Wonder: The Andrews Forest* (Corvallis: Oregon State University Press, 2021), 30–32.

3. Brooks, *Law and Ecology*, 3.

4. Spencer Weart, *The Discovery of Global Warming*, rev. and expanded ed. (Cambridge, UK: Harvard University Press, 2008); Joshua Howe, *Behind the Curve: Science and the Politics of Global Warming* (Seattle: University of Washington Press, 2014).

5. Syukuro Manabe and Richard T. Wetherald, "The Effects of Doubling the CO_2 Concentration on the Climate of a General Circulation Model," *Journal of the Atmospheric Sciences* 32, no. 1 (January 1, 1975): 3–15; Syukuro Manabe and Richard T. Wetherald, "Thermal Equilibrium of the Atmosphere with a Given Distribution of Relative Humidity," *Journal of the Atmospheric Sciences* 24, no. 3 (May 1, 1967): 241–259.

6. Weart, *The Discovery of Global Warming*, 114.

7. John R. Ware, Stephen V. Smith, and Marjorie L. Reaka-Kudla, "Coral Reefs: Sources or Sinks of Atmospheric CO_2?" *Coral Reefs* 11, no. 3 (September 1, 1992): 127–130.

8. David M. Hart and David G. Victor, "Scientific Elites and the Making of US Policy for Climate Change Research, 1957–74," *Social Studies of Science* 23, no. 4 (1993): 643–680, 668.

9. Hart and Victor, "Scientific Elites," 646.

10. Howe, *Behind the Curve*, 82.

11. 92 Stat. 601 (1978).

12. Howe, *Behind the Curve*, 105.

13. Weart, *The Discovery of Global Warming*, 141.

14. 101 Stat. 1407 (1987).

15. 104 Stat. 3096 (1990).

16. Budget numbers are found in *Our Changing Planet*, the annual report of the U.S. Global Climate Change Research Program, in reports for fiscal years 1990 to 1999. The budget reached $1.81 billion in FY1996 and FY1997.

17. Howe, *Behind the Curve*, 151.

18. Joyeeta Gupta, *The History of Global Climate Governance* (Cambridge, UK: Cambridge University Press, 2014), xv.

19. John Dernbach, *Acting as If Tomorrow Matters: Accelerating the Transition to Sustainability* (Washington, DC: Environmental Law Institute, 2012), 9.

20. Pamela Wexler et al., *Cool Tools* (Baltimore: Center for Global Change at University of Maryland, 1992).

21. Wexler et al., *Cool Tools*.

22. Carmen Sirianni, *Sustainable Cities in American Democracy: From Postwar Urbanism to a Civic New Deal* (Lawrence: University Press of Kansas, 2020), 200.

23. ICLEI USA, "Who We Are," n.d., https://icleiusa.org/about/who-we-are.

24. Stephen M. Wheeler, "State and Municipal Climate Change Plans: The First Generation," *Journal of the American Planning Association* 74, no. 4 (October 21, 2008): 481–496; Pamela Wexler and Susan Conbere, "States Fight Global Warming," *EPA Journal* 18, no. 4 (October 1992); Gupta, *The History of Global Climate Governance*.

25. Garth Lindseth, "The Cities for Climate Protection Campaign (CCPC) and the Framing of Local Climate Policy," *Local Environment* 9, no. 4 (August 1, 2004): 325–336, 328.

26. Lindseth, "The Cities for Climate Protection Campaign," 333.

27. The EPA also had a grant program for cities to inventory greenhouse gas emissions and create mitigation plans. Wheeler, "State and Municipal Climate Change Plans," 481–482.

28. Wheeler, 485–486.

29. Wheeler, 487.

30. Gupta, *The History of Global Climate Governance*, 2–14, 53, 174.

31. Gerrard discusses in addition decisions by the Environmental Appeals Board within the EPA considering whether the agency could consider the impact of un-regulated pollutants (like CO_2) when granting permits under the Clean Air Act. Michael Gerrard, *Global Climate Change and U.S. Law*, 1st ed. (Chicago: American Bar Association, 2007), 151.

32. 912 F.2d 478 (D.D.C. 1990).

33. 83 Stat. 852 (1970).

34. 912 F.2d 478, 481.

35. 912 F.2d 478, 483.

36. 60 Stat. 237 (1946).

37. *Foundation on Economic Trends v. Watkins*, 794 F. Supp. 395 (D.D.C. 1992), 398–399. This restrictive approach to standing in the D.C. Circuit was further

reinforced by a 1996 decision, *Florida Audubon Society v Bentsen*, 94 F.3rd 658 (D.C. Cir. 1996), which explicitly rejected *L.A. v. NHTSA*'s argument in favor of standing based on informational harms. 94 F.3rd 658, 669. This restrictive view of standing was not endorsed by all federal courts, however. The Ninth Circuit, for example, continued to take a broader approach. See *Ctr. for Biological Diversity v. Nat'l Highway Traffic Safety Admin.*, 538 F.3d 1172 (9th Cir 2008), 1225.

38. *Seattle Audubon Society v. Lyons*, 871 F. Supp. 1291 (W.D.Wash. 1994), 1324.

39. 126 F3d 1158 (9th Cir 1997).

40. 126 F3d 1158, 1187.

41. 578 N.W.2d 794 (Minn. Ct. of Appeals 1998).

42. 1991 Minn. Laws ch. 315, §1.

43. 578 N.W.2d 794, 796.

44. In American law, "comity" refers to the principle that courts in different political jurisdictions will recognize one another's legal acts. More broadly, it refers to a court's respect for another court's or government's legal authority over an issue.

45. 578 N.W.2d 794, 800.

46. 499 S.W.3d 793 (Tex. 2016).

47. 499 S.W.3d 793, 807.

48. 499 S.W.3d 793, 810.

49. Gupta, *The History of Global Climate Governance*, 49–50.

50. Howland interview.

51. John P. Joergensen, "Second Tier Law Reviews, Lexis and Westlaw: A Pattern of Increasing Use," *Legal Reference Services Quarterly* 21, no. 1 (2002): 43–74, 44–45.

52. A search for "greenhouse effect" did not generate substantially different results. I also searched NexisUni, but it has limited coverage of the 1980s and did not yield additional references.

53. Edith Brown Weiss, *The International Political and Legal Problems of Weather and Climate Modification* (Berkeley: University of California, 1973).

54. Edith Brown Weiss et al., *Regimes for the Ocean: Outer Space & Weather* (Washington, DC: Brookings Institution Press, 1977).

55. Brown Weiss interview.

56. Edith Brown Weiss, "A Resource Management Approach to Carbon Dioxide During the Century of Transition," *Denver Journal of International Law & Policy* 10 (1981): 487–509, 489.

57. Brown Weiss, "A Resource Management Approach to Carbon Dioxide," 490.

58. Brown Weiss, 509. Brown Weiss did advocate for research to find strategies to manage carbon emissions so that action could be taken sooner rather than later.

59. Edith Brown Weiss, "The Planetary Trust: Conservation and Intergenerational Equity," *Ecology Law Quarterly* 11, no. 4 (1984): 495–582; Edith Brown Weiss, "Global Warming: Legal Implications for the Arctic," *Georgetown International Environmental Law Review* 2, no. 2 (1989): 81–98.

60. Rafe Pomerance, "The Dangers from Climate Warming: A Public Awakening," *EPA Journal* 12, no. 10 (1986): 15–16.

61. Allene Zanger, "Carbon Dioxide's Threat to Global Climate: An International Solution Note," *Stanford Journal of International Law* 17, no. 2 (1981): 389–412; Margot B. Peters, "An International Approach to the Greenhouse Effect: The Problem of Increased Atmospheric Carbon Dioxide Can Be Approached by an Innovative International Agreement," *California Western International Law Journal* 20, no. 1 (1989): 67–90.

62. David A. Einhorn and R. Alta Charo, "Carbon Dioxide and the Greenhouse Effect: Possibilities for Legislative Action Special Issue: Legal Issues Arising from the Audubon Energy Plan 1984," *Columbia Journal of Environmental Law* 11, no. 2 (1986): 495–516, 507.

63. Einhorn and Charo, "Carbon Dioxide and the Greenhouse Effect," 499.

64. Ved P. Nanda, "Global Warming and International Environmental Law—A Preliminary Inquiry," *Harvard International Law Journal* 30, no. 2 (1989): 375–392; Mohamed Munavvar, "Greenhouse Effect and Sea Level Rise—Threat to Small Island States: A Perspective of International Legal Responsibility," 1 *African Journal of International & Comparative Law* (1989): 484–499.

65. Indeed, the first Brown Weiss article on global warming has been largely, and unjustifiably, forgotten. I searched these articles on Google Scholar; Zaelke and Cameron were cited 125 times, most recently in 2021. Brown Weiss received 16 citations, most of them before 1990.

66. Robert Fischman, "Global Warming and Property Interests," 19 *Hofstra Law Review* 19 (1991): 565–602; Robert Stavins, "National Policy Instruments for Climate Change?" *University of Chicago Legal Forum* (1997): 293–329; Tracy Hester and Ann Cole, "New World, New Laws: Preparing to Advise Clients on Global Warming Legal Policies and Strategies," *Houston Lawyer* 36 (1999): 18–22; Jay Michaelson, "Geoengineering: A Climate Change Manhattan Project," *Stanford Environmental Law Journal* 17 (1998): 73–140.

67. Joseph Sax, "Environmental Law in the Law Schools: What We Teach and How We Feel About It," *ELR* 19 (1989): 10251–10253, 10253.

68. David Wirth, "Teaching and Research in International Environmental Law," *Harvard Environmental Law Review* 23 (1999): 423–440, 423–424.

69. Richard Lazarus, "Environmental Scholarship and the Harvard Difference," *Harvard Environmental Law Review* 23 (1999): 327–356; Daniel Farber, "Taking Slippage Seriously," *Harvard Environmental Law Review* 23 (1999): 297–325; Alison Rieser, "Prescriptions for the Commons," *Harvard Environmental Law Review* 23 (1999): 393–421.

70. Zygmunt Plater, "Environmental Law and the Three Economies," *Harvard Environmental Law Review* 23 (1999): 359–392, 363–364.

71. Plater, "Environmental Law and the Three Economies," 364.

72. Parenteau interview.

73. Brown Weiss interview.

74. Heinzerling interview.

75. Johnson interview.

76. Tarlock interview.

77. Lazarus interview; Parker interview; Dernbach interview.

78. Funk interview.

79. Buzbee interview.

80. Craig interview; Panarella interview; LaPlante interview.

81. Civins interview, Haragan interview.

82. Giannini interview.

83. Roger Findley and Daniel Farber, *Cases and Materials on Environmental Law*, 1st ed. (St. Paul, MN: West, 1981), 466–470.

84. Richard Stewart and James Krier, *Cases and Materials on Environmental Law and Policy*, 2nd ed. (Indianapolis: Bobbs-Merrill, 1978); Richard Stewart and James Krier, *Cases and Materials on Environmental Law and Policy*, 1982 update (Indianapolis: Bobbs-Merrill, 1982), 10, 13, 17.

85. Clean Air Act §202(a)(1).

86. Clean Air Act §7602(g).

87. Farber interview; Buzbee interview; Lazarus interview; Heinzerling interview.

88. *Massachusetts v. EPA*, 549 U.S. 497 (2007). The lead author of Massachusetts's brief happened to be Lisa Heinzerling.

89. Heinzerling interview; Tolan interview.

90. Farber interview.

91. Buzbee interview.

92. David Getches, *Water Law in a Nutshell* (St. Paul, MN: West, 1984).

93. William Goldfarb, *Water Law*, 1st ed. (Boston: Butterworth Publishing, 1984), 118.

94. Craig interview; Thompson interview. Abrams's 1989 article on the impact of climate change on riparian doctrine is one of the first treatments of this subject in the law review literature, but the article didn't get much attention until the late 1990s, when citations to it began to increase. Robert Abrams, "Charting the Course of Riparianism: An Instrumentalist Theory of Change," *Wayne Law Review* 35, no. 4 (1989): 1381–1446.

95. William Rodgers, *Energy and Natural Resources Law*, 1st ed. (St. Paul, MN: West, 1979), xv; Michael Blumm and David Becker, "From Martz to the Twenty-First Century: A Half-Century of Natural Resource Law Casebooks and Pedagogy," *University of Colorado Law Review* 78 (2007): 647–694, 651.

96. Fred Bosselman, "Symposium on Energy Law: A Brief History of Energy Law In United States Law Schools: An Introduction to the Symposium," *Chicago–Kent*

Law Review 86 (2011): 3–8; Donald Zillman, "30th Anniversary Special Section Evolution of Modern Energy Law: A Personal Retrospective," *Journal of Energy & Natural Resources Law* 30 (2012): 485–493.

97. John Carroll, "Pennsylvania's Natural Gas Boom: Gas Boom Triggers a Boom in Legal Education," *Pennsylvania Lawyer* 34 (March/April 2012): 32–35.

98. Zillman, "30th Anniversary Special Section Evolution of Modern Energy Law."

99. Kraham interview.

100. William Buzbee, for example, began focusing on climate change because of his theoretical interest in regulatory federalism. Buzbee interview.

101. Buzbee interview.

102. Babcock interview.

103. Lazarus interview; Kysar interview.

104. Buzbee interview.

105. Tolan interview; Connolly interview.

106. Fershee interview.

107. Babich interview.

108. Kysar interview.

109. Farber interview.

110. Osofsky interview; Hari Osofsky, "Is Climate Change 'International'? Litigation's Diagonal Regulatory Role," *Virginia Journal of International Law* 49 (2009): 585–650.

111. John Nolon, "Considering the Trend Toward Local Environmental Law," *Pace Environmental Law Review* 20 (2002): 3–18, 3–4.

112. Panarella interview; Davis interview; Craig interview; Haragan interview; Parker interview. Vincent Johnson did mention the lack of a textbook as one challenge of teaching his early global warming course. Johnson interview.

113. Tarlock interview; Blumm interview.

114. Gerrard interview; Davis interview.

115. Seiger interview; Klass interview.

116. Burns interview.

117. Burns interview; Klass interview.

118. Fershee interview; Haragan interview.

119. Babich interview; Kraham interview.

120. For example, the American Association of University Professors issued a report in 2017 on the threat to academic freedom posed by the attacks on climate science. American Association of University Professors, Committee A on Academic Freedom and Tenure, *National Security, the Assault on Science, and Academic Freedom* (Washington, DC: The Association, 2017). The attacks are not limited to natural science, as *Inside Higher Ed* has reported. Colleen Flaherty, "Standing Up to Trolls," *Inside Higher Ed*, February 2, 2017.

Chapter 3. The Changing Landscape

1. The campaign resulted in some state legislation limiting affirmative action and judicial decisions, further shaping the admissions landscape. See *Grutter v. Bollinger*, 539 U.S. 306 (2003).

2. American Bar Association, ABA Statistics Archive, www.americanbar.org/groups/legal_education/resources/statistics.

3. ABA Statistics Archive. I did not adjust these numbers for inflation, since inflation was very low between 2001 and 2012. After 2012, the ABA changed the question wording, and no statistics are reported after 2013.

4. Paul F. Campos, "The Extraordinary Rise and Sudden Decline of Law School Tuition: A Case Study of Veblen Effects in Higher Education," *Seton Hall Law Review* 48, no. 1 (2017): 167–192, 172.

5. Campos, "Extraordinary Rise and Sudden Decline"; ABA Statistics Archive.

6. Brian Tamanaha, *Failing Law Schools* (Chicago: University of Chicago Press, 2012); Campos, "Extraordinary Rise and Sudden Decline"; Amy Li, "Dollars and Sense: Student Price Sensitivity to Law School Tuition," *Journal of Law, Business & Ethics* 26 (2020): 47–70.

7. Allison C. Reeve and Travis Weller, "Empirical Legal Research Support Services: A Survey of Academic Law Libraries," *Law Library Journal* 107, no. 3 (2015): 399–420.

8. Robert B. Archibald and David H. Feldman, *Why Does College Cost So Much?* (New York: Oxford University Press, 2010), 97–98. The authors also note the lack of empirical evidence that increased administrative staff is driving tuition increases.

9. ABA Statistics Archive.

10. Li, "Dollars and Sense."

11. Campos, "Extraordinary Rise and Sudden Decline," 174.

12. Wendy Nelson Espeland and Michael Sauder, *Engines of Anxiety: Academic Rankings, Reputation, and Accountability* (New York: Russell Sage Foundation, 2016).

13. Referring to the Law School Admission Test, administered by the Law School Admission Council and until recently used by virtually all law schools in admissions decisions.

14. Mary Lu Bilek et al., *Twenty Years After the MacCrate Report: A Review of the Current State of the Legal Education Continuum and the Challenges Facing the Academy, Bar, and Judiciary* (Chicago: American Bar Association, 2013), 6.

15. Tamanaha, *Failing Law Schools*, 71–77; Campos, "Extraordinary Rise and Sudden Decline," 185.

16. Some law schools have recently refused to participate in the rankings. It remains to be seen whether that decision will transform administrative decision-making. Anemona Hartocollis, "Yale and Harvard Law Schools Withdraw from the U.S. News Rankings," *New York Times*, November 16, 2022.

17. Tamanaha, *Failing Law Schools*, 47–52; see also Edward Rubin, "Should Law Schools Support Faculty Research?" *Journal of Contemp. Legal Issues* 17 (2008): 139–169.

18. Tamanaha, *Failing Law Schools*, 39–43; Osofksy interview.

19. Tamanaha, *Failing Law Schools*, 11–12.

20. Tamanaha, 11.

21. Tamanaha, 18.

22. Brent Newton, "Preaching What They Don't Practice: Why Law Faculties' Preoccupation with Impractical Scholarship and Devaluation of Practical Competencies Obstruct Reform in the Legal Academy," *South Carolina Law Review* 62 (2010): 105–156.

23. Bilek et al., *Twenty Years After the MacCrate Report*, 12.

24. American Bar Association, *Legal Education and Professional Development— An Educational Continuum: Report of the Task Force on Law Schools and the Profession: Narrowing the Gap* (Chicago: American Bar Association, 1992).

25. Bilek reports that "the publication of the MacCrate Report set off a wide-ranging discussion among academics, practitioners, bar examiners, and the judiciary in a variety of contexts including: statewide conclaves, held in 25 states, that brought together local bar associations, representatives of local law schools, and the judiciary, to discuss means to improve the state's legal educational continuum; meetings, in various law schools, of special faculty committees and sometimes the entire faculty to discuss reforms of the curriculum; law school conferences to discuss the Report; and numerous law review articles discussing the Report and/or issues identified by the Report." Bilek et al., *Twenty Years After the MacCrate Report*, 2.

26. American Bar Association, 2005–2006 Standards: Rules of Procedure for Approving Law Schools (Chicago: American Bar Association 2005), Standard 302.

27. Roy Stuckey and et al., *Best Practices for Legal Education* (Columbia: CLEA, 2007), vii.

28. Catherine Carpenter et al., *A Survey of Law School Curricula: 2002–2010* (Chicago: American Bar Association, 2012), 14; see also Bilek et al., *Twenty Years After the MacCrate Report*, 7.

29. Catherine Carpenter et al., *1992–2002 Survey of Law School Curricula* (Chicago: American Bar Association, 2004), 44; see also William Sullivan et al., *Educating Lawyers: Preparation for the Profession of Law* (Stanford, CA: Carnegie Foundation for the Advancement of Teaching, 2007); Roy Stuckey et al. *Best Practices for Legal Education*.

30. Carpenter et al., *1992–2002 Survey of Law School Curricula*, 45.

31. Carpenter et al., 43.

32. Martha F. Davis, "Institutionalizing Legal Innovation: The (Re)Emergence of the Law Lab," *Journal of Legal Education* 65, no. 1 (2015): 190–206.

33. Student interviews.

34. Tamanaha, *Failing Law Schools*, 57; Newton, "Preaching What They Don't Practice."

35. Indeed, apparently it is one of the most-cited law review articles of all time. Ronald K. L. Collins and Harry T. Edwards, "On Legal Scholarship: Questions for Judge Harry T. Edwards," *Journal of Legal Education* 65, no. 3 (2016): 637–660, 638.

36. Harry T. Edwards, "Another Look at Professor Rodell's Goodbye to Law Reviews," *Virginia Law Review* 100 (2014): 1483–1511.

37. Edward Rubin, "Should Law Schools Support Faculty Research?" *Journal of Contemporary Legal Issues* 17 (2008): 139–169, 151 (emphasis added).

38. Rubin, "Should Law Schools Support Faculty Research?" 163.

39. Kim Diana Connolly, "Elucidating the Elephant: Interdisciplinary Law School Classes," *Washington University Journal of Law & Policy* 11 (2003): 11–63, 13–14.

40. Connolly, "Elucidating the Elephant," 33.

41. Thomas S. Ulen, "The Impending Train Wreck in Current Legal Education: How We Might Teach Law as the Scientific Study of Social Governance," *University of St. Thomas Law Journal* 6 (2008): 302–336, 315.

42. Ulen, "The Impending Train Wreck in Current Legal Education," 315.

43. Ulen, 319.

44. Michael I. Meyerson, "Law School Culture and the Lost Art of Collaboration: Why Don't Law Professors Play Well with Others," *Nebraska Law Review* 93 (2014): 547–590, 554.

45. Andrew T. Hayashi, "The Small and Diversifying Network of Legal Scholars: A Study of Co-Authorship from 1980–2020," *Virginia Law Review Online* 108 (December 2022): 343–379, 374.

46. Stephen Daniels, Martin Katz, and William Sullivan, "Analyzing Carnegie's Reach: The Contingent Nature of Innovation," *Journal of Legal Education* 63, no. 4 (2014): 585–611, 605.

47. Edward Rubin, "The Future and Legal Education: Are Law Schools Failing and, If So, How?" *Law & Social Inquiry* 39 (Spring 2014): 499–518, 509.

48. Rubin, "The Future and Legal Education," 510–512.

49. Connolly interview.

50. Ulen interview.

51. Osofsky interview.

52. Macdougald interview.

53. Macdougald interview; student interviews.

54. The Trump administration withdrew from the treaty in 2020, but the Biden administration rejoined it a few months later.

55. Energy Independent and Security Act of 2007, 42 U.S.C. ch. 152, §17001 et seq.

56. Patrick Parenteau, "Lead, Follow, or Get Out of the Way: States Tackle Climate Change with Little Help from Washington," *Connecticut Law Review* 40 (2008): 1453–1475, 1467–1471.

57. Stephen M. Wheeler, "State and Municipal Climate Change Plans: The First Generation," *Journal of the American Planning Association* 74, no. 4 (October 21, 2008): 481–496.

58. Parenteau, "Lead, Follow, or Get Out of the Way," 1462–1463.

59. *California Chamber of Commerce v. California Air Resources Board*, 10 Cal. App.5th 604 (2017).

60. Augusta Wilson, "Linking Across Borders," *Columbia Journal of Environmental Law* 43 (2018): 227–267, 248–256.

61. Steven Ferrey, "Auctioning the Building Blocks of Life: Carbon Auction, the Law, and Global Warming," *Notre Dame Journal of Legal Ethics & Public Policy* 23 (2009): 317–379; *Rocky Mountain Farmers Union v. Corey*, 730 F.3d 1040 (9th Cir 2013).

62. Low Carbon Fuel Standard §95481(a)(11).

63. Michael Gerrard, "What the Law and Lawyers Can and Cannot Do About Global Warming," *Southeastern Environmental Law Journal* 16 (2007): 33–64, 52–54.

64. *California Chamber of Commerce v. California Air Resources Board*, 10 Cal. App.5th 604 (2017); *Rocky Mountain Farmers Union v. Corey*, 730 F.3d 1040 (9th Cir 2013).

65. Ethan Elkind, Ted Lamm, and Katie Segal, *Seeding Capital: Policy Solutions to Accelerate Investment in Nature-Based Climate Action* (UC Berkeley Center for Law, Energy & the Environment/UCLA Emmett Institute on Climate Change & the Environment, June 2021).

66. Wheeler, "State and Municipal Climate Change Plans," 485.

67. Carmen Sirianni, *Sustainable Cities in American Democracy: From Postwar Urbanism to a Civic New Deal* (Lawrence: University Press of Kansas, 2020), 205–206.

68. John Dernbach, *Acting as If Tomorrow Matters: Accelerating the Transition to Sustainability* (Washington, DC: Environmental Law Institute, 2012), 86.

69. Markell and Ruhl, using the Sabin database, identify only 201 of those lawsuits as "climate litigation." David Markell and J. B. Ruhl, "An Empirical Assessment of Climate Change in the Courts: A New Jurisprudence of Business as Usual?" *Florida Law Review* 56 (2012): 15–85.

70. Markell and Ruhl, "An Empirical Assessment of Climate Change in the Courts," 76.

71. Michael Gerrard, *Global Climate Change and U.S. Law*, 1st ed. (Chicago: American Bar Association, 2007).

72. Markell and Ruhl, "An Empirical Assessment of Climate Change in the Courts," 85.

73. Richard Hildreth et al., *Climate Change Law: Mitigation and Adaptation* (St.

Paul, MN: West, 2009); Chris Wold, David Hunter, and Melissa Powers, *Climate Change and the Law* (New York: Matthew Bender/Lexis Nexis, 2009).

Chapter 4. The Great Transformation, 2000–2010

1. Specifically, Randall S. Abate, *Directory of Environmental Law Education Opportunities at American Law Schools*, 2nd ed. (Durham, NC: Carolina Academic Press 2008); brochures and websites that law schools use concerning their environmental programs; and responses received to a fall 2008 inquiry that Dernbach posted on the environmental law professors listserv.

2. John C. Dernbach, "The Essential and Growing Role of Legal Education in Achieving Sustainability," *Journal of Legal Education* 60, no. 3 (2011): 489–518, 505.

3. Dernbach, "Essential and Growing," 506–507.

4. Dernbach, "Essential and Growing," 509. His numbers are lower than mine for the early 1990s because he searched only for articles with "climate change" or "global warming" in the title.

5. Dernbach, "Essential and Growing," 510. The Washington and Lee journal apparently lasted only until 2015, but the San Diego journal is still active. Hein Online finds two other journals focused on climate, but both are published outside the United States: *Climate Law* (published by Brill) and *Carbon & Climate Law Review* (published by Lexxion).

6. Dernbach, "Essential and Growing," 512.

7. Student interviews.

8. Buzbee interview.

9. Adam Buzbee, "Recognizing the Regulatory Commons: A Theory of Regulatory Gaps," *Iowa Law Review* 89 (2003): 1–64.

10. Zimmermann interview; Doremus interview.

11. Haragan interview; Kraham interview.

12. Kraham interview.

13. Kraham interview.

14. Davis interview.

15. Macdougald interview.

16. Klass interview.

17. Klass interview.

18. *Native Village of Kivalina v ExxonMobil*, 696 F.3d 849 (9th Cir. 2012).

19. 434 F.Supp.2d 957 (D.Ore. 2006).

20. 663 F.Supp.2d 983 (D.Ore. 2009).

21. LaPlante interview.

22. Lyman interview.

23. Tolan interview.

24. Dernbach interview; 2008 syllabus retrieved from International Union for the Conservation of Nature database.

25. Benjamin interview; Burns interview; Fershee interview.

26. Civins interview; Babich interview; Benjamin interview.

27. This was a graduate course which used a textbook by Stanley Manahan, published in 1972.

28. Lazarus interview.

29. Infelise interview.

30. Dernbach interview.

31. Babich interview.

32. Doremus interview.

33. Yang syllabus, retrieved from IUCN database.

34. Parenteau interview.

35. Gerrard interview.

36. Macdougald interview.

37. Burns interview.

38. Parenteau interview; Blumm interview; Thompson interview; Funk interview; Tolan interview.

39. enr [pseudonym], "The Science of Global Warming: Oops, There Goes Another Ice Sheet," Environmental Law Prof Blog (August 11, 2006), https://law professors.typepad.com/environmental_law/2006/08/the_science_of__1.html; enr, "Ocean Temperatures are not Declining," Environmental Law Prof Blog (June 23, 2007); https://lawprofessors.typepad.com/environmental_law/2007/06/ocean -temperatu.html.

40. enr, "Here's a Good Climate Change Overview for Class," Environmental Law Prof Blog (January 22, 2009), https://lawprofessors.typepad.com/environment al_law/2009/01/worldwatch-clim.html.

41. enr, "Mixed Reaction to Bush Administration Gagging Climate Scientist," Environmental Law Prof Blog (January 30, 2006), https://lawprofessors.typepad .com/environmental_law/2006/01/bush_administra.html.

42. Burns interview; Haragan interview; Blumm interview; "Blogs and Discussion Lists," Envirolawteachers.com, www.envirolawteachers.com/blogs-and-discuss ion-lists.html.

43. IUCN Academy of Environmental Law, "Climate Law Teaching Resources," www.iucnael.org/en/online-resources/climate-law-teaching-resources, n.d.; Burns interview.

44. Civins interview; Tolan interview.

45. American College of Environmental Lawyers, "About Us," n.d., https://aco el.org/about-us.

46. Higgins/Chandler interview.

47. Higgins/Chandler interview.

48. Robert V. Percival, "Environmental Law in the Twenty-First Century," *Virginia Environmental Law Journal* 25 (2007): 1–35, 32.

49. The book, originally published by Aspen, was taken over by Wolters-Kluwer in the 2011 fifth edition.

50. Robert Glicksman et al., *Environmental Protection: Law and Policy*, 5th ed. (Blue Springs, MO: Aspen Publishing Co., 2007), xxix.

51. Buzbee interview.

52. Buzbee interview.

53. J. B. Ruhl, John Copeland Nagle, and James Salzman, *The Practice and Policy of Environmental Law*, 1st ed. (Mineola, NY: Foundation Press, 2008).

54. Robert Beck and Amy Kelly, *Water and Water Rights*, 2nd ed. (New York: LexisNexis, 2007).

55. Beck and Kelly, *Water and Water Rights*, sec. 1.04.

56. Beck and Kelly, sec. 9.01.

57. Dan Tarlock, James Corbridge, and David Getches, *Water Resource Management*, 5th ed. (Mineola, NY: Foundation Press, 2002).

58. Dan Tarlock, James Corbridge, and David Getches, *Water Resource Management*, 7th ed. (Mineola, NY: Foundation Press, 2014).

59. Fred Bosselman et al., *Energy, Economics and the Environment*, 3rd ed. (Mineola, NY: Foundation Press, 2010).

60. Chandler/Higgins interview.

61. Gerrard interview.

62. Michael Gerrard, *Global Climate Change and U.S. Law*, 1st ed. (Chicago: American Bar Association, 2007), 25.

63. Chris Wold, David Hunter, and Melissa Powers, *Climate Change and the Law* (New York: Matthew Bender/Lexis Nexis, 2009).

64. Richard Hildreth et al., *Climate Change Law: Mitigation and Adaptation* (St. Paul, MN: West, 2009), vi.

65. Hildreth et al., *Climate Change Law*, vii.

66. Klass interview.

67. Osofsky interview; Miller interview.

68. Miller interview.

69. Zimmermann interview.

70. Farber interview.

71. Doremus interview.

72. Kysar interview.

73. Connolly interview.

74. Byrne interview.

75. Macdougald interview; Osofsky interview.

76. Craig interview.

77. Gordon interview.

78. Thompson interview.

Chapter 5. Making Climate Lawyers, 2011–2020

1. Cary Funk and Brian Kennedy, "How Americans See Climate Change and the Environment in Seven Charts," Pew Research Center (April 21, 2020), www.pewre search.org/fact-tank/2020/04/21/how-americans-see-climate-change-and-the-envi ronment-in-7-charts.

2. Sabin Center for Climate Change Law, Climate ReRegulation Tracker, n.d., https://climate.law.columbia.edu/content/climate-reregulation-tracker.

3. Erin C. Pischke, Barry D. Solomon, and Adam M. Wellstead, "A Historical Analysis of US Climate Change Policy in the Pan-American Context," *Journal of Environmental Studies and Sciences* 8, no. 2 (June 1, 2018): 225–232.

4. Energy Policy Act of 2005, PL 108-58; Energy Independence and Security Act of 2007, PL 110–140; American Reinvestment and Recovery Act of 2009, PL 111-5.

5. White House Briefing Room, "Fact Sheet: The Bipartisan Infrastructure Deal Boosts Clean Energy Jobs, Strengthens Resilience, and Advances Environmental Justice," November 8, 2021, www.whitehouse.gov/briefing-room/statements-releas es/2021/11/08/fact-sheet-the-bipartisan-infrastructure-deal-boosts-clean-energy -jobs-strengthens-resilience-and-advances-environmental-justice.

6. Jennifer Cronin, Gabrial Anandarajah, and Olivier Dessens, "Climate Change Impacts on the Energy System: A Review of Trends and Gaps," *Climatic Change* 151, no. 2 (November 1, 2018): 79–93.

7. Meetpal S. Kukal and Suat Irmak, "Climate-Driven Crop Yield and Yield Variability and Climate Change Impacts on the U.S. Great Plains Agricultural Production," *Scientific Reports* 8, no. 1 (February 22, 2018): 3450–3468.

8. M. Barange et al., "Impacts of Climate Change on Fisheries and Aquaculture: Synthesis of Current Knowledge, Adaptation and Mitigation Options," FAO Fisheries and Aquaculture Technical Paper (FAO) Eng No. 627. 2018 (Rome: Food and Agriculture Organization of the United Nations, 2018).

9. Reza Marsool et al., "Climate Change Exacerbates Hurricane Flood Hazards along US Atlantic and Gulf Coasts in Spatially Varying Patterns," *Nature Communications* 10, no. 1 (August 22, 2019): 3785–3794.

10. A. Park Williams et al., "Observed Impacts of Anthropogenic Climate Change on Wildfire in California," *Earth's Future* 7, no. 8 (2019): 892–910.

11. Matthew L. Kirwan and Keryn B. Gedan, "Sea-Level Driven Land Conversion and the Formation of Ghost Forests," *Nature Climate Change* 9 (June 2019): 450–457.

12. Robert McLeman et al., "Conceptual Framing to Link Climate Risk Assessments and Climate-Migration Scholarship," *Climatic Change* 165, no. 1 (March 19, 2021): 24–31.

13. Katie Hayes et al., "Climate Change and Mental Health: Risks, Impacts and Priority Actions," *International Journal of Mental Health Systems* 12, no. 1 (June 1, 2018): 28–40.

14. Cronin, Anandarajah, and Dessens, "Climate Change Impacts on the Energy System."

15. Tomoko Hasegawa et al., "Risk of Increased Food Insecurity Under Stringent Global Climate Change Mitigation Policy," *Nature Climate Change* 8 (August 2018): 699–703.

16. Michael Gerrard and John Dernbach, *Legal Pathways to Deep Decarbonization in the United States* (Washington, DC: Environmental Law Institute, 2018).

17. Daniel Farber, "The Emergence of Climate Law Courses," LegalPlanet Blog, August 19, 2014, https://legal-planet.org/2014/08/19/the-emergence-of-climate-law-courses.

18. Robin Kundis Craig, "Learning to Think About Complex Environmental Systems in Environmental and Natural Resource Law and Legal Scholarship: A Twenty-Year Retrospective," *Fordham Environmental Law Review* 24 (2013): 87–102, 87.

19. Doremus interview.

20. Inara Scott, "Is It Time to Say Goodbye to Environmental Law?" Environmental Law Prof Blog, November 17, 2018, https://lawprofessors.typepad.com/environmental_law/2018/11/is-it-time-to-say-goodbye-to-environmental-law.html.

21. Scott, "Is it Time to Say Goodbye to Environmental Law?"

22. Lazarus interview.

23. Connolly interview.

24. Blumm interview, Doremus interview, Thompson interview.

25. J. B. Ruhl et al., *The Practice and Policy of Environmental Law*, 2nd ed. (Mineola, NY: Foundation Press, 2010).

26. J. B. Ruhl et al., *The Practice and Policy of Environmental Law*, 3rd ed. (Mineola, NY: Foundation Press, 2014); J. B. Ruhl et al., *The Practice and Policy of Environmental Law*, 4th ed. (Mineola, NY: Foundation Press, 2016).

27. Daniel Farber, William Boyd, and Ann Carlson, *Cases and Materials on Environmental Law*, 10th ed. (St. Paul, MN: West, 2019), v.

28. Farber, Boyd, and Carlson, *Cases and Materials on Environmental Law*, 10th ed., 111–117.

29. David Driesen, Robert Adler, and Kirsten Engel, *Environmental Law: A Conceptual and Pragmatic Approach*, 2nd ed. (Blue Springs, MO: Aspen Publishing Co., 2011).

30. Zygmunt Plater et al., *Environmental Law and Policy: Nature, Law and Society*, 5th ed. (Blue Springs, MO: Aspen Publishing Co., 2016), 70–71.

31. Plater et al., *Environmental Law and Policy*, 5th ed., 96, 156.

32. Plater et al., 327–332.

33. Plater et al., 345, 413–417.

34. Plater et al., 429, 451–453.

35. Plater et al., 513–518.

36. Plater et al., 629–643.

37. Robert V. Percival et al., *Environmental Regulation*, 9th ed. (Blue Springs, MO: Aspen Publishing Co., 2021), 2.

38. Robert Glicksman et al., *Environmental Protection: Law and Policy*, 8th ed. (Blue Springs, MO: Aspen Publishing Co., 2019).

39. Amy J. Wildermuth, "The Next Step: The Integration of Energy Law and Environmental Law," *Utah Environmental Law Review* 31, no. 2 (2011): 369–388, 369.

40. Osofsky interview.

41. Klass interview; University of Minnesota Law School, "Environment and Energy Law Concentration," n.d., https://law.umn.edu/academics/concentrations /environmental-energy-law-concentration.

42. George Washington University Law School, "Environmental & Energy Law," n.d., www.law.gwu.edu/environmental-energy-law.

43. UC Berkeley Law School, "For Prospective Students: Environmental Law Program," n.d., www.law.berkeley.edu/research/clee/environmental-and-energy -law-programs.

44. Talus interview.

45. Byrne interview.

46. Kysar interview.

47. Parker interview.

48. Haragan interview.

49. Fershee interview.

50. Talus interview.

51. Talus interview.

52. Talus interview.

53. Gerrard interview.

54. Connolly interview.

55. Sanders interview.

56. Harvard Law School, "HumanRights@Harvard," n.d., https://hrp.law.harva rd.edu/areas-of-focus/human-rights-the-environment.

57. Giannini interview.

58. Giannini interview.

59. Giannini interview.

60. Byrne interview.

61. Davis interview.

62. Verchick interview.

63. Parker interview.

64. Sabin Center for Climate Change Law, "Searchable Library," n.d., https:// climate.law.columbia.edu/content/searchable-library.

65. Sabin Center for Climate Change Law, *Winter/Spring 2016: A Summary of the Key Activities of the Sabin Center for Climate Change Law* (2016), https://cli

mate.law.columbia.edu/sites/default/files/content/Sabin-Center-Semiannual-Re
port-2016H1.pdf>>.

66. Center for Law, Energy & the Enviroment, *2019 Snapshot* (2019), www.law
.berkeley.edu/wp-content/uploads/2019/06/CLEE-2019-Snapshot-Spread.pdf.

67. Sabin Center for Climate Change Law, *Summer/Fall 2016: A Summary of the
Key Activities of the Sabin Center for Climate Change*, https://issuu.com/earthinstitu
te/docs/101996_sabin_center-ws16_report_web?e=4098028/41891402.

68. Widener University Environmental Law and Sustainability Center, "Model
Sustainability Ordinances," n.d., https://widenerenvironment.com/students/ordin
ances.

69. Talus interview; Seiger interview.

70. Dernbach interview.

71. Macdougald interview.

72. Stanford Law School, "Only-at-SLS," n.d., https://law.stanford.edu/educa
tion/only-at-sls.

73. Sanders interview.

74. Sanders interview.

75. Seiger interview.

76. Cullenward interview.

77. Dave Owen and Caroline Noblet, "Interdisciplinary Research and Environmental Law," *Ecology Law Quarterly* 41, no. 4 (2019): 887–938, 891.

78. Owen and Noblet, "Interdisciplinary Research and Environmental Law,"
904.

79. Owen and Noblet, 909–921, 914.

80. Owen and Noblet, 919–924.

81. Mance interview. Mance, I'm pleased to report, has been hired by SMU Ded-
man School of Law in Dallas, Texas.

82. Buzbee interview.

83. Gordon interview.

84. Daniel Farber and Cinnamon Carlane, *Climate Change Law: Concepts and
Insights* (Mineola, NY: Foundation Press, 2016).

85. Farber interview.

86. Sieger interview.

87. Kysar interview.

88. Kysar interview.

89. Giannini interview. Giannini notes, and Richard Lazarus confirms, that
Lazarus is now offering a course on climate lawyering that examines the role that
lawyers can play in addressing climate change in almost every legal practice area.

90. Craig, "Learning to Think About Complex Environmental Systems," 87–
102, 92.

91. Davis interview.

92. Verchick interview.

93. Snjolaug Arnadottir, *Climate Change and Maritime Boundaries* (Cambridge, UK: Cambridge University Press, 2021).

94. Kysar interview.

Conclusion

1. 549 U.S. 547 (2007).

2. Byrne interview.

3. Craig interview.

4. Farber interview.

5. Kysar interview.

6. Doremus interview.

7. Lazarus, Climate Lawyering syllabus, 2023 (on file with author).

8. Student interview.

9. Student interview.

Appendix B

1. This chart was compiled by Moses Jehng. The list compiled by Edward P. Richards at LSU helped significantly in assembling this list. See https://sites.law.lsu .edu/coast/2016/02/law-school-environmental-and-energy-programs. Environmental law–adjacent centers and institutes (such as land use or sea law centers) were listed only when environmental law centers did not exist at that law school. Clinics were excluded.

2. Slashes indicate that the center is the product of re-founding or merging of a no longer existing center. The first date represents when the first, now subsumed, center was founded.

3. I was unable to find the founding date of some centers.

Bibliography

Casebooks

Adler, Robert, Robin Craig, and Noah Hall. *Modern Water Law: Private Property, Public Rights, and Environmental Protections.* 1st ed. Mineola, NY: Foundation Press, 2013.

Anderson, Fred, Daniel Mandelker, and Dan Tarlock. *Environmental Protection: Law and Policy.* 1st ed. Boston: Little, Brown & Co., 1984.

———. *Environmental Protection: Law and Policy.* 2nd ed. Boston: Little, Brown & Co., 1990.

———. *Environmental Protection: Law and Policy.* 3rd ed. Boston: Little, Brown & Co., 1999.

Beck, Robert, and Amy Kelly. *Water and Water Rights.* New York: LexisNexis, 1991.

Bonine, John, and Thomas McGarity. *The Law of Environment and Pollution: Cases, Statutes, and Materials.* 1st ed. N.p., 1980.

———. *The Law of Environment and Pollution: Cases, Statutes, and Materials.* 2nd ed. St. Paul, MN: West, 1984.

Bosselman, Fred, Jim Rossi, and Jacqueline Lang Weaver. *Energy, Economics and the Environment.* 1st ed. Mineola, NY: Foundation Press, 2000.

Bosselman, Fred, et al. *Energy, Economics and the Environment.* 2nd ed. Mineola, NY: Foundation Press, 2006.

Bosselman, Fred, et al. *Energy, Economics and the Environment.* 3rd ed. Mineola, NY: Foundation Press, 2010.

Coggins, G. C., and Charles Wilkinson. *Federal Public Land and Resources Law.* 1st ed. Mineola, NY: Foundation Press, 1981.

Coggins, G. C., Charles Wilkinson, and John Leshy. *Federal Public Land and Resources Law.* 3rd ed. Westbury, NY: Foundation Press, 1993.

———. *Federal Public Land and Resources Law.* 4th ed. Mineola, NY: Foundation Press, 2001.

———. *Federal Public Land and Resources Law.* 5th ed. Mineola, NY: Foundation Press, 2002.

Craig, Robin [Kundis]. *Environmental Law in Context.* 1st ed. St. Paul, MN: West, 2005.

Currie, David. *Pollution: Cases and Materials.* St. Paul, MN: West, 1975.

Davies, Lincoln, Alexandra Klass, and Hari Osofsky. *Energy Law and Policy*. 1st ed. St. Paul, MN: West Academic, 2015.

Doremus, Holly, Albert Lin, and Ronald Rosenberg. *Environmental Policy Law: Problems, Cases and Readings*. 6th ed. Mineola, NY: Foundation Press, 2012.

Driesen, David, and Robert Adler. *Environmental Law: A Conceptual and Pragmatic Approach*. Alphen aan den Rijn, Netherlands: Wolters Kluwer, 2007.

Driesen, David, Robert Adler, and Kirsten Engel. *Environmental Law: A Conceptual and Pragmatic Approach*. 2nd ed. Blue Springs, MO: Aspen Publishing Co., 2011.

Farber, Daniel, and Cinnamon Carlane. *Climate Change Law: Concepts and Insights*. Mineola, NY: Foundation Press, 2016.

Farber, Daniel, William Boyd, and Ann Carlson. *Cases and Materials on Environmental Law*. 10th ed. St. Paul, MN: West, 2019.

Ferrey, Steven. *Environmental Law*. 8th ed. Alphen aan den Rijn, Netherlands: Wolters Kluwer, 2019.

Findley, Roger, and Farber, Daniel. *Cases and Materials on Environmental Law*. 1st ed. St. Paul, MN: West, 1981.

———. *Cases and Materials on Environmental Law*. 3rd ed. St. Paul, MN: West, 1991.

———. *Cases and Materials on Environmental Law*. 4th ed. St. Paul, MN: West, 1995.

———. *Cases and Materials on Environmental Law*. 5th ed. St. Paul, MN: West, 1999.

———. *Environmental Law in a Nutshell*. St. Paul, MN: West, 1983.

Geltman, Elizabeth Glass. *Environmental Law and Business*. New York: LexisNexis, 1994.

———. *Modern Environmental Law*. St. Paul, MN: West, 1997.

Gerrard, Michael. *Global Climate Change and U.S. Law*. 1st ed. Chicago: American Bar Association, 2007.

Gerrard, Michael, and Jody Freeman, eds. *Global Climate Change and U.S. Law*. 2nd ed. Chicago: American Bar Association, 2014.

Getches, David. *Water Law in a Nutshell*. St. Paul, MN: West, 1984.

Glicksman, Robert, et al. *Environmental Protection: Law and Policy*. 5th ed. Blue Springs, MO: Aspen Publishing Co., 2007.

Glicksman, Robert, et al. *Environmental Protection: Law and Policy*. 6th ed. Blue Springs, MO: Aspen Publishing Co., 2011.

Glicksman, Robert, et al. *Environmental Protection: Law and Policy*. 7th ed. Blue Springs, MO: Aspen Publishing Co., 2015.

Glicksman, Robert, et al. *Environmental Protection: Law and Policy*. 8th ed. Blue Springs, MO: Aspen Publishing Co., 2019.

Goldfarb, William. *Water Law*. 1st ed. Boston: Butterworth Publishing, 1984.

———. *Water Law*. 2nd ed. Chelsea, MI: Lewis Publishers, 1988.

Gray, Oscar. *Environmental Law: Cases and Materials*. 1st ed. Washington, DC: Bureau of National Affairs, 1970.

———. *Environmental Law: Cases and Materials*. 2nd ed. Washington, DC: Bureau of National Affairs, 1973.

Hanks, Eva, Dan Tarlock, and John Hanks. *Environmental Law and Policy: Cases and Materials.* St. Paul, MN: West, 1974.

Hildreth, Richard, David Hodas, Nicholas Robinson, and James Speth. *Climate Change Law: Mitigation and Adaptation.* St. Paul, MN: West, 2009.

Hovenkamp, Herbert, and Sheldon Kurtz. *The Law of Property.* 5th ed. St. Paul, MN: West, 2001.

Johnston, Craig, and Victor Flatt. *Legal Protection of the Environment.* St. Paul, MN: Thomson/West, 2005.

———. *Legal Protection of the Environment.* 2nd ed. St. Paul, MN: West, 2007.

———. *Legal Protection of the Environment.* 3rd ed. St. Paul, MN: West, 2010.

Klein, Christine, Fred Cheever, and Bret Birdsong. *Natural Resources Law: A Place-Based Book of Problems and Cases.* 3rd ed. Alphen aan den Rijn, Netherlands: Wolters Kluwer, 2013.

Meyers, Charles, and Dan Tarlock. *Selected Legal and Economic Aspects of Environmental Protection.* Mineola, NY: Foundation Press, 1971.

———. *Water Resource Management.* Mineola, NY: Foundation Press, 1971.

———. *Water Resource Management.* 2nd ed. Mineola, NY: Foundation Press, 1980.

Meyers, Charles, Dan Tarlock, and David Getches. *Water Resource Management.* 3rd ed. Mineola, NY: Foundation Press, 1988.

Osofsky, Hari, William C. G. Burns, and Lesley McAllister. *Climate Change Law and Policy.* Blue Springs, MO: Aspen Publishing Co., 2012.

Percival, Robert V., Alan Miller, and James Leape. *Environmental Regulation.* 6th ed. Blue Springs, MO: Aspen Publishing Co., 2009.

Percival, Robert V., et al. *Environmental Regulation.* 1st ed. Boston: Little, Brown & Co., 1992.

———. *Environmental Regulation.* 2nd ed. Blue Springs, MO: Aspen Publishing Co., 1996.

———. *Environmental Regulation.* 3rd ed. Blue Springs, MO: Aspen Publishing Co., 2000.

———. *Environmental Regulation.* 4th ed. Blue Springs, MO: Aspen Publishing Co., 2003.

———. *Environmental Regulation.* 5th ed. Blue Springs, MO: Aspen Publishing Co., 2006.

———. *Environmental Regulation.* 7th ed. Blue Springs, MO: Aspen Publishing Co., 2013.

———. *Environmental Regulation.* 8th ed. Blue Springs, MO: Aspen Publishing Co., 2018.

———. *Environmental Regulation.* 9th ed. Blue Springs, MO: Aspen Publishing Co., 2021.

Plater, Zygmunt, et al. *Environmental Law and Policy: Nature, Law, and Society.* 1st ed. St. Paul, MN: West, 1992.

———. *Environmental Law and Policy: Nature, Law, and Society*. 2nd ed. St. Paul, MN: West, 1998.

———. *Environmental Law and Policy: Nature, Law and Society*. 5th ed. Blue Springs, MO: Aspen Publishing Co., 2016.

Revesz, Richard. *Environmental Law and Policy*. 2nd ed. Mineola, NY: Foundation Press, 2012.

Rodgers, William. *Energy and Natural Resources Law*. 1st ed. St. Paul, MN: West, 1979.

———. *Handbook on Environmental Law*. St. Paul, MN: West, 1977.

Ruhl, J. B., John Copeland Nagle, and James Salzman. *The Practice and Policy of Environmental Law*. 1st ed. Mineola, NY: Foundation Press, 2008.

Ruhl, J. B., et al. *The Practice and Policy of Environmental Law*. 2nd ed. Mineola, NY: Foundation Press, 2010.

———. *The Practice and Policy of Environmental Law*. 3rd ed. Mineola, NY: Foundation Press, 2014.

———. *The Practice and Policy of Environmental Law*. 4th ed. Mineola, NY: Foundation Press, 2016.

Salzman, James, and Barton Thompson. *Environmental Law and Policy*. 5th ed. Mineola, NY: Foundation Press, n.d.

Sax, Joseph, and Robert Abrams. *Legal Control of Water Resources*. 1st ed. St. Paul, MN: West, 1986.

Sax, Joseph, Robert Abrams, and Barton Thompson. *Legal Control of Water Resources*. 2nd ed. St. Paul, MN: West, 1991.

Schoenbaum, Thomas. *Environmental Policy Law: Cases, Readings, and Text*. 1st ed. Mineola, NY: Foundation Press, 1982.

Schoenbaum, Thomas, and Ronald Rosenberg. *Environmental Policy Law: Cases, Readings, and Text*. 2nd ed. Mineola, NY: Foundation Press, 1991.

———. *Environmental Policy Law: Cases, Readings, and Text*. 3rd ed. Mineola, NY: Foundation Press, 1996.

Schoenbaum, Thomas, Ronald Rosenberg, and Holly Doremus. *Environmental Policy Law: Cases, Readings, and Text*. 4th ed. Mineola, NY: Foundation Press, 1996.

Stewart, Richard, and James Krier. *Cases and Materials on Environmental Law and Policy*. 2nd ed. Indianapolis: Bobbs-Merrill, 1978.

Tabb, William Murray, and Linda Malone. *Environmental Law: Cases and Materials*. 1st ed. Charlottesville, NC: Michie Co., 1992.

———. *Environmental Law: Cases and Materials*. 2nd ed. Charlottesville, NC: LexisLaw Publishing, 1997.

Tarlock, Dan, James Corbridge, and David Getches. *Water Resource Management*. 5th ed. Mineola, NY: Foundation Press, 2002.

Trelease, Frank, and George Gould. *Cases and Materials on Water Law*. 4th ed. St. Paul, MN: West, 1986.

Wold, Chris, David Hunter, and Melissa Powers. *Climate Change and the Law*. New York: Matthew Bender/Lexis Nexis, 2009.

Other Sources

Abate, Randall. *Directory of Environmental Law Opportunities at American Law Schools*. 2nd ed. Durham, NC: Carolina Academic Press, 2008.

Abrams, Robert. "Charting the Course of Riparianism: An Instrumentalist Theory of Change." *Wayne Law Review* 35, no. 4 (1989): 1381–1446.

ACOEL. "A Truly Global Community of Environmental Law Scholars." July 16, 2021. https://acoel.org/a-truly-global-community-of-environmental-law-scholars.

Allan, Bentley B. "Producing the Climate: States, Scientists, and the Constitution of Global Governance Objects." *International Organization* 71, no. 1 (2017): 131–162.

Almanza, Paul. "Review of The Challenge of Global Warming." *Ecology Law Quarterly* 17, no. 2 (1990): 449–451.

American Association for the Advancement of Science. "Finding Aid to the AAAS Climate Program Records." n.d. www.aaas.org/archives/finding-aid-aaas-climate-program-records.

American Association of University Professors. Committee A on Academic Freedom and Tenure. *National Security, the Assault on Science, and Academic Freedom*. Washington, DC: The Association, 2017.

American Bar Association. *ABA Standards and Rules of Procedure for Approval of Law Schools, 2014–2021*. Chicago: American Bar Association, 2014.

———. "Report Accompanying Resolution on Sustainable Development." 2003. www.americanbar.org/groups/environment_energy_resources/resources/section_sponsored_resolutions.

American Bar Association, Task Force on Sustainable Development. "Final Report of the American Bar Association Task Force on Sustainable Development." July 30, 2015.

Antadze, Nino. "The Role of Leadership in Depleting Institutional Ethos: The Case of Scott Pruitt and the Environmental Protection Agency." *Journal of Environmental Studies and Sciences* 9, no. 2 (June 1, 2019): 187–195.

Archibald, Robert B., and David H. Feldman. *Why Does College Cost So Much?* New York: Oxford University Press, 2010.

Ariens, Michael. "Modern Legal Times: Making a Professional Legal Culture." *The Journal of American Culture* 15, no. 1 (1992): 25–35.

Association of American Law Schools. "Spotlight: Environmental Law." N.d. www.aals.org/about/publications-2/newsletters/summer-2018/spotlight-environmental-law.

Attanasio, Donna. "Energy Law Education in the U.S.: An Overview and Recommendations." *Energy Law Journal* 36 (2015): 217–259.

Auerbach, Jerold S. *Unequal Justice Lawyers and Social Change in Modern America*. New York: Oxford University Press, 1976.

Auerbach, Jerold S., and Eugene Bardach. "'Born to an Era of Insecurity': Career Patterns of Law Review Editors, 1918–1941." *American Journal of Legal History* 17, no. 1 (1973): 3–26.

Babich, Adam. "The Apolitical Law School Clinic." *Clinical Review* 11 (2005): 447–472.

Baldwin, Malcolm and James Paige. *Law and the Environment*. Washington, DC: Conservation Foundation, 1970.

Barange, M., et al. "Impacts of Climate Change on Fisheries and Aquaculture: Synthesis of Current Knowledge, Adaptation and Mitigation Options." FAO Fisheries and Aquaculture Technical Paper (FAO) Eng No. 627. 2018.

Barnes, Katherine Y., and Elizabeth Mertz. "Law School Climates: Job Satisfaction Among Tenured US Law Professors." *Law & Social Inquiry* 43, no. 2 (2018): 441–467.

Bilek, Mary Lu, et al. *Twenty Years After the MacCrate Report: A Review of the Current State of the Legal Education Continuum and the Challenges Facing the Academy, Bar, and Judiciary*. Committee on the Professional Educational Continuum, Section on Legal Education and Admissions to the Bar, American Bar Association, March 20, 2013.

Bintliff, Barbara. "What Can the Faculty Expect from the Library of the Twenty-First Century?" *Law Library Journal* 96, no. 3 (2004): 507–512.

Blomquist, Robert. "Government's Role Regarding Industrial Pollution Prevention in the United States." *Georgia Law Review* 29 (Winter 1995): 349–448.

Blumm, Michael, and David Becker. "From Martz to the Twenty-First Century: A Half-Century of Natural Resource Law Casebooks and Pedagogy." *University of Colorado Law Review* 78 (2007): 647–694.

Bolin, B. *A History of the Science and Politics of Climate Change: The Role of the Intergovernmental Panel on Climate Change*. Cambridge, UK: Cambridge University Press, 2008.

Bonica, Adam. "Why Are There So Many Lawyers in Congress?" *Legislative Studies Quarterly* 45, no. 2 (May 2020): 253–289.

Börk, Karrigan, and Kurtis Burmeister. "Cases and Places: A Field-Based Approach to Teaching Natural Resource and Environmental Law." *Journal of Legal Education* 68, no. 2 (October 1, 2019): 338–356.

Bosselman, Fred. "A Brief History of Energy Law in United States Law Schools: An Introduction to the Symposium." *Chicago–Kent Law Review* 86 (2011): 3–8.

Brecht, Albert. "Introduction Symposium on Automation and the Changing Environment of Legal Scholarship." *Law Library Journal* 83, no. 4 (1991): 623–626.

Brooks, Richard Oliver. *Law and Ecology: The Rise of the Ecosystem Regime*. Ecology and Law in Modern Society. Aldershot, Hants, UK: Ashgate, 2002.

Brown Weiss, Edith. "The Future of the Planetary Trust in a Kaleidoscopic World." *Environmental Policy and Law* 50, no. 6 (2020): 449–456.

———. "Global Warming: Legal Implications for the Arctic." *Georgetown International Environmental Law Review* 2, no. 2 (1989): 81–98.

———. "Intergenerational Equity in a Kaleidoscopic World." *Environmental Policy and Law* 49, no. 1 (2019): 3–11.

———. "International Law in a Kaleidoscopic World." *Asian Journal of International Law* 1 (2011): 21–32.

———. *The International Political and Legal Problems of Weather and Climate Modification*. Berkeley: University of California, 1973.

———. "The Planetary Trust: Conservation and Intergenerational Equity." *Ecology Law Quarterly* 11, no. 4 (1984): 495–582.

———. "A Resource Management Approach to Carbon Dioxide During the Century of Transition." *Denver Journal of International Law & Policy* 10 (1981): 487–509.

Bulkeley, Harriet, and Peter Newell. *Governing Climate Change*. London: Routledge, 2010.

Bunn, Isabella D. "Linkages between Ethics and International Economic Law." *University of Pennsylvania Journal of International Economic Law* 19 (1998): 319–327.

Campos, Paul [F.]. "The Crisis of the American Law School Perspectives on Legal Education Reform." *University of Michigan Journal of Law Reform* 46, no. 1 (2012): 177–224.

———. "The Extraordinary Rise and Sudden Decline of Law School Tuition: A Case Study of Veblen Effects in Higher Education." *Seton Hall Law Review* 48, no. 1 (2017): 167–192.

Carlson, Ann. "Regulatory Capacity and State Environmental Leadership: California's Climate Policy." *Fordham Environmental Law Review* 24 (2013): 63–86.

Carnes, Nicholas. "Does the Numerical Underrepresentation of the Working Class in Congress Matter?" *Legislative Studies Quarterly* 37, no. 1 (2012): 5–34.

Carney, William. "Curricular Change in Legal Education." *Indiana Law Review* 53 (2020): 245–282.

Carpenter, Catherine, et al. "1992–2002 Survey of Law School Curricula." Chicago: American Bar Association, 2004.

———. "A Survey of Law School Curricula: 2002–2010." Chicago: American Bar Association, 2012.

Carpenter, Daniel. *The Forging of Bureaucratic Autonomy*. Princeton: Princeton University Press, 2001.

Carroll, John. "Pennsylvania's Natural Gas Boom: Gas Boom Triggers a Boom in Legal Education." *Pennsylvania Lawyer* 34 (March/April 2012): 32–35.

Cass, Loren R. *The Failures of American and European Climate Policy: International Norms, Domestic Politics, and Unachievable Commitments*. Albany, NY: SUNY Press, 2012.

Clark, W. C., et al. *Learning to Manage Global Environmental Risk*. Cambridge, MA: MIT Press, 2003.

Clinton, Joshua D., et al. "Separated Powers in the United States: The Ideology of Agencies, Presidents, and Congress." *American Journal of Political Science* 56, no. 2 (2012): 341–354.

Collins, Ronald K. L., and Harry T. Edwards. "On Legal Scholarship: Questions for Judge Harry T. Edwards." *Journal of Legal Education* 65, no. 3 (2016): 637–660.

Connolly, Kim Diana. "Elucidating the Elephant: Interdisciplinary Law School Classes." *Washington University Journal of Law & Policy* 11 (2003): 11–63.

Cook, Jetta. "Greater Than the Sum: Sub-National Renewable Energy Policy During the Trump Administration." LegalPlanet. May 19, 2021. https://legal-planet .org/2021/05/19/guest-contributor-jetta-cook-greater-than-the-sum-sub-nation al-renewable-energy-policy-during-the-trump-administration.

Coquillette, Daniel R., and Bruce A. Kimball. *On the Battlefield of Merit: Harvard Law School, the First Century*. Cambridge, MA: Harvard University Press, 2015.

Craig, Robin Kundis. "Learning to Think About Complex Environmental Systems in Environmental and Natural Resource Law and Legal Scholarship: A Twenty-Year Retrospective." *Fordham Environmental Law Review* 24 (2013): 87–102.

Cronin, Jennifer, Gabrial Anandarajah, and Olivier Dessens. "Climate Change Impacts on the Energy System: A Review of Trends and Gaps." *Climatic Change* 151, no. 2 (November 1, 2018): 79–93.

Cullenward, Danny, and David G. Victor. *Making Climate Policy Work*. Cambridge, MA: Polity, 2020.

Currie, Brainerd. "The Materials of Law Study." *Journal of Legal Education* 8, no. 1 (1955): 1–78.

Daly, Gail [M.]. "Library-Vendor Cooperation in Cataloging Legal Research Databases: The Minnesota/WESTLAW Experience." *Law Library Journal* 82 (1990): 331–340.

———. "There's No Law Library on the Starship 'Enterprise.'" *Journal of Legal Education* 58, no. 3 (2008): 455–462.

Dana, David. "One Green America: Continuities and Discontinuities In Environmental Federalism in the United States." *Fordham Environmental Law Review* 24 (2013): 103–124.

Daniels, Stephen, Martin Katz, and William Sullivan. "Analyzing Carnegie's Reach: The Contingent Nature of Innovation." *Journal of Legal Education* 63, no. 4 (2014): 585–611.

Davis, Martha F. "Institutionalizing Legal Innovation: The (Re)Emergence of the Law Lab." *Journal of Legal Education* 65, no. 1 (2015): 190–206.

Decker, Jefferson. *The Other Rights Revolution*. New York: Oxford University Press, 2016.

Dernbach, John [C.]. *Acting as If Tomorrow Matters: Accelerating the Transition to Sustainability*. Washington, DC: Environmental Law Institute, 2012.

———. "Call to the Bar." March 15, 2019.

———. "The Essential and Growing Role of Legal Education in Achieving Sustainability." *Journal of Legal Education* 60, no. 3 (2011): 489–518.

Dickinson, Gerald, and Sheila Foster. "Foreword: Stasis and Change In Environmental Law: The Past, Present and Future of the Fordham Environmental Law Review." *Fordham Environmental Law Review* 24 (2013): 1–24.

Doren, Jack Van, and Christopher Roederer. "McDougal–Lasswell Policy Science: Death and Transfiguration." *Richmond Journal of Global Law & Business* 11, no. 2 (2012): 125–157.

Edley, Christopher Jr. "Fiat Flux: Evolving Purposes and Ideals of the Great American Public Law School." *California Law Review* 100 (2012): 313–330.

Edwards, Harry T. "Another Look at Professor Rodell's Goodbye to Law Reviews." *Virginia Law Review* 100 (2014): 1483–1511.

———. "The Growing Disjunction Between Legal Education and the Legal Profession." *Michigan Law Review* 91 (October 1992): 34–78.

Edwards, Paul N. *A Vast Machine: Computer Models, Climate Data, and the Politics of Global Warming*. Cambridge, MA: MIT Press, 2010.

Einhorn, David A., and R. Alta Charo. "Carbon Dioxide and the Greenhouse Effect: Possibilities for Legislative Action." Special Issue: Legal Issues Arising from the Audubon Energy Plan 1984. *Columbia Journal of Environmental Law* 11, no. 2 (1986): 495–516.

Elkind, Ethan, Ted Lamm, and Katie Segal. *Seeding Capital: Policy Solutions to Accelerate Investment in Nature-Based Climate Action.* UC Berkeley Center for Law, Energy & the Environment/UCLA Emmett Institute on Climate Change & the Environment, June 2021.

Ernst, Daniel R. "Common Laborers? Industrial Pluralists, Legal Realists, and the Law of Industrial Disputes, 1915–1943." *Law and History Review* 11, no. 1 (1993): 59–100.

———. "Law and American Political Development, 1877–1938." *Reviews in American History* 26, no. 1 (1998): 205–219.

———. "Willard Hurst and the Administrative State: From Williams to Wisconsin." *Law and History Review* 18, no. 1 (2000): 1–36.

Espeland, Wendy Nelson, and Michael Sauder. *Engines of Anxiety: Academic Rankings, Reputation, and Accountability*. New York: Russell Sage Foundation, 2016.

Farber, Daniel. "The Emergence of Food Law." LegalPlanet. May 26, 2013. https://legal-planet.org/2013/05/26/the-emergence-of-food-law.

———. "Principles of Climate Governance." LegalPlanet. August 19, 2019. https://legal-planet.org/2019/08/19/principles-of-climate-governance.

———. "Taking Slippage Seriously." *Harvard Environmental Law Review* 23 (1999): 297–325.

———. "The Trajectory of Environmental Law Scholarship: 1975–2018." Legal Planet. April 22, 2109. https://legal-planet.org/2019/04/22/the-trajectory-of-environmental-law-scholarship-1975-2018.

Feldman, Stephen M. "The Transformation of an Academic Discipline: Law Professors in the Past and Future (or *Toy Story Too*)." *Journal of Legal Education* 54 (2004): 471–498.

Ferrey, Steven. "Auctioning the Building Blocks of Life: Carbon Auction, the Law, and Global Warming." *Notre Dame Journal of Legal Ethics & Public Policy* 23 (2009): 317–379.

Fetner, Gerald. "The Law Teacher as Legal Reformer: 1900–1945." *Journal of Legal Education* 28, no. 4 (1977): 508–529.

Fischman, Robert. "What Is Natural Resources Law?" *University of Colorado Law Review* 78 (Spring 2007): 717–749.

Fisher, Dana. *National Governance and the Global Climate Change Regime*. Lanham, MD: Rowman & Littlefield, 2004.

Flaherty, Colleen. "Standing Up to Trolls." *Inside Higher Ed*, February 2, 2017.

Flatt, Victor. "Frozen in Time: The Ossification of Environmental Statutory Change and the Theatre of the (Administrative) Absurd." *Fordham Environmental Law Review* 24 (2013): 125–148.

Foote, Gregory. "Considering Alternatives: The Case for Limiting $CO[2]$ Emissions From New Power Plants Through New Source Review." *Environmental Law Reporter* 34 (2004): 10642–10672.

Friedman, Lawrence. "Taking Law and Society Seriously." *Chicago–Kent Law Review* 74 (1999): 529–542.

Frye, Richard. "Climatic Change and Fisheries Management." *Natural Resources Journal* 23, no. 1 (1983): 77–96.

Funk, William. "Recent Environmental Law Casebooks: Searching for a Pedagogical Principle." *Environmental Law* 15 (1984): 201–216.

Gaille, S. Scott. "The ABA Task Force Report on the Future of Legal Education: The Role of Adjunct Professors and Practical Teaching in the Energy Sector." *Energy Law Journal* 35 (2014): 199–213.

Garth, Bryant G. "From MacCrate to Carnegie: Very Different Movements for Curricular Reform." *Legal Writing: Journal of Legal Writing Institute* 17 (2011): 261–278.

Gaylord, Tonya R. "Analyzing International Commitment to Mitigate Global Climate Change: The Choice between Fossil Fuel Use and Environmental Concerns Note." *Georgetown International Environmental Law Review* 2, no. 2 (1989): 185–208.

Gerrard, Michael. "What the Law and Lawyers Can and Cannot Do About Global Warming." *Southeastern Environmental Law Journal* 16 (2007): 33–64.

Gordon, Robert W. "The Case for (and Against) Harvard." *Michigan Law Review* 93, no. 6 (1995): 1231–1260.

———. "The Geologic Strata of the Law School Curriculum." *Vanderbilt Law Review* 60 (2007): 339–369.

Gupta, Joyeeta. *The History of Global Climate Governance*. Cambridge, UK: Cambridge University Press, 2014.

Hain, P., and J. Pierson. "Lawyers and Politics Revisited: Structural Advantages of Lawyers-Politicians." *American Journal of Political Science* 19, no. 1 (1975): 41–51.

Hamilton, Neil. "Ethical Leadership in Professional Life." *University of St. Thomas Law Journal* 6 (2009): 358–396.

Harrington, William G. "A Brief History of Computer-Assisted Legal Research." *Law Library Journal* 77, no. 3 (1984): 543–556.

Harris, Cyril M., and Albert J. Rosenthal. "The Interdisciplinary Course in the Legal Aspects of Noise Pollution at Columbia University." *Journal of Legal Education* 31, no. 1/2 (1981): 128–133.

Hart, David M., and David G. Victor. "Scientific Elites and the Making of US Policy for Climate Change Research, 1957–74." *Social Studies of Science* 23, no. 4 (1993): 643–680.

Hartocollis, Anemona. "Yale and Harvard Law Schools Withdraw from the U.S. News Rankings." *New York Times*, November 16, 2022.

Hartog, Hendrik. "Snakes in Ireland: A Conversation with Willard Hurst." *Law and History Review* 12, no. 2 (1994): 370–390.

Hasegawa, Tomoko, et al. "Risk of Increased Food Insecurity Under Stringent Global Climate Change Mitigation Policy." *Nature Climate Change* 8 (August 2018): 699–703.

Hayashi, Andrew T. "The Evolving Network of Legal Scholars." SSRN Scholarly Paper. Rochester, NY: Social Science Research Network, April 25, 2021.

———. "The Small and Diversifying Network of Legal Scholars: A Study of Co-Authorship from 1980–2020." *Virginia Law Review Online* 108 (December 2022): 343–379. https://virginialawreview.org/articles/the-small-and-diversifying-network-of-legal-scholars-a-study-of-co-authorship-from-1980-2020.

Hayes, Katie, et al. "Climate Change and Mental Health: Risks, Impacts and Priority Actions." *International Journal of Mental Health Systems* 12, no. 1 (June 1, 2018): 28–40.

Hayhoe, Katherine. "Here's How Long We've Known About Climate Change." Ecowatch. November 25, 2016. www.ecowatch.com/katharine-hayhoe-climate-change-2103671842.html.

Hoffman, Peter. "Law Schools and the Changing Face of Practice." *New York Law School Law Review* 56 (2011–2012): 203–231.

Hoover, James L. "Legal Scholarship and the Electronic Revolution." *Law Library Journal* 83, no. 4 (1991): 643–652.

Hornsby, David J., Alastair J. S. Summerlee, and Kenneth B. Woodside. "NAFTA's Shadow Hangs Over Kyoto's Implementation." *Canadian Public Policy/Analyse de Politiques* 33, no. 3 (2007): 285–297.

Houck, Oliver. "Land Loss in Coastal Louisiana: Causes, Consequences, and Remedies." *Tulane Law Review* 58 (October 1983): 3–168.

Howe, Joshua. *Behind the Curve: Science and the Politics of Global Warming*. Seattle: University of Washington Press, 2014.

———. *Making Climate Change History*. Seattle: University of Washington Press, 2017.

Huffman, James L. "The Past and Future of Environmental Law." *Environmental Law* 30 (2000): 23–33.

International Bar Association. "Achieving Justice and Human Rights in an Era of Climate Disruption." 2014. www.ibanet.org/MediaHandler?id=0f8cee12-ee56 -4452-bf43-cfcab196cc04.

Irwin, Frances. "The Law School and the Environment." *Natural Resources Journal* 12 (1972): 278–285.

Jacobi, Dan, and Caitlin Andersen. "Agriculture and the Law: Can the Legal Profession Power the Next Green Revolution." *Drake Journal of Agricultural Law* 21 (2016): 177–192.

Jasanoff, Sheila. *The Fifth Branch: Science Advisers as Policymakers*. Cambridge, MA: Harvard University Press, 1990.

Joergensen, John P. "Second Tier Law Reviews, Lexis and Westlaw: A Pattern of Increasing Use." *Legal Reference Services Quarterly* 21, no. 1 (2002): 43–74.

Kalman, Laura. *Legal Realism at Yale, 1927–1960*. Chapel Hill: University of North Carolina Press, 1986.

Kaswan, Alice. "Environmental Justice and Environmental Law." *Fordham Environmental Law Review* 24 (2013): 149–179.

Keohane, Robert O., and David G. Victor. "The Regime Complex for Climate Change." *Perspectives on Politics* 9, no. 1 (2011): 7–23.

Kift, Sally. "21st Century Climate for Change: Curriculum Design for Quality Learning Engagement in Law." *Legal Education Review* 18 (2008): 1–30.

Kimball, Bruce. "Before the Paper Chase: Student Culture at Harvard Law School, 1895–1915." *Journal of Legal Education* 61, no. 1 (August 1, 2011): 30–67.

———. "Charity, Philanthropy and Law School Fundraising: The Emergence and the Failure, 1880–1930." *Journal of Legal Education* 63, no. 2 (November 1, 2013): 247–281.

———. *The Inception of Modern Professional Education: C. C. Langdell, 1826–1906*. Chapel Hill: University of North Carolina Press, 2009.

Kirwan, Matthew L., and Keryn B. Gedan. "Sea-Level Driven Land Conversion and the Formation of Ghost Forests." *Nature Climate Change* 9 (June 2019): 450–457.

Klass, Alexandra. "The Current State of Environmental Law, Part II: Climate Change and the Convergence of Environmental and Energy Law." *Fordham Environmental Law Review* 24 (2013): 180–204.

Konefsky, Alfred S., and John Henry Schlegel. "Mirror, Mirror on the Wall: Histories of American Law Schools." *Harvard Law Review* 95, no. 4 (1982): 833–851.

Krakoff, Sarah. "Keeping an Eye on the Golden Snitch: Implications of the Interdisciplinary Approach in the Fourth Generation of Natural Resources Law Casebooks." *University of Colorado Law Review* 78 (Spring 2007): 751–765.

Kukal, Meetpal S., and Suat Irmak. "Climate-Driven Crop Yield and Yield Variability and Climate Change Impacts on the U.S. Great Plains Agricultural Production." *Scientific Reports* 8, no. 1 (February 22, 2018): 3450–3468.

Lang, Isa. "Wrestling with an Elephant: A Selected Bibliography and Resource Guide on Global Climate Change." *Law Library Journal* 100 (2008): 675–713.

LaPiana, William P. *Logic and Experience the Origin of Modern American Legal Education*. New York: Oxford University Press, 1994.

Lavey, Warren. "Toolkit for Integrating Climate Change into Ten High-Enrollment Law School Courses." *Environmental Law* 49 (2019): 513–586.

Lazarus, Richard. "Environmental Law at the Crossroads." *University of Michigan Journal of Environmental & Administrative Law* 2 (2013): 267–284.

———. "Environmental Scholarship and the Harvard Difference." *Harvard Environmental Law Review* 23 (1999): 327–356.

———. *The Making of Environmental Law*. Chicago: University of Chicago Press, 2004.

Lemos, Margaret H. "Aggregate Litigation Goes Public: Representative Suits by State Attorneys General." *Harvard Law Review* 126, no. 2 (2012): 486–549.

Li, Amy. "Dollars and Sense: Student Price Sensitivity to Law School Tuition." *Journal of Law, Business & Ethics* 26 (2020): 47–70.

Lindseth, Gard. "The Cities for Climate Protection Campaign (CCPC) and the Framing of Local Climate Policy." *Local Environment* 9, no. 4 (August 1, 2004): 325–336.

Linnekin, Baylen, and Emily Broad Leib. "Food Law & Policy: The Fertile Field's Origins and First Decade." *Wisconsin Law Review* 2014 (2014): 555–611.

Luterbacher, Urs, and Detlef F. Sprinz. *International Relations and Global Climate Change*. Cambridge, MA: MIT Press, 2001.

Magallanes, Catherine J. Iorns. "Teaching for Transnational Lawyering." *Journal of Legal Education* 55, no. 4 (2005): 519–524.

Manabe, Syukuro, and Richard T. Wetherald. "The Effects of Doubling the CO_2 Concentration on the Climate of a General Circulation Model." *Journal of the Atmospheric Sciences* 32, no. 1 (January 1, 1975): 3–15.

———. "Thermal Equilibrium of the Atmosphere with a Given Distribution of Relative Humidity." *Journal of the Atmospheric Sciences* 24, no. 3 (May 1, 1967): 241–259.

Markell, David, and J. B. Ruhl. "An Empirical Assessment of Climate Change in the Courts: A New Jurisprudence of Business as Usual?" *Florida Law Review* 56 (2012): 15–85.

Marsooli, Reza, et al. "Climate Change Exacerbates Hurricane Flood Hazards along US Atlantic and Gulf Coasts in Spatially Varying Patterns." *Nature Communications* 10, no. 1 (August 22, 2019): 3785–3794.

Martin, Patrick. "Preface—LSU Journal of Energy Law and Resources." *LSU Journal of Energy Law & Resources* 1 (Fall 2012): 1–3.

Martin, Peter W. "How New Information Technologies Will Change the Way Law Professors Do and Distribute Scholarship." *Law Library Journal* 83, no. 4 (1991): 633–642.

Martz, Clyde O. "The Study of Natural Resource Law." *Journal of Legal Education* 1, no. 4 (1949): 588–589.

Matter, Ulrich, and Alois Stutzer. "The Role of Lawyer-Legislators in Shaping the Law: Evidence from Voting on Tort Reforms." *Journal of Law & Economics* 58, no. 2 (2015): 357–384.

McCrary, Justin, Joy Milligan, and James Phillips. "The Ph.D. Rises in American Law Schools, 1960–2011: What Does It Mean for Legal Education?" *Journal of Legal Education* 65, no. 3 (February 1, 2016): 543–579.

McGarity, Thomas. "EPA at Helm's Deep: Surviving the Fourth Attack on Environmental Law." *Fordham Environmental Law Review* 24 (Spring 2013): 205–241.

McLeman, Robert, et al. "Conceptual Framing to Link Climate Risk Assessments and Climate-Migration Scholarship." *Climatic Change* 165, no. 1 (March 19, 2021): 24–31.

Mehling, Michael, et al. "Teaching Climate Law: Trends, Methods, and Outlook." *Journal of Environmental Law* 32, no. 3 (2020): 417–440.

Mersky, Roy M., and John E. Christensen. "Computer-Assisted Legal Research Instruction in Texas Law Schools." *Law Library Journal* 73, no. 1 (1980): 79–98.

Meyerson, Michael I. "Law School Culture and the Lost Art of Collaboration: Why Don't Law Professors Play Well with Others?" *Nebraska Law Review* 93 (2015): 547–590.

Miller, Clark A., Alastair Iles, and Christopher F. Jones. "The Social Dimensions of Energy Transitions." *Science as Culture* 22, no. 2 (June 2013): 135–148.

Miller, Mark. *The High Priests of American Politics: The Role of Lawyers in American Political Institutions*. Knoxville: University of Tennessee Press, 1995.

Mintz, Joel A. "Teaching Environmental Law: Some Observations on Curriculum and Materials." *Journal of Legal Education* 33, no. 1 (1983): 94–110.

Mintzer, Irving M. "A Matter of Degrees: Energy Policy and the Greenhouse Effect." *Environmental Policy and Law* 17, no. 6 (1987): 247–254.

Morag-Levine, Noga. *Chasing the Wind*. Princeton, NJ: Princeton University Press, 2003.

Morant, Blake D. "Benefits from Challenge: The Continual Evolution of American Legal Education." *Journal of Legal Education* 64, no. 4 (May 2015): 523–529.

Munavvar, Mohamed. "Greenhouse Effect and Sea Level Rise—Threat to Small Island States: A Perspective of International Legal Responsibility." *African Journal of International & Comparative Law* 1 (1989): 484–499.

Nanda, Ved P. "Global Warming and International Environmental Law—A Preliminary Inquiry." *Harvard International Law Journal* 30, no. 2 (1989): 375–392.

———. "Symposium: Global Climate Change: An Introduction." *Denver Journal of International Law & Policy* 10, no. 3 (1981): 463–468.

Nasi, Michael. "Greening the Bar Through Sustainability Initiatives." *Texas Bar Journal* 72 (2009): 262–267.

NeJaime, Douglas. "Cause Lawyers Inside the State." *Fordham Law Review* 81 (2012): 649–704.

Newton, Brent. "Preaching What They Don't Practice: Why Law Faculties' Preoccupation with Impractical Scholarship and Devaluation of Practical Competencies Obstruct Reform in the Legal Academy." *South Carolina Law Review* 62 (2010): 105–156.

Nolon, John. "Considering the Trend Toward Local Environmental Law." *Pace Environmental Law Review* 20 (2002): 3–18.

———. "Shifting Paradigms Transform Environmental and Land Use Law: The Emergence of the Law of Sustainable Development." *Fordham Environmental Law Review* 24 (2013): 242–274.

Organ, Jerome M. "Net Tuition Trends by LSAT Category from 2010 to 2014 with Thoughts on Variable Return on Investment." *Journal of Legal Education* 67, no. 1 (2017): 51–85.

Osofsky, Hari. "Is Climate Change 'International'? Litigation's Diagonal Regulatory Role." *Virginia Journal of International Law* 49 (2009): 585–650.

Osofsky, Hari, William C. G. Burns, and Lesley McAllister. *Climate Change Law and Policy*. 1st ed. Blue Springs, MO: Aspen Publishing Co., 2012.

Owen, Dave, and Caroline Noblet. "Interdisciplinary Research and Environmental Law." *Ecology Law Quarterly* 41, no. 4 (2019): 887–938.

Parenteau, Patrick. "Lead, Follow, or Get Out of the Way: States Tackle Climate Change with Little Help from Washington." *Connecticut Law Review* 40 (2008): 1453–1475.

Paulk, John, and Lynn Hodges. "Environmental Education: The Future Environmental Education." *EPA Journal* 14, no. 6 (1988): 36–37.

Percival, Robert V. "Green Briefs and Toxic Torts: Educating Lawyers with Environmental Savvy." *Environment* 35, no. 3 (April 1993): 6–37.

———. "Matching the Supply and Demand for Environmental, Energy, and Natural Resources Lawyers—How the Environment Has Changed Legal Education." Paper presented to the annual fall meeting, Section on Environment, Energy, and Resources, American Bar Association, Hilton Head, SC, October 10, 1998.

Pertschuk, Michael. *When the Senate Worked for Us: The Invisible Role of Staffers in Countering Corporate Lobbies*. Nashville, TN: Vanderbilt University Press, 2017.

Peters, Margot B. "An International Approach to the Greenhouse Effect: The Problem of Increased Atmospheric Carbon Dioxide Can Be Approached by an Innovative International Agreement Comment." *California Western International Law Journal* 20, no. 1 (1989): 67–90.

Pipek, Volmar, and Volker Wulf. "Infrastructuring: Toward an Integrated Perspective on the Design and Use of Information Technology." *Journal of the Association for Information Systems* 10, no. 5 (May 2009): 447–473.

Pischke, Erin C., Barry D. Solomon, and Adam M. Wellstead. "A Historical Analysis of US Climate Change Policy in the Pan-American Context." *Journal of Environmental Studies and Sciences* 8, no. 2 (June 1, 2018): 225–232.

Pistone, Michele. "Law Schools and Technology: Where We Are and Where We Are Heading." *Journal of Legal Education* 64, no. 4 (2015): 586–604.

Plater, Zygmunt. "Environmental Law and the Three Economies." *Harvard Environmental Law Review* 23 (1999): 359–392.

Pomerance, Rafe. "The Dangers from Climate Warming: A Public Awakening." *EPA Journal* 12, no. 10 (1986): 15–16.

Reeve, Allison C., and Travis Weller. "Empirical Legal Research Support Services: A Survey of Academic Law Libraries." *Law Library Journal* 107, no. 3 (2015): 399–420.

Reitze, Arnold. "Environmental Policy: It's Time for a New Beginning." *Columbia Journal of Environmental Law* 14, no. 1 (1989): 111–156.

Rhode, Deborah L. "Leadership in Law." *Stanford Law Review* 69 (2017): 1603–1666.

———. *The Trouble with Lawyers*. New York: Oxford University Press, 2015.

Ribes, David, and Thomas Finholt. "The Long Now of Technology Infrastructure: Articulating Tensions in Development." *Journal of the Association for Information Systems* 10, no. 5 (May 2009): 375–398.

Ricker, Darlene. "The Coming Storm." *ABA Journal* 105, no. 8 (2019): 34–41.

Rieser, Alison. "Prescriptions for the Commons." *Harvard Environmental Law Review* 23 (1999): 393–421.

Robbins, William. *A Place for Inquiry, a Place for Wonder: The Andrews Forest*. Corvallis: Oregon State University Press, 2021.

Robertson, Heidi. "Methods for Teaching Environmental Law: Some Thoughts on Providing Access to the Environmental Law System." *Columbia Journal of Environmental Law* 23 (1998): 237–278.

Robinson, Marshall. "The Ford Foundation: Sowing the Seeds of a Revolution." *Environment* 35, no. 3 (April 1993): 10–41.

Robinson, Nicholas. "After a Decade: 'Theory as Practice' at the Center for Environmental Legal Studies." *Pace Environmental Law Review* 11 (1993): 3–10.

Robinson-Dorn, Michael. "Teaching Environmental Law in the Era of Climate

Change: A Few Whats, Whys, and Hows." *Washington Law Review* 82 (2007): 619–648.

Rogers, E. M. *Diffusion of Innovations*. 5th ed. New York: Free Press, 2003.

Rosan, Richard. "On the Fiftieth Anniversary of the Federal Energy Bar Association." *Energy Law Journal* 17 (1996): 1–26.

Rosenbloom, Jonathan, and John Dernbach. "Teaching Applied Sustainability: A Practicum Based on Drafting Ordinances." *Texas A&M Journal of Property Law* 4 (2017): 83–116.

Rubin, Edward. "The Future and Legal Education: Are Law Schools Failing and, If So, How?" *Law & Social Inquiry* 39 (Spring 2014): 499–518.

———. "Should Law Schools Support Faculty Research?" *Journal of Contemporary Legal Issues* 17 (2008): 139–169.

Ruhl, J. B. "Climate Change Adaptation and the Structural Transformation of Environmental Law." *Environmental Law* 40 (2010): 363–435.

———. "Complexity Theory as a Paradigm for the Dynamical Law-And-Society System: A Wake-Up Call for Legal Reductionism and the Modern Administrative State." *Duke Law Journal* 45 (March 1996): 849–928.

Ruhl, J. B., and James Salzmann. "Climate Change Meets the Law of the Horse." *Duke Law Journal* 62 (February 2013): 975–1027.

Sabin, Paul. "Environmental Law and the End of the New Deal Order." *Law and History Review* 33, no. 4 (November 2015): 965–1003.

Sarat, Austin, and Stuart A. Scheingold. *Cause Lawyering: Political Commitments and Professional Responsibilities*. New York: Oxford University Press, 1998.

Savoy, Paul. "Towards a New Politics of Legal Education." *Yale Law Journal* 79 (1970): 444–504.

Sax, Joseph [L.]. "Environmental Law in the Law Schools: What We Teach and How We Feel About It." *Environmental Law Reporter* 19 (1989): 10251–10253.

———. "The Public Trust Doctrine in Natural Resource Law: Effective Judicial Intervention." *Michigan Law Review* 68, no. 3 (January 1970): 471–566.

Scheiber, Harry N. *The State and Freedom of Contract*. Stanford, CA: Stanford University Press, 1998.

Scheingold, Stuart A. *Something to Believe in: Politics, Professionalism, and Cause Lawyering*. Stanford, CA: Stanford Law and Politics, 2004.

Schlegel, John Henry. *American Legal Realism and Empirical Social Science*. Chapel Hill: University of North Carolina Press, 1995.

Schneider, Claudine. "Changing Our Ways or Changing the Earth's Climate Dialogues." *Environmental Law Reporter News & Analysis* 19, no. 5 (1989): 10208–10210.

Schneider, Susan. "A Reconsideration of Agricultural Law." *William & Mary Environmental Law & Policy Review* 34 (2010): 935–963.

Scott, Inara. "Is It Time to Say Goodbye to Environmental Law?" Environmental Law Prof Blog, November 17, 2018. https://lawprofessors.typepad.com/environmental_law/2018/11/is-it-time-to-say-goodbye-to-environmental-law.html.

Seligman, Joel. *The High Citadel: The Influence of Harvard Law School.* Boston: Houghton Mifflin, 1978.

Shapiro, Martin. "Recent Developments in Political Jurisprudence." *Western Political Quarterly* 36, no. 4 (1983): 541–548.

Shaw, Christopher, and Brigitte Nerlich. "Metaphor as a Mechanism of Global Climate Change Governance: A Study of International Policies, 1992–2012." *Ecological Economics* 109 (January 1, 2015): 34–40.

Sheppard, Steve. *The History of Legal Education in the United States: Commentaries and Primary Sources.* 2 vols. Pasadena, CA: Salem Press, 1999.

Short, Aric. "New Beginnings." *Texas Bar Journal* 77 (March 2014): 232–237.

Sirianni, Carmen. *Sustainable Cities in American Democracy: From Postwar Urbanism to a Civic New Deal.* Lawrence: University Press of Kansas, 2020.

Skocpol, Theda. *Protecting Soldiers and Mothers.* Cambridge, MA: Belknap Press, 1992.

Skowronek, Stephen. *Building a New American State.* Cambridge, UK: Cambridge University Press, 1982.

Smith, Kimberly. *The Conservation Constitution.* Lawrence: University Press of Kansas, 2019.

Sohn, Louis B., and Edith Brown Weiss. "Intergenerational Equity in International Law." *Proceedings of the Annual Meeting of the American Society of International Law* 81 (1987): 126–133.

Sörlin, Sverker, and Melissa Lane. "Historicizing Climate Change—Engaging New Approaches to Climate and History." *Climatic Change* 151, no. 1 (November 2018): 1–13.

Southworth, Ann. *Lawyers of the Right: Professionalizing the Conservative Coalition.* Chicago Series in Law and Society. Chicago: University of Chicago Press, 2008.

Speth, Gus. "Global Energy Futures and the Carbon Dioxide Problem." *Boston College Environmental Affairs Law Review* 9, no. 1 (1980): 1–12.

Stake, Jeffrey Evans. "The Interplay between Law School Rankings, Reputations, and Resource Allocation: Ways Rankings Mislead." *Indiana Law Journal* 81, no. 1 (2006): 229–270.

Stephen, Ninian. "Once and Future Law Schools." *Griffith Law Review* 1 (1992): 10–14.

Stevens, Robert Bocking. *Law School: Legal Education in America from the 1850s to the 1980s.* Chapel Hill: University of North Carolina Press, 1983.

Strauss, Peter. "Review Essay: Christopher Columbus Langdell and the Public Law Curriculum." *Journal of Legal Education* 66, no. 1 (September 1, 2016): 157–185.

Stuckey, Roy, et al. *Best Practices for Legal Education.* Columbia: CLEA, 2007.

Stumpf, Harry P. "The Recent Past." *Western Political Quarterly* 36, no. 4 (1983): 534–541.

Sturm, Susan. "Law Schools, Leadership, and Change." *Harvard Law Review Forum* 127 (2013): 49–53.

Sullivan, William. "After Ten Years: The Carnegie Report and Legal Education." *University of St. Thomas Law Journal* 14 (2018): 331–344.

Sullivan, William, et al. "Educating Lawyers: Preparation for the Profession of Law." Stanford, CA: Carnegie Foundation for the Advancement of Teaching, 2007.

Sweeney, Joseph C. "International Law at Fordham Law School." *Fordham International Law Journal* 29 (2006): 1139–1154.

Tai, Stephanie. "Food Systems Law from Farm to Fork and Beyond." *Seton Hall Law Review* 45 (2015): 109–171.

Talbott, Kirk, Sera Song, and Janis Alcorn. "Edith Brown Weiss as a Pathfinder: Strengthening Property Rights and Community-Based Resource Governance for Indigenous Peoples Worldwide" *Georgetown Environmental Law Review* 32 (2020): 533–567.

Tamanaha, Brian. *Failing Law Schools*. Chicago: University of Chicago Press, 2012.

Tarlock, Dan. "The Airlie House Conference and the Dawn of Environmental Law." In *Pioneers of Environmental Law*, ed. Jan Laitos and John Copeland Nagle, 83–102. Northport, NY: Twelve Tables Press, 2020.

———. "Why There Should Be No Restatement of Environmental Law." *Brooklyn Law Review* 79 (2014): 663–678.

Tejani, Riaz. "Professional Apartheid: The Racialization of US Law Schools after the Global Economic Crisis." *American Ethnologist* 44, no. 3 (2017): 451–463.

Tomlins, Christopher. "Framing the Field of Law's Disciplinary Encounters: A Historical Narrative." *Law & Society Review* 34, no. 4 (2000): 911–972.

Tushnet, Mark. "The Legitimation of the Administrative State: Some Aspects of the Work of Thurgood Marshall." *Studies in American Political Development* 5, no. 1 (1991): 94–118.

Ulen, Thomas S. "The Impending Train Wreck in Current Legal Education: How We Might Teach Law as the Scientific Study of Social Governance." *University of St. Thomas Law Journal* 6 (2009): 302–336.

Victor, David G. *The Collapse of the Kyoto Protocol and the Struggle to Slow Global Warming*. Princeton, NJ: Princeton University Press, 2004.

———. "What the Framework Convention on Climate Change Teaches Us About Cooperation on Climate Change." *Politics and Governance* 4, no. 3 (September 8, 2016): 133–141.

Walker, Anders. "Bramble Bush Revisited: Llewellyn, the Great Depression, and the First Law School Crisis, 1929–1939." *Journal of Legal Education* 64 (2014): 145–180.

Ware, John R., Stephen V. Smith, and Marjorie L. Reaka-Kudla. "Coral Reefs:

Sources or Sinks of Atmospheric CO2?" *Coral Reefs* 11, no. 3 (September 1, 1992): 127–130.

Weart, S. [Spencer] R. *The Discovery of Global Warming*. Cambridge, MA: Harvard University Press, 2003.

———. *The Discovery of Global Warming*. Rev. and expanded ed. Cambridge, MA: Harvard University Press, 2008.

Wegner, Judith Welch. "Law School Assessment in the Context of Accreditation: Critical Questions, What We Know and Don't Know, and What We Should Do Next." *Journal of Legal Education* 67, no. 2 (2018): 412–461.

Weis, Janice. "A 35 Year Perspective." Lewis & Clark Law School blog. 2005. https://law.lclark.edu/programs/environmental_and_natural_resources_law/perspectives.

Wenger, Etienne. *Communities of Practice: Learning, Meaning, and Identity*. 6th ed. Cambridge, UK: Cambridge University Press, 1999.

Wexler, Pamela, and Susan Conbere. "States Fight Global Warming." *EPA Journal* 18, no. 4 (October 1992): 18–19.

Wexler, Pamela, et al. "Cool Tools." Center for Global Change at University of Maryland. 1992.

Wheeler, Stephen M. "State and Municipal Climate Change Plans: The First Generation." *Journal of the American Planning Association* 74, no. 4 (October 21, 2008): 481–496.

Wildermuth, Amy J. "The Next Step: The Integration of Energy Law and Environmental Law." *Utah Environmental Law Review* 31, no. 2 (2011): 369–388.

Williams, A. Park, et al. "Observed Impacts of Anthropogenic Climate Change on Wildfire in California." *Earth's Future* 7, no. 8 (2019): 892–910.

Williams, R. W. "Additions to the List of the Birds of Leon County." *Auk* 46, no. (1) (1929): 122.

Williamson, Jennifer, and Michael Rooke-Ley. "SALT History: Founding of SALT." *SALT Equalizer* (April 2000): 19–23.

Wilson, Augusta. "Linking Across Borders." *Columbia Journal of Environmental Law* 43 (2018): 227–267.

Wirth, David. "Teaching and Research in International Environmental Law." *Harvard Environmental Law Review* 23 (1999): 423–440.

Wizner, Stephen. "The Law School Clinic: Legal Education in the Interests of Justice." *Fordham Law Review* 70 (2002): 1929–1937.

———. "The Way to Carnegie: Practice, Practice, Practice." *Boston College Journal of Law & Social Justice* 32 (Spring 2012): 345–355.

Woodward, Jennifer. "Turning Down the Heat: What United States Laws Can Do to Help Ease Global Warming Comment." *American University Law Review* 39, no. 1 (1989): 203–238.

Yang, Tseming, and Robert V. Percival. "The Emergence of Global Environmental Law." *Ecology Law Quarterly* 36 (2009): 615–664.

Yochim, Jordan. "Climate Change and a Changing Profession: What Future Will We Choose?" American Bar Association, January 8, 2019. www.americanbar.org /groups/bar_services/publications/bar_leader/2017-18/january-february/clima te-change-and-a-changing-profession-what-future-will-we-choose.

Zaelke, Durwood, and James Cameron. "Global Warming and Climate Change—An Overview of the International Legal Process." *American University International Law Review* 5 (1990): 249–290.

Zanger, Allene. "Carbon Dioxide's Threat to Global Climate: An International Solution Note." *Stanford Journal of International Law* 17, no. 2 (1981): 389–412.

Zillman, Donald. "30th Anniversary Special Section Evolution of Modern Energy Law: A Personal Retrospective." *Journal of Energy & Natural Resources Law* 30 (2012): 485–493.

Index

Abrams, Robert, 74, 76
Adler, Robert, 127, 150
Administrative Procedure Act (1946), 28, 34, 39, 60
Agran, Larry, 56–57
Airlie House Conference on Law and the Environment, 34–35
Air Quality Act (1967), 36
American Bar Association (ABA)
  accreditation, 90–91
  antitrust litigation, 90
  bar exams, 21–22, 80
  Curriculum Committee, 93–94
  Environment, Energy, and Resources section, 109, 126
  MacCrate Report, 92–93, 203n25
American College of Environmental Lawyers, 126
American Recovery and Reinvestment Act (2009), 108, 143
American University International Law Review, 69
Anderson, Fred, 42–43, 73, 74, 129
Anton, Don, 126
Asia-Pacific Partnership for Clean Development and Climate (2005), 104
Aspen Institute of Humanistic Studies, 66
Aspen Publishing, 22
Association of American Law Schools (AALS), 22
Association of Legal Writing Directors, 22, 93
Association of Public Agency Customers v. Bonneville Power Administration, 61
Audubon Energy Plan (1984), 68
author's experiences, vii, 1–2, 45–46
author's methodology, 11–13, 65

Babcock, Hope, 48, 79
Babich, Adam, 122, 123, 173
Baldwin, Malcolm, 35
bar exams, 21–22, 80
Barry University School of Law, 120
Beck, Robert, 131
Benedick, Richard, 123
Benjamin, Lisa, 119
Biber, Eric, 114
Biden, Joe, 123, 142, 143
Bilek, Mary Lu, 88
Birdsong, Bret, 131
Blumm, Michael, 39, 47, 75–76, 147, 154
Bonica, Adam, 16
Bonine, John, 43, 73, 126
Bonneville Power Administration, 61
Bosselman, Fred, 77, 127, 131–132
Boston College Environmental Affairs Law Review, 65
Bowman, Wallace, 35
Boxer, Barbara, 89
Boyd, William, 127, 148
Brown Weiss, Edith, 48, 66–68, 69, 71, 72, 79, 113
Bureau for Biological Survey, 33
Burns, Wil, 82, 124–125, 126
Bush, George H. W., 105
Bush, George W., 4, 103
Buzbee, Adam, 166
Buzbee, William, 72, 74, 79, 113, 129, 171
Byrd-Stevens Climate Change Strategy and Technology Innovation Act, 103
Byrne, Peter, 137, 154, 159, 175, 177

CAFE standards (Corporate Average Fuel Efficiency), 59–60, 104

California
  California Environmental Quality Act (CEQA), 107
  Center for Law, Energy & the Environment (CLEE), 106–107, 161
  energy policies, 56, 104
  fuel efficiency standards, 104
  Global Warming Solutions Act (2006), 105–106
  Irvine, 56–57
  local emission reduction goals, 107
Cameron, James, 69
Campos, Paul, 86, 87
Cannon, Jonathan, 17
cap-and-trade regulation, 46, 75, 105
carbon emissions
  carbon trading programs, 104–106
  and international law, 66–67
Carlarne, Cinnamon, 153, 167
Carlson, Ann, 127, 148
Carnegie Report, 93–94, 99
Carolina Academic Press, 22
Carpenter, Catherine, 93
Carson, Rachel, 34
Carter, Jimmy, 73
Cascades National Park, 36
casebooks
  climate change as integrative framework, 128, 129–130, 147–148
  curricular trends, 147
  energy law, 131–132
  faculty use of, 132
  natural resources, 131
  water law, 131
case method of legal education, 20–21, 28–29, 43, 161
Cases and Materials on Environmental Law (Farber), 147–150
Cases and Materials on Environmental Law (Gray), 41
Cases and Materials on Environmental Law and Policy (Stewart & Krier), 41, 73
Cases and Materials on Natural Resources and Energy (Rodgers), 77
Cases and Materials on the Law of Natural Resources (Martz), 39
Cases and Materials on Water Law (Gould et al.), 131

Cases and Materials on Water Law (Trelease & Gould), 76
Center for Energy Law, Tulane, 153–154
Center for Global Change, 38
Center for Law, Energy, & the Environment (CLEE), 106–107, 161
Center for Law and Social Policy, 36, 37
Chandler, Pamela, 127–128, 132
Charo, R. Alta, 68
Cheever, Frederico, 131
Chevron refinery case study, 46–47
Chicago Climate Exchange, 105
Cities for Climate Protection Campaign (CCPC), 57
Citizens to Preserve Overton Park v. Volpe, 35
city-level climate action, 56–57, 107
Civins, Jeff, 72, 119, 173
Clean Air Acts (1963/1970), 36, 43, 46, 74, 103, 109, 113, 119, 175
Clean Power Plan (2015), 17, 103, 123, 161
Clean Water Act (1972), 36, 43
Clean Water Restoration Act (1966), 36
climate change
  climate denialism, 83, 155, 156
  federal regulation, lack of, 80–82
  and food system, 115–116
  as international vs. state/local issue, 64
  as pervasive problem, 142–146
  state and local policies, 142–143
Climate Change and the Law (Wold et al.), 127, 133–134
Climate Change Law: Mitigation and Adaptation (Hildreth et al.), 127, 134–135
Climate Change Law & Policy Works-in-Progress Symposium, 127
climate law
  climate change as disruptive force, 166–172
  climate-related litigation, 144
  and human rights, 159
  importance of, 145
  international, 121
  international cooperation, need for, 6
  multi-scalar policy, 121
  overview, 3–5, 120–125
  as part of environmental law, 139
  pedagogical approaches, 155–166

policy, state and local, 104–108
political aspects, 83–84
state vs. federal authority, 113
climate policy, development and evolution of, 53–64, 103–110
climate science
complexity of, 98, 121–122, 138
coverage in law school curricula, 121–122
current impacts, 106, 143
development of, 1–2
importance of understanding, 178–179
and legal scholarship, 64–69
litigation strategies and court cases, 58–64, 108–110, 118–119
overview, 52–53
Clinical Legal Education Association, 22, 92, 93
Clinton, Bill, 103
coal, 117, 119
Coastal Zone Management Act (1972), 36
Coburn, Tom, 89
Coggins, George, 76, 131
Cole, Daniel, 131
Cole, Luke, 116
Columbia Journal of Environmental Law, 68
Columbia University
Earth Institute, 124
Law School, 26, 72, 77, 114, 124
Legislative Drafting Research Fund, 26, 68
Sabin Center, 3–4, 108, 115, 142, 144, 160–161
Conference of Parties (Copenhagen 2009), 119
Connolly, Kim Diana, 39, 96, 100, 137, 146–147, 157–158
conservation movement, 32–33
Cooley Law School, 120
Cool Tools (University of Maryland Center for Global Change), 55–56
Corbridge, James, 76, 131
Corporate Average Fuel Efficiency (CAFE) standards, 59–60, 104
Council on Environmental Quality, 71, 73
Council on Legal Education for Professional Responsibility, 29
court cases and climate governance, 58–64
Craig, Robin Kundis, 76, 119, 127, 138, 145, 169, 176–177

Creighton School of Law, 80
Cullenward, Danny, 5, 163–164
Currie, Brainerd, 26
Currie, David, 35, 41

Daniels, Stephen, 99
databases, 126
HeinOnline, 65
LexisNexis, 65
NexisUni, 69
Sabin Center climate litigation database, 144
Westlaw, 65, 124
Davies, Lincoln, 152
Davis, Mark, 116–117, 119–120, 135, 160, 170
Davis, Martha, 95
Defending the Environment (Sax), 37
Denver Journal of International Law & Policy, 66
Department of Agriculture, 60–61
Department of Energy, 60–61, 108
Department of Housing and Urban Development, 41
Department of Justice, 90–91
Department of the Interior, 60–61
Department of Transportation, 41
Dernbach, John, 72, 111, 112, 121, 122, 144, 161
diffusion of innovations theory, 8–9
disaster law, 116, 170
Docherty, Bonnie, 158–159
Doremus, Holly, 114, 123, 136, 145, 147, 171, 177
Driesen, David, 127, 150
Dwyer, John, 45, 46–47, 114
Dwyer, Judge William, 61
Dynamic Sociology (Ward), 24

EarthRights International, 158–159
Earth Summit (1992), 55, 70
Earthwise Law Center, Lewis & Clark, 118
Echevarria, John, 137
Ecology Law Quarterly, 2, 39
ecosystems, theories of, 52
Edwards, Harry, 96
Einhorn, David, 68
Electric Power in a Carbon Constrained World conference, 145

INDEX 239

Elkind, Ethan, 107
emissions allowance markets, 104–106. *See also* greenhouse gas emission policies
Emory Law School, 113
Endangered Species Act (1973), 36, 138
endangered species law, 76
Energy, Economics, and the Environment (Bosselman et al.), 77, 127, 131–132
energy law, 5, 77, 151–154
Energy Law and Policy (Osofsky et al.), 152
Energy Policy Act (2005), 143
Energy Policy and Conservation Act (1975), 36
Energy Security and Independence Act (2007), 143
Engel, Kirsten, 150
Environmental Defense Fund, 36, 55
environmental justice movement, 49, 135, 151
and lawyers, 17–18
environmental law
casebooks, 1980s–1990s, 73–74, 76
casebooks, early, 41–43, 44
climate law as subset of, 139, 146–151
education, development of, 39–49
emerging challenges of, 138–140
energy law, 77, 151–154
history of, 31–39
international vs. domestic, 70, 78–79, 81–82
law school curricula, 4, 48–49, 70–78
utility of, 145–146
water law, 76
Environmental Law (Driesen et al.), 127, 150
Environmental Law (Reitze), 41
Environmental Law (Shaw), 39
Environmental Law: Cases and Materials (Findley & Farber), 43, 73–74, 78–79
Environmental Law: Cases and Materials (Tabb & Malon), 74
Environmental Law: Cases and Materials (Weinberg), 73
Environmental Law and Policy (Hanks et al.), 41, 42
Environmental Law and Policy (Krier), 41
Environmental Law and Policy (Mennell & Stewart), 74
Environmental Law and Policy (Plater et al.), 74, 150

Environmental Law and Policy (Salzman & Thompson), 127
Environmental Law in Context (Craig), 127
Environmental Law Institute (ELI), 35, 38, 126
Environmental Law Prof Blog, 126
Environmental Law Review, 39
Environmental Policy Law (Schoenbaum), 43, 73
Environmental Policy Project, 137
Environmental Protection (Anderson et al.), 42–43, 73, 129–130
Environmental Protection Agency (EPA), 17, 37
regulation of pollutants, 74
See also greenhouse gas emission policies; *Massachusetts v. EPA*
Environmental Regulation: Law Science and Policy (Percival et al.), 74, 128–129, 150–151
EPA Journal, 68
experiential learning, 157–160, 181–182

Failing Law Schools (Tamanaha), 90
Farber, Daniel
casebooks by, 43, 73–74, 75, 78
on defining climate law and curricula, 167, 177
Harvard Law Review symposium, 70
survey of American law schools, 144–145, 147–150
University of California, Berkeley Law School, 114, 136, 153
University of Illinois Law School, 100
University of Minnesota Law School, 47–48, 79, 81
Federal Public Land and Resources Law (Coggins et al.), 76, 131
Ferrey, Steven, 105
Fershee, Joshua, 77, 80, 120, 156
Findley, Roger, 43, 73, 74, 78, 148
Flatt, Victor, 127, 130
flood control, 62
Florida State University College of Law, 119
Ford Foundation, 29, 36, 40
Foundation on Economic Trends, 60–61
Frankfurter, Felix, 24–25, 97
Freeman, Jody, 110

Freund, Ernst, 25
Freyfogle, Eric, 131
Friends of the Earth, 71
fuel efficiency standards, 104, 142
Funk, William, 44–45, 72, 127, 130

Gabrielson, Ira, 34
Garrison, Lloyd, 27
geoengineering, 69, 178
Georgetown University Law Center, 45, 48, 66, 79, 112–113, 153, 159
George Washington University Law School, 39, 40, 45, 126, 152–153
Gerrard, Michael
  Columbia Law School climate courses taught by, 119, 124, 125, 157
  on defining climate law, 106
  Global Climate Change and U.S. Law, 109–110, 127, 132–133
  Legal Pathways to Deep Decarbonization in the United States, 144
  Sabin Center, started by, 115
Getches, David, 76, 131
Giannini, Tyler, 73, 158, 159, 169
Ginsburg, Douglas H., 59–60
Ginsburg, Ruth Bader, 59–60, 64
Glicksman, Robert, 129, 151
Global 2000 Report, 73
Global Alliance for Animals and the Environment, 118
Global Change Research Act (1990), 54
Global Climate Change and U.S. Law (Gerrard), 109–110, 124, 125, 132–133
Global Climate Protection Act (1987), 54
Global Environment Facility, 38
Global Methane Initiative (2004), 104
Global Warming: The Complete Briefing (Houghton), 123
Global Warming Solutions Act (California), 105
Goldfarb, William, 74, 76
Gordon, Kate, 139, 163, 167
Gordon, Robert, 25
Gore, Al, 55
Gould, George, 76, 131
Grad, Frank, 72, 113
Grant, Douglas, 131
Gray, Oscar, 41

greenhouse gas emission policies, 56, 57, 104–106, 118, 133, 142–143. *See also* Environmental Protection Agency (EPA)
Gupta, Joyeeta, 58

Hanks, Eva, 41, 42
Hanks, John, 41, 42
Haragan, Kelly, 73, 114, 155–156
Harris, Cyril, 41
Harris County Flood Control District v. Kerr, 62
Harvard Law Review, 70
Harvard Model, 19–23
  criticism and challenges of, 23–30
Harvard University
  Human Rights Clinic, 158
  Law School, 39
Hayashi, Andrew, 99
Hayhoe, Katharine, 1–2
HeinOnline, 65
Heinzerling, Lisa, 45–46, 47, 72, 74, 75, 79, 113
Heller, Thomas, 163
Higgins, Louis, 127–128, 132
Hildreth, Richard, 127, 134
Hodas, David, 127, 134
Houghton, John, 123
Howe, Joshua, 2
Hubert H. Humphrey School of Public Affairs, 152
Hull, Eric, 120
human rights and climate law, 115, 159, 169
Hunter, David, 121, 127, 133–134
Hurricane Katrina, 114–115, 116–117, 174
Hurst, Willard, 25, 27–28, 29, 46

Index to Legal Periodicals, 65
Indiana University School of Law, 39
Infelise, Robert, 122, 153
Inflation Reduction Act (2022), 143
Institute for Resilience and Climate Adaptation, 101
Institute for Sustainable Investment (Columbia), 115
Institute for the Study of Law, Johns Hopkins University, 26–27
Institute on Water Resources Law & Policy, Tulane, 153

interdisciplinary centers and institutes, 100–103

interdisciplinary research, 95–100

International Council for Local Environmental Initiatives (ICLEI), 56

and CCPC, 57

International Environmental Law and Policy (Hunter et al.), 121

International Panel on Climate Change, 4, 55

International Partnership for Hydrogen Economy (2003), 104

International Relations and Climate Change (Luterbacher & Sprintz), 123

International Union for the Conservation of Nature's Academy of Law, 126

Irvine, California, 56–57

Irwin, Frances, 39, 40

Islands First, 119

Jehng, Moses, 160

Johns Hopkins University, Institute for the Study of Law, 26–27

Johnson, Vincent, 72

Johnston, Craig, 127, 130

Journal of Climate and Energy Law, 111

Journal of Energy, Climate, and the Environment, 111

Kagan, Robert, 46

Kalman, Laura, 25, 27

Katz, Martin, 99

Keeling, Charles, 54

Kelly, Amy, 131

Klass, Alexandra, 77, 117, 147, 152, 154

Klein, Christine, 131

knowledge infrastructure, 7–8, 168, 173–174

Kraham, Susan, 77, 114–115, 135

Krakoff, Sarah, 127

Krier, James, 41, 46, 73, 75

Kyoto Protocol, 4, 55, 58, 103, 109

Kysar, Douglas, 80, 120, 127, 134, 136–137, 154, 168, 171, 177

Laitos, Jan, 131

Lake Pontchartrain Basin Foundation, 116

Lamm, Ted, 107

Landis, James, 25

land use policy, 5, 42, 56, 81, 117, 150

Langdell, Christopher Columbus, 20, 24

LaPlante, Allison, 118–119

Lasswell, Harold, 27

Law of Environmental Protection, The (Bonine & McGarity), 43, 73

law schools

accreditation (ABA), 9, 15–16, 21–22, 90–91

case method of legal education, 20–21, 28–29, 43, 123, 161

centers and institutes, 100–103, 160–164, 187–188

climate change curricula, 70–78, 112–120

climate change curricula, evolution of, 122–123

climate change curricula, obstacles and challenges, 78–84, 120–125

climate change curricular gaps, 178

climate law, challenges of, 63

climate law, overview, 3–5, 8–10

climate law curriculum development, 120–125

clinical courses, 93, 118–119

clinics, 92–95

competition and inequality among, 88–90, 102–103, 180

curricular reform, 90–92, 93–94, 102–103

doctrine-focused, 174

elective coursework, 94

environmental law education, 39–49, 127–136

experiential learning, 157–160, 181–182

faculty, 48, 95–100

faculty networks, 125–127

Harvard Model, 19–23, 95

Harvard Model, criticism and challenges, 23–30, 45

innovative academic methods, 9–10, 71, 89–90, 163, 165–166, 169–171, 174–175

interdisciplinary teaching/scholarship, 136–138, 164–166, 178–179

law reviews, 64–65

legal education, history of, 19–30

and "legal ideology," 18–19

legal writing courses, 22, 92

overview of curricula, 30–31

and policy innovation, 3

private vs. public law, 20–21, 23
problem-based learning, 78–79, 94, 128–129, 175
seminar-style coursework, 46–47
skills-based education, 21, 29, 45, 92, 102–103
statute-based courses, 22, 43, 45
teaching strategies, 123–125
tuition and financial aspects of attendance, 86–88
Lazarus, Richard, 34–35, 70, 72, 74, 122, 146, 178
Leape, James, 74
Learner, Howard, 154
Lefcoe, George, 35
legal clinics
environmental law clinics, 77
law labs, 95
in underserved communities, 21, 22, 29
Legal Control of Water Resources (Sax & Abrams), 76
Legal Education and Public Policy (Lasswell & Myres), 27
Legal Pathways to Deep Decarbonization in the U.S. (Gerrad & Dernbach), 144
LegalPlanet blog, 148, 160–161
Legal Protection of the Environment (Johnston et al.), 127, 130
Legal Realist movement, 24, 97
legal research, interdisciplinary, 95–100
Leopold, Aldo, 33, 34
Leshy, John, 76, 131
Lewis & Clark Law School, 39, 47, 72, 76, 158
Earthwise Law Center, 118
Global Alliance for Animals and the Environment, 119
International Environmental Law Project, 119
LexisNexis, 65. *See also* NexisUni
Lindseth, Gard, 57
lobbyists, 17, 36
Los Angeles v. National Highway Traffic Safety Administration (NHTSA), 59–60
Loyola University, 47, 116
Center for Environmental Law, 160
Luterbacher, Urs, 123
Lyman, Erica, 118, 119

MacCrate Report (ABA), 92–93, 203n25
Macdougald, Joseph, 101, 102, 117, 124, 137, 161
Malon, Linda, 74
Manabe, Syukuru, 52
Managing Our Urban Environment (Mandelker), 39
Mance, Anna, 165–166
Mandelker, Daniel, 39, 41, 42–43, 73
marine law, 170
Markell, David, 109–110, 129
Martin Daniel Gould Center for Conflict Resolution, 101
Martz, Clyde, 39, 76
Massachusetts Attorney General, 74
Massachusetts v. EPA (2007), 75, 108–109, 114, 129, 130, 174. *See also* Environmental Protection Agency (EPA)
Mayors Climate Protection Agreement, 58, 107
McCain-Lieberman Climate Stewardship Act, 103
McDougal, Myres, 27
McGarity, Thomas, 43, 73
Menell, Peter, 74, 114
Meyer, Charles, 76
Meyerson, Michal, 99
Michigan Law Review, 96
Miller, Alan, 37–38, 74, 136
Miller, Mark, 18–19, 23
Minnesota, Public Utility Commission (PUC), 61–62
Mintz, Joseph, 43–44, 45
Missouri, energy policies, 56
Montreal Protocol (1987), 55

Nagle, John Copeland, 127, 130, 147
Nanda, Ved, 66, 68–69
National Climate Program Act (1978), 54
National Conference of Bar Examiners, 22
National Environmental Policy Act (NEPA), 35, 36, 43, 59, 60
National Resources Defense Council (NRDC), 59–60
natural resource law, 31, 147
natural resources casebooks, 131
Natural Resources Defense Council (NRDC), 36, 38, 46, 55

Natural Resources Law (Freyfogle), 131
Natural Resources Law (Klein et al.), 131
Natural Resources Law (Laitos et al.), 131
nature, views of, 52
NeJaime, Douglas, 18
New Orleans and Hurricane Katrina,
  114–115, 116–117
Newton, Brian, 91
NexisUni, 69
Noblet, Caroline, 165
Nolon, John, 81–82
Northwest Environmental Defense
  Center, 118
*Northwest Environmental Defense Center v.
  Owens Corning Corp.*, 118
Northwestern Pritzker School of Law, 81
nuisance law, 31, 117–118, 149

Obama, Barack, 103, 123
Oliphant, Herman, 26
online research strategies, 124. *See also*
  databases
Osofsky, Hari, 77, 81, 101, 137, 152
Ossom, Aminta, 159
Owen, Dave, 165
Ozone Diplomacy (Benedick), 123

Pacala, Stephen, 124
Panarella, Samuel, 77
Parenteau, Patrick, 39, 71, 78, 104, 112, 123
Paris Agreement (2016), 103
Parker, Richard, 72, 154, 160
Pennsylvania State University Law School
  Center for Energy Law and Policy, 101
Penttinen, Sirja-Leena, 153
Percival, Robert, 74, 113, 150–151
Peters, Margot, 68
Pinchot, Gifford, 33
Plager, Sheldon, 35
Plater, Zygmunt, 70, 74, 150
pollution policies, 31–32, 34–35, 41–43,
  48–53, 128, 130, 148–149
Pomerance, Rafe, 71
Portland, Oregon, 56, 107–108
Pound, Roscoe, 24
Powers, Melissa, 119, 127, 133–134
*Practice and Policy of Environmental Law,
  The* (Ruhl et al.), 127, 130–131, 147

Princeton University, climate research,
  53–54
Progressive Era conservation movement,
  32–33
public interest law firms, 36
public land law, 76
public policy
  centers and institutes, 160–164
  and law, 171–172
Public Utility Commission (PUC),
  Minnesota, 61–62
publishing industry, legal academic, 22
Purdy, Jed, 127

Reagan, Ronald, 37
Reed, Alfred, 24
Regional Greenhouse Gas Initiative
  (RGGI), 104–105
Reitze, Arnold, 39, 41, 45, 126
Renewable Energy and Energy Efficiency
  Partnership (2004), 104
renewable energy policies, 142–143
Restoring the Quality of Our Environment
  (1965), 54
Revercomb, George, 60
Rieser, Alison, 70
Robinson, Nicholas, 35, 127, 134
Rocky Mountain Mineral Institute, 126
Rodgers, William, 41, 77
Rose, Carol, 47
Rosenthal, Alfred, 41
Rossi, Jim, 77
Rubin, Edward, 96, 99
Ruhl, J. B., 39, 109–110, 127, 130, 147
Russell Sage Foundation, 29
Rutgers Law School, 77

Sabin, Paul, 34
Sabin Center for Climate Change Law,
  Columbia University, 3–4, 108, 115,
  142, 144, 160–161
Salim, Oday, 77
Salzman, James, 121, 127, 130, 134, 147
A Sand County Almanac (Leopold), 33
Sanders, Matthew, 158, 162
Santa Clara University School of Law,
  82, 124
Sax, Joseph, 35–38, 41, 45, 46, 70, 76, 114

Schlegel, John Henry, 26
Schoenbaum, Thomas, 43, 73
Schroeder, Christopher, 74
Scott, Inara, 145–146
Section on Environment, Energy, and
    Resources (SEER), 109
Securities and Exchange Act (1934), 144
Seeding Capital (CLEE), 107
Segal, Katie, 107
Seiger, Alicia, 162–163, 165, 167–168
Shaw, Bill, 39
Sierra Club, 54
    Cool Cities program, 58, 107
    Legal Defense Fund, 36
Sierra Club v. Hickel, 35
Sierra Club v. Portland General Electric, 119
Silent Spring (Carson), 34
Sirianni, Carmen, 107–108
social justice. *See* environmental justice
    movement
social learning theory, 7–8
Society of American Law Teachers, 22
Socolow, Robert, 124
Socratic dialogue, 20. *See also* case method
    of legal education
Southeastern Association of Law Schools, 126
Spence, David, 77, 127
Speth, James Gustave, 65–66, 71, 73, 127, 134
Sprintz, Detlef, 123
Squillace, Mark, 127
Stanford University
    Center for Internet and Society, 101
    Law School, 39, 161–164
    Mills Legal Clinic, 158
    Steyer-Taylor Center for Energy Policy
        and Finance, 162
Stewart, Richard, 41, 46, 47, 73, 74, 75
Steyer-Taylor Center for Energy Policy and
    Finance, Stanford, 162
St. Mary's University School of Law
    (Innsbruck, Austria), 72
Stuckey, Roy, 93
Sullivan, William, 93, 99
sustainable development, 72

Tabb, William Murray, 74
Talus, Kim, 153–154, 156–157, 161
Tamanaha, Brian, 90, 91

Tarlock, Dan, 35, 41–43, 72, 73, 76, 131
Texas Environmental Superconference, 126
Thompson, Barton "Buzz," 76, 122–123,
    127, 139, 146, 147
Tolan, Patrick, 46, 75, 120
Tomain, Joseph, 152
Trelease, Frank, 76
Trump, Donald, 37, 142
Tulane Institute on Water Resources Law
    & Policy, 116–117
Tulane University School of Law, 116, 120,
    153–154, 160

Ulen, Thomas, 97–98, 100, 119, 135
United Nations
    Earth Summit (1972), 54
    Earth Summit, Rio de Janeiro (1992), 55
    Framework Convention on Climate
        Change (1992), 55
United States
    legal system, overview, 7
    political system, role of lawyers, 15–19
    state development, overview, 5–6
University at Buffalo School of Law, 137
University of California, Berkeley, vii, 136, 153
    Center for Law, Energy & the
        Environment, 106–107, 148, 160
    School of Law, 39, 45, 113–114
University of California, Davis, 136
University of California, Los Angeles
    Center for Law, Energy & the
        Environment (CLEE), 106–107, 161
    Law School, 40
University of Chicago Law School, 28, 75
University of Colorado Law School, 127
University of Connecticut Law School, 72,
    101, 117, 160
    Center for Energy and Environmental
        Law, 101, 161
University of Denver College of Law, 40, 66
University of Illinois College of Law, 97,
    98, 119
University of Maryland, Center for Global
    Change, 55–56
University of Michigan Law School, 39,
    75, 154
University of Minnesota Law School, 48,
    117, 145, 152

University of North Dakota, 120
University of San Diego Law School, 144–145
University of South Carolina
   School of Law, 96, 100
   School of the Environment, 137
University of Southern California Law Center, 40
University of Texas School of Law, 72–73, 114, 119, 155–156
University of the Bahamas, 119
University of Utah S. J. Quinney College of Law, 145
University of Virginia School of Law, 73
University of Wisconsin Law School, 27–28, 29
urban planning, 159–160
USDA (Department of Agriculture), 17, 33
US Forest Service, 33, 61
U.S. News & World Report law school rankings, 88
Utah Law Review, 145

Van Ness, William, Jr., 35
Verchick, Robert, 47, 116, 135, 160, 170
Vermont Law School, 39, 71, 112, 126
Victor, David, 5
Vienna Convention (1985), 4

Wald, Patricia, 59–60
Ward, Lester Frank, 24
Washington University School of Law, 72
Water and Water Rights (Beck & Kelly), 131
water law, 76, 116–117, 170
   casebooks, 131
Water Law (Goldfarb), 76
Water Law in a Nutshell (Getches), 76
Water Quality Act (1965), 36
Water Resource Management (Meyer & Tarlock), 76
Water Resource Management (Tarlock et al.), 131
Weart, Spencer, 2, 53
Weaver, Jacqueline, 77
Weber, Gregory, 131

Weinberg, Philip, 73
Weissman, Steven, 114
West Academic, 22, 127
Western Climate Initiative, 105
Westlaw (legal resource platform), 65, 124
Wetherhald, Richard, 52
Wheeler, Stephen, 58, 104–105, 107
Whittier Law School, 81
Widener University
   Environmental Law & Sustainability Center, 111, 160–161
   Widener Law Commonwealth, 72, 112
Wild and Free-Roaming Horses Act (1971), 36
Wild and Scenic Rivers Act (1968), 36
Wildermuth, Amy, 151–152
Wilderness Act (1964), 35
Wilkinson, Charles, 76, 131
William Mitchell College of Law, 117
Williams, Robert White, 32–34, 37
Williston, Samuel, 25
Wilson, Elizabeth, 152
Wilson, Woodrow, 25
Wirth, David, 4, 70
Wold, Chris, 119, 127, 133–134
Wood, Mary, 131
World Bank Group, 38
World Climate Conference (1979), 54
World Meteorological Organization (WMO), 52
   World Climate Research Program, 54
World Resources Institute, 38

Yale University
   Center for Environmental Law & Policy, 154
   Law School, 27
Yang, Tseming, 112, 123, 126

Zaelke, Durwood, 69, 121, 134
Zanger, Allene, 68
Zellmer, Sandra, 39, 131
Zillman, Donald, 77
Zimmermann, Scott, 114, 136

Printed in the USA
CPSIA information can be obtained
at www.ICGtesting.com
CBHW031402210524
8885CB00008B/81/J